THE NEW
Oxford Book
of Canadian Verse
IN ENGLISH

THE NEW
Oxford Book
of Canadian Verse
IN ENGLISH

Chosen and with an Introduction by
MARGARET ATWOOD

TORONTO   LONDON   NEW YORK
Oxford University Press

PUBLICATION OF THIS BOOK WAS ASSISTED BY
THE CANADA COUNCIL
THE TORONTO ARTS COUNCIL
THE MUNICIPALITY OF METROPOLITAN TORONTO

Oxford University Press, 70 Wynford Drive, Don Mills,
Ontario M3C 1J9

Toronto   Oxford   New York
Delhi   Bombay   Calcutta   Madras   Karachi   Petaling Jaya
Singapore   Hong Kong   Tokyo   Nairobi   Dar es Salaam
Cape Town   Melbourne   Auckland

and associated companies in
Berlin   Ibadan

CANADIAN CATALOGUING IN PUBLICATION DATA

Main entry under title:
The New Oxford book of Canadian verse in English

ISBN 0-19-540396-7

1. Canadian poetry (English).* I. Atwood, Margaret,
1939-

PS8273.N47   C811'.008   C82-095151-X
PR9195.23.N47

CONTENTS

NOTE. *The date of first book publication is given at the end of each poem, except where it is more useful to give the date of first periodical publication, which appears in square brackets. No date is given for previously unpublished poems.*

ACKNOWLEDGEMENTS

PATRICK ANDERSON. 'Cold Colloquy' reprinted by permission of Orlando Gearing. 'House Burning: Quebec' from *The Colour as Naked* by Patrick Anderson reprinted by permission of The Canadian Publishers, McClelland and Stewart Limited, Toronto. MARGARET ATWOOD. Reprinted by permission of Margaret Atwood and Oxford University Press Canada: 'Death of a Young Son by Drowning' from *The Journals of Susanna Moodie*; 'There is Only One of Everything' and 'November' from *Your Are Happy*; 'Marrying the Hangman' and 'You Begin' from *Two-headed Poems*; and 'Notes Towards a Poem That Can Never Be Written' and 'Variations on the Word *Sleep*' from *True Stories*. MARGARET AVISON. 'In a Season of Unemployment', 'The Dumbfounding', 'A Nameless One', and 'Unspeakable' reprinted from *The Dumbfounding, poems by Margaret Avison*, by permission of W.W. Norton & Company, Inc. Copyright © 1966 Margaret Avison; 'The Swimmer's Moment', 'Snow', 'New Year's Poem', 'Civility a Bogey', 'Thaw', and 'Meeting Together of Poles and Latitudes' from *Winter Sun and other poems* by Margaret Avison reprinted by permission of The Canadian Publishers, McClelland and Stewart Limited, Toronto. KEN BELFORD. 'Turn' and 'Carrier Indians' from *Fireweed* (Talonbooks, 1967). EARLE BIRNEY. Reprinted by permission of The Canadian Publishers, McClelland and Stewart Limited, Toronto: 'David' and 'Slug in Woods' from *The Collected Poems of Earle Birney* by Earle Birney; 'Bushed', 'Can. Lit.', and 'The Bear on the Delhi Road' from *Ghost in the Wheels: Selected Poems*, by Earle Birney; 'Anglosaxon Street' from *Selected Poems 1940-1966* by Earle Birney; and 'My Love is Young' from *Fall by Fury and Other Makings* by Earle Birney. BILL BISSETT. Reprinted by permission of the author: 'dont worry yr hair' and 'christ i wudint know normal if i saw it when' from *nobody owns th earth* (House of Anansi Press, Toronto); and 'th wundrfulness uv th mountees our secret police' from *Sailor* (Talonbooks, Vancouver). E.D. BLODGETT. All poems reprinted by permission of NeWest Publishers Limited. ROO BORSON. All poems reprinted from *A Sad Device* by Roo Borson by permission of the author. GEORGE BOWERING. Reprinted by permission of the author: 'The Envies', 'Dobbin', and 'The House'. Reprinted by permission of The Canadian Publishers, McClelland and Stewart Limited, Toronto: 'In the Forest' from *Another Mouth* by George Bowering; 'Grandfather' from *Touch: Selected Poems 1960-1970* by George Bowering; and 'From "Summer Solstice" ' from *The Catch* by George Bowering. MARILYN BOWERING. 'Russian Asylum', 'Seeing Oloalok', and 'Wishing Africa' from *Sleeping with Lambs* by Marilyn Bowering reprinted by permission of Press Porcépic Ltd. ELIZABETH BREWSTER. 'Anti-Love Poems' by Elizabeth Brewster is reprinted from *Sometimes I Think of Moving* by permission of Oberon Press; 'Death by Drowning', 'Great-Aunt Rebecca', and 'If I Could Walk Out Into the Cold Country' from *Passage of Summer* (Ryerson Press) reprinted by permission of Elizabeth Brewster. ROBERT BRINGHURST. Reprinted by permission of Robert Bringhurst: 'Deuteronomy' from *Deuteronomy* (Sono Nis Press, 1974) and 'Notes to the Reader' from *Bergschrund* (Sono Nis Press, 1975); 'These Poems, She Said' from *The Beauty of the Weapons* by Robert Bringhurst reprinted by permission of The Canadian Publishers, McClelland and Stewart Limited, Toronto. VICTOR COLEMAN. 'How the Death of a City . . .' and 'Day Twenty-three'

ACKNOWLEDGEMENTS

from *one/eye/love* (Coach House Press, 1967) reprinted by permission of the author.
DON COLES. 'Photograph in a Stockholm Newspaper' from *Sometimes All Over*
by Don Coles and 'Natalya Nikolayevna Goncharov' from *The Prinzhorn Collection*
by Don Coles reprinted by permission of Macmillan of Canada, a Division of Gage
Publishing Limited. LEONARD COHEN. Reprinted by permission of The Cana-
dian Publishers, McClelland and Stewart Limited, Toronto: 'The killers that run
. . .' from *The Energy of Slaves* by Leonard Cohen; 'Heirloom', 'You Have the
Lovers', 'I Have Not Lingered in European Monasteries', and 'A Kite Is a Victim'
from *Selected Poems 1956-1968* by Leonard Cohen. FRANK DAVEY. All poems
reprinted by permission of the author. CHRISTOPHER DEWDNEY. All poems
reprinted by permission of the author. PIER GIORGIO DI CICCO. Reprinted by
permission of The Canadian Publishers, McClelland and Stewart Limited, Toronto:
'The Head Is a Paltry Matter' and 'Errore' from *The Tough Romance* by Pier Giorgio
di Cicco; 'Male Rage Poem' and 'Flying Deeper into the Century' from *Flying
Deeper into the Century* by Pier Giorgio di Cicco. MARY DI MICHELE. From
Mimosa and Other Poems (Mosaic Press/Valley Editions, 1981) reprinted by permis-
sion. DON DOMANSKI. 'Three Songs from the Temple' and 'Deadsong' from
Heaven (Toronto: House of Anansi Press, 1978) reprinted by permission. DAVID
DONNELL. All poems reprinted by permission of the author. LOUIS DUDEK.
'The Dead' and 'Coming Suddenly to the Sea' from *Collected Poetry* reprinted by
permission of the author; 'Garcia Lorca' from *East of the City* (The Ryerson Press,
Toronto, 1946), copyright Louis Dudek, reprinted by permission. RONALD
EVERSON. All poems reprinted by permission of the author. DOUG FETHER-
LING. All poems reprinted by permission of the author. ROBERT FINCH. 'Last
Visit' and 'Silverthorn Bush' from *Silverthorn Bush & Other Poems* by Robert Finch,
reprinted by permission of Macmillan of Canada, a Division of Gage Publishing
Limited. R.A.D. FORD. 'Twenty Below' from *A Window on the North* by R.A.D.
Ford reprinted by permission of the author; 'Sakhara' and 'Earthquake' from *The
Solitary City* by R.A.D. Ford reprinted by permission of The Canadian Publishers,
McClelland and Stewart Limited, Toronto. GAIL FOX. All poems from *In Search of
Living Things* (Oberon, 1980) reprinted by permission of the author. GARY
GEDDES. All poems reprinted by permission of the author and Talonbooks.
JOHN GLASSCO. All poems reprinted from *Selected Poems* by permission of
Oxford University Press Canada. ARTIE GOLD. All poems from *before Romantic
Words* (Véhicule Press, 1979) reprinted by permission of the author. PHYLLIS
GOTLIEB. All poems reprinted by permission of the author. ELDON GRIER. All
poems from *Selected Poems 1955-1970*, copyright 1971 by Eldon Grier, reprinted by
permission of the author. KRISTJANA GUNNARS. 'wakepick I' and 'changeling
VIII' from *Wake-Pick Poems* (Toronto: House of Anansi Press, 1981) reprinted by
permission. RALPH GUSTAFSON. Reprinted by permission of The Canadian
Publishers, McClelland and Stewart Limited, Toronto: 'Mothy Monologue' and
'Wednesday at North Hatley' from *Corners in the Glass* by Ralph Gustafson; and
'Columbus Reaches Juana, 1492' from *Sift in an Hour Glass* by Ralph Gustafson.
DAVID HELWIG. 'A Dead Weasel', 'For Edward Hicks' by David Helwig are
reprinted from *Figures in a Landscape* by permission of Oberon Press; 'Drunk Poem',
'Considerations', and 'Words from Hell' by David Helwig are reprinted from *The
Best Name of Silence* by permission of Oberon Press. DARYL HINE. 'Fabulary Sat-
ire IV,' 'A Bewilderment at the Entrance of the Fat Boy into Eden,' and 'Point
Grey,' in *Selected Poems* by Daryl Hine (copyright © 1980 Daryl Hine) reprinted
with the permission of Atheneum Publishers. 'Fabulary Satire IV' and 'A Bewilder-
ment at the Entrance of the Fat Boy into Eden,' first published in *The Carnal and the*

Crane, copyright © 1957 Daryl Hine; 'Point Grey,' first published in *Minutes*, copyright © 1968 Daryl Hine. PAULETTE JILES. All poems reprinted by permission of the author. GEORGE JOHNSTON. Reprinted by permission of the author: 'Cathleen Sweeping' from *The Cruising Auk* by George Johnston and 'Veterans' and 'Bliss' from *Home Free* by George Johnston, 'War on the Periphery', reprinted by permission, © 1951, 1979 The New Yorker Magazine, Inc. GEORGE JONAS. All poems reprinted by permission of the author. D.G. JONES. All poems reprinted by permission of the author. LIONEL KEARNS. All poems, from *By the Light of the Silvery McLune*, reprinted by permission of Lionel Kearns. A.M. KLEIN. All poems from *The Collected Poems of A.M. Klein* reprinted by permission of McGraw-Hill Ryerson Limited. RAYMOND KNISTER. All poems from *Collected Poems of Raymond Knister* reprinted by permission of McGraw-Hill Ryerson Limited. ROBERT KROETSCH. 'Stone Hammer Poem' from *Field Notes* by Robert Kroetsch reprinted by permission of General Publishing Co. Limited. PATRICK LANE. All poems reprinted by permission of the author. IRVING LAYTON. All poems from *Collected Poems* by Irving Layton reprinted by permission of The Canadian Publishers, McClelland and Stewart Limited, Toronto. DENNIS LEE. 'From "Civil Elegies" ' by Dennis Lee from *Civil Elegies and Other Poems* (Toronto: House of Anansi Press, 1972) reprinted by permission; 'The Gods' from *The Gods* by Dennis Lee reprinted by permission of The Canadian Publishers, McClelland and Stewart Limited, Toronto. DOUGLAS LePAN. All poems reprinted by permission of the author. CHARLES LILLARD. All poems reprinted by permission of the author. DOROTHY LIVESAY. All poems from *Collected Poems: The Two Seasons* by Dorothy Livesay, reprinted by permission of McGraw-Hill Ryerson Limited. MALCOLM LOWRY. All poems reprinted by permission of Literistic Ltd, © 1962 Margerie Lowry. PAT LOWTHER. All poems from *A Stone Diary* reprinted by permission of Oxford University Press Canada. GWENDOLYN MacEWEN. 'Dark Pines Under Water' 'The Discovery', 'Manzini: Escape Artist', 'A Breakfast for Barbarians', and 'The Thing is Violent' from *Magic Animals: Collected Poems Old and New*, reprinted by permission of Macmillan of Canada, a Division of Gage Publishing Limited; 'The Void' and 'There is No Place to Hide' from *The T.E. Lawrence Poems* (Mosaic Press/Valley Editions, 1982) reprinted by permission. DAVID McFADDEN. Reprinted by permission of The Canadian Publishers, McClelland and Stewart Limited, Toronto: 'House Plants' from *A Knight in Dried Plums* by David McFadden; 'A Form of Passion' from *On the Road Again* by David McFadden; and 'Lennox Island' from *My Body Was Eaten by Dogs* by David McFadden. DON McKAY. All poems reprinted by permission of the author. BARRY McKINNON. All poems reprinted by permission of the author. JAY MACPHERSON. All poems reprinted from *Poems Twice Told* by permission of Oxford University Press Canada. ELI MANDEL. All poems reprinted by permission of the author. DAPHNE MARLATT. All poems reprinted from *Net Work: Selected Writing* (Talonbooks, 1980), edited by Fred Wah, by permission of Daphne Marlatt. ANNE MARRIOTT. All poems from *The Circular Coast: Poems New and Selected* (Mosaic Press/Valley Editions, 1981) reprinted by permission. TOM MARSHALL. All poems are reprinted from *The Elements* by Tom Marshall by permission of Oberon Press. SID MARTY. 'In the Dome Car of the "Canadian" ' from *Nobody Danced With Miss Rodeo* by Sid Marty reprinted by permission of The Canadian Publishers, McClelland and Stewart Limited, Toronto. SEYMOUR MAYNE. By permission of Seymour Mayne: 'Roots' reprinted from *Mouth* (The Quarry Press, 1970); and 'Before Passover' reprinted from *The Impossible Promised Land* (Mosaic Press/Valley Editions, 1981). RONA MURRAY. From *Selected Poems* by Rona Murray reprinted by permission of the author. SUSAN MUSGRAVE. All poems from *A Man to Marry a Man to Bury* by Susan Musgrave reprinted by permission of The Canadian Publishers, McClelland and Stewart Limited, Toronto. JOHN NEWLOVE. Reprinted by permission of The Canadian Publishers, McClelland and Stewart Limited, Toronto: 'America', 'Samuel Hearne in Wintertime', 'What Do You Want?' from *Selected Poems 1962-1972* by John Newlove; and 'The Pride' from *Black Night Window* by John Newlove. bp NICHOL. All poems reprinted by permission of the author. ALDEN NOWLAN. 'The Bull Moose' and 'Beginning' reprinted by permission of the author. 'In the Operating Room', 'Suppose This Moment', and 'For Jean Vincent d'Abbadie' from *Bread Wine and Salt* by Alden Nowlan © 1967 by Clarke, Irwin & Company Limited. Used by permission. MICHAEL ONDAATJE. All poems reprinted by permission of the author: 'The Cinnamon Peeler' from *Running in the Family* (1982) (U.S.A., W.W. Norton & Co; Canada, McClelland and Stewart Limited), © Michael Ondaatje, reprinted by permission. P.K. PAGE. All poems reprinted by permission of the author. E.J. PRATT. All poems reprinted by permission of University of Toronto Press. AL PURDY. 'Remains of an Indian Village' and 'Night Song for a Woman' reprinted by permission of the author; reprinted by permission of The Canadian Publishers, McClelland and Stewart Limited, Toronto: 'The Country North of Belleville', 'Poem', 'Wilderness Gothic', 'The Cariboo Horses' and 'Alive or Not' from *Selected Poems* by Al Purdy; 'The Dead Poet' and 'Spinning' from *The Stone Bird* by Al Purdy. JAMES REANEY. For permission to reprint 'The School Globe', 'The Upper Canadian', 'Granny Crack', and 'The Lost Child', from *Poems*, by James Reaney, copyright Canada 1972, thanks are due to the author; to New Press, Toronto, publisher; and to Sybil Hutchison, literary agent. CHARLES G.D. ROBERTS. All poems reprinted from *Poems* by Charles G.D. Roberts by permission of Lady Joan Roberts. DOROTHY ROBERTS. Reprinted by permission of Dorothy Roberts: 'Cold' from *Twice to Flame* (Ryerson Press, Toronto) and 'Dazzle' from *The Self of Loss* (Fiddlehead Books, University of New Brunswick). T.G. ROBERTS. From *The Lost Shipmate* by T.G. Roberts, reprinted by permission of McGraw-Hill Ryerson Limited. JOE ROSENBLATT. Reprinted by permission of the author: 'Fish', 'Of Dandelions & Tourists', 'The Ant Trap', and 'It's in the Egg' first published in *The Blind Photographer* (Press Porcépic, 1973); 'Cat' and 'Ichthycide' from *Top Soil* (Press Porcépic, 1976). W.W.E. ROSS. All poems reprinted by permission of Academic Press. D.C. SCOTT. The work of Duncan Campbell Scott is reprinted with the permission of John G. Aylen, Ottawa, Canada. F.G. SCOTT. Reprinted by permission of F.R. Scott. F.R. SCOTT. 'Night Club' reprinted by permission of F.R. Scott. All other poems from *Collected Poems* by F.R. Scott reprinted by permission of The Canadian Publishers, McClelland and Stewart Limited, Toronto. ROBERT SERVICE. From *The Collected Poems of Robert Service*, reprinted by permission of McGraw-Hill Ryerson Limited, Dodd, Mead & Company, Inc., and Ernest Benn Ltd. ROBIN SKELTON. All poems from *Timelight* by Robin Skelton reprinted by permission of The Canadian Publishers, McClelland and Stewart Limited, Toronto. A.J.M. SMITH. 'The Common Man' and 'The Dead' reprinted by permission of William Toye. 'The Resurrection of Arp' and 'The Lonely Land' from *The Classic Shade* by A.J.M. Smith reprinted by permission of The Canadian Publishers, McClelland and Stewart Limited, Toronto. RAYMOND SOUSTER. All poems are reprinted from *Collected Poems of Raymond Souster, Volume 3* by permission of Oberon Press. FRANCIS SPARSHOTT. All poems reprinted by permission of the author. ANDREW SUKNASKI. Reprinted by permission of Andrew Suknaski: 'Chinese Camp, Kamloops (circa 1883)' from *The Ghosts Call You Poor* (copyright 1978) and 'The Snake' from

Wood Mountain Poems (copyright 1976). ANNE SZUMIGALSKI. By permission of the author and publisher: 'A Midwife's Story: Two' and 'Angels' first appeared in *A Game of Angels* (Turnstone Press, 1980); 'Visitors' Parking' first appeared in *Woman Reading in Bath* (Doubleday 1974). SHARON THESEN. All poems reprinted by permission of the author. COLLEEN THIBAUDEAU. All poems reprinted by permission of the author. JOHN THOMPSON. Reprinted by permission: 'The Onion', 'The Bread Hot from the Oven' from *At the Edge of the Chopping There Are No Secrets* (Toronto: House of Anansi Press, 1973); 'Now you have burned . . .' from *Stilt Jack* (Toronto: House of Anansi Press, 1978). PETER VAN TOORN. All poems from *Mountain Tea* by permission of the author. MIRIAM WADDING-TON. 'Ten Years and More' © Miriam Waddington from *The Price of Gold* (Oxford University Press, 1976) reprinted by permission; all other poems reprinted from *Driving Home* by Miriam Waddington by permission of Oxford University Press Canada. FRED WAH. 'Breathe dust . . .' from *Breathin' My Name with a Sigh* (Talonbooks, 1981). BERTRAM WARR. From *Acknowledgement to Life: The Collected Poems of Bertram Warr*, reprinted by permission of McGraw–Hill Ryerson Limited. WILFRED WATSON. Reprinted by permission of Faber and Faber Ltd. from *Friday's Child* by Wilfred Watson. TOM WAYMAN. Reprinted by permission of Macmillan of Canada, a Division of Gage Publishing Limited: 'Another Poem About the Madness of Women' from *Free Time: Industrial Poems* by Tom Wayman and 'The Chilean Elegies: 5. The Interior' from *Money and Rain: Tom Wayman Live*; 'Wayman in Love' from *Wayman in Love* by Tom Wayman is reprinted by permission of The Canadian Publishers, McClelland and Stewart Limited, Toronto. PHYLLIS WEBB. All poems reprinted by permission of the author. ANNE WIL-KINSON. All poems from *Collected Poems of Anne Wilkinson* by Anne Wilkinson are reprinted by permission of Macmillan of Canada, a Division of Gage Publishing Limited. GEORGE WOODCOCK. All poems reprinted by permission of the author. J. MICHAEL YATES. From *The Great Bear Lake Meditations* (Oberon, 1970) and *Nothing Speaks for the Blue Moraines* (Sono Nis Press, 1973) reprinted by permission of the author. DALE ZIEROTH. Reprinted by permission: 'Baptism' from *Mid-River* (Toronto: House of Anansi Press, 1981); 'The Hunter of the Deer' and 'Beautiful Woman' from *Clearing: Poems From a Journey* (Toronto: House of Anansi Press, 1973).

There are a few poems whose copyright owners have not been located after diligent inquiry. The publishers would be grateful for information enabling them to make suitable acknowledgements in future printings.

INTRODUCTION

I

I first came to Canadian poetry through two collections edited by A.J.M. Smith: the third edition of his *Book of Canadian Poetry* (1957) and *The Oxford Book of Canadian Verse* (1960). At that time I was an extremely young poet, and Smith's books were for me the first indication that there was anything resembling a Canadian tradition in poetry, not to mention the fact that there were living as well as dead practitioners of it. Thus, some twenty years later, I undertook the editing of *The New Oxford Book of Canadian Verse in English* both with the sense of making a personal memorial tribute to someone who had contributed greatly to my education as a poet, and, I hope, with the same sense of cultural mission that Smith himself pursued through his tireless collecting and elucidating. All cultures are, to some extent, retrospective: we see where we are and where we're going partly by where we've been, and an anthology such as this one is not only gathered from the past but aimed towards the future. Furthermore, as a Canadian born in 1939 I had 'In Flanders Fields' hammered into my head at an early age, and will doubtless never be able to shake the notion that what one properly does with torches is to hold them high: otherwise you get haunted. Consider what follows, then, as the propitiation of both a collective ancestral ghost, and of the individual spirit of a sage and generous man.

Smith's book was more ambitious in scope than the present volume, since it was a survey of poetry in French as well as in English. The yeast-like growth of poetry in both languages since 1960 has meant that considerations of length, as well as the ignorance of the present editor, have limited this collection to poetry in English only. This in no way denies the existence or worth of the poetry that has been written in languages other than English, including native languages, as well as many European and Asian ones. The title of this book indicates its scope: its contents record the collision between a particular language and a certain environment, each of which has affected the other.

It would be well to say, at the outset, that this anthology is not fully representative formally. While I have not hesitated to include examples of the prose poem, leaving it to theorists to define the borders, sound poetry, performance poetry, and concrete poetry— all of which have flourished in the past fifteen years—could not by their nature be well represented here. Similarly the increasingly popular book-length poem—the journal-entry sequence, the docu- drama poem that mixes lyrics with factual accounts, the radio poem-for-voices, in fact any long poem whose segments depend for their effect on their position within a book-length whole—was excluded to avoid chopping it up for the purposes of this anthol- ogy, exceptions being made for extracts from book-length poems by some Victorian poets and for E.J. Pratt. Certain long poems, such as Earle Birney's *David* and John Newlove's *The Pride,* have been included whole.

I am aware that 'regional' has changed in recent years from a bad word to a good word, in Canada at any rate, and I have attempted to behave accordingly. But regional representation was not a deter- minant when the chips were down. In other words I feel that the poems in this book are here not because they are regional but be- cause they are readable, and more than that. Luckily, good poets have shown a tendency to live in places other than Toronto, thus enabling me to satisfy the head-counters without having to com- promise the principles of selection.

In addition to its other internal deficiencies, this collection does not claim to represent the cutting edge. Being in the Oxford an- thology is like getting your baby boots bronzed: the aim is durabil- ity. This may explain why established poets are not always repre- sented by their most recent work: I would have had to leave out earlier poems that have already, to some extent, entered the canon. For this reason too the reader acquainted with Canadian poetry may come across more than one poem he has read before. Old chestnuts are old chestnuts because they have survived the other chestnuts, and there's usually good reason for that. I have followed Smith's example in including some poets of recent germination, not just because they are recent but because—based on their accom- plishments so far—I'm putting my money on them as probable chestnut-producers of the future. But the list is by no means com- plete: an anthology of the 100 most promising Canadian poets would have been a different kind of book.

While on this ticklish subject, let me say a word about sex. It is an indication of one of the major changes that have taken place be- tween 1960 and 1982 that I feel compelled to do so. A.J.M. Smith felt no such necessity: when commenting on the woman poets in his anthology he made no overt distinctions, nor did he note their relative scarcity. Woman poets were included as poets, not as woman poets.

We are now more conscious and less innocent. However, despite gains made elsewhere, this book does not contain an equal number of male and female poets. One reading of this might be that men dominate poetry publishing and tend to exclude women; another that my taste is skewed by prevailing male critical standards. My own view is that there are more male poets in this book because there are more in Canada. There is no reason why equality should be present in the field of poetry when it is absent everywhere else. *Why* there are more male poets is a matter for fascinating speculation. (In Canadian fiction, for instance, there is more balance.) My guess is that the process starts long before any poet gets to the point of submitting to a little magazine, and has something to do with that unfortunate term 'socialization'.

There is another view of this question, however, and it's usually put forward by observers from outside the country. I have been asked, many times, why there are so many good woman poets in Canada. Whether the glass is two-thirds empty or a third full depends on how thirsty you are, and it is possible to see woman poets in Canada not in terms of their scantiness but in terms of their relative prominence and excellence. In the nineteenth century a woman Canadian poet was the equivalent, say, of a white Anglo-Saxon Protestant Innuit shaman—yet we have several of them. Some might explain the presence of female achievement in discriminatory periods as tokenism. But it would be a vast and inaccurate insult to claim that twentieth-century poets of the calibre of P.K. Page, Margaret Avison, Phyllis Webb, Dorothy Livesay, Miriam Waddington, Elizabeth Brewster, Phyllis Gotlieb, and Jay Macpherson made it into print as part of somebody's quota. The truth appears to be that, although Canada was and is no Utopia for women, it has historically and for mysterious reasons favoured the production of good women poets to a greater extent than have England, the United States, or Australia. The reader of this anthology, however, may rest assured: no poet has been excluded because he is male.

II

Editing an anthology of poetry in a relatively new country such as Canada or Australia presents problems quite different in kind from those involved in compiling a similar volume in, say, England or France. Time itself, in the older countries, has been the great anthologizer. Originally 'anthology' meant a collection of the flowers of verse; and when the sorting process has been long at work, there is little dispute about which are the flowers and which the weeds until one reaches the present century. Canadian poetry, however, is a different kind of organism. There are 120 poets represented in this book; 88 are living, of whom 65 have been added since Smith's collection of 1960. Considered as a plant, the creature is clearly top-heavy.

One cannot have flowers without roots. New cultures—made uneasy, perhaps, by their sensed absence of substructures—are constantly grubbing around in the soil. In English-Canadian poetry, geology and archeology are far more dominant as motifs than is botany: the images of permafrost and granite bedrock, blizzard, mountain, and glacier are repeatedly set against the state of being human and made to take its measure. Perhaps Canada should abandon the term 'anthology' altogether and adopt another, signifying 'a collection of rocks, roots, pottery shards and skull fragments'. Like the poetry of Al Purdy, which in so many ways epitomizes it, English-Canadian poetry has been very fond of digging things up.

III

The present editor might be accused of a similar excavationism for her decision to include some of the material at the beginning of this book. The poems by Hayman, Stansbury, O'Grady, Goldsmith, and McLachlan, however, are presented with as much delight as one would take in presenting, for instance, the Norse inscription found recently at a copper mine north of Lake Superior. These poets are important not for their elegance or originality but because they were there, they were there first, and they said something. There is no more need to apologize for their presence than there would be for beginning a survey of American poetry with Anne Bradstreet. We read them as we would read travel writers, for their reports of a strange country that later became our own.

English Canada was settled by displaced persons who brought their language and their preconceptions with them. Not surprisingly, the poetry they wrote does not differ formally from that of the times in which they wrote. Poetry is a form of human speech and it is used to express, among other things, sentiments that the writer considers appropriate to the occasion. Apart from Hayman—who seems to have liked Newfoundland, not so much for itself but as a contrast to England—these poets, very early on, sound two notes that have sunk deeply into the Canadian poetic tradition:

the elegaic, a mourning of homes left and things lost; and the satiric, a bitter account of dismal surroundings, both social and geographical. It should be remembered that English Canada was settled later than either French Canada or New England. No religious mission inspired the emigrants: they did not seek to convert the heathen to the greater glory of God, or to found a model 'city upon a hill'. Most left New England because they were expelled, or Britain because they were poor and hoped to better themselves. What Canada had to offer was seen, when anything was seen at all, not as the kingdom of God upon earth but as a chance at economic independence and pastoral domestic tranquillity, as evidenced by Goldsmith's *Rising Village*. From this perspective anything that interfered with the reproduction of a European tamed nature was best got rid of: hence the savage tribes and gloomy shades. McLachlan's noteworthy and false assertion that Canadian birds don't sing is more a product of culture shock than of direct observation; and his account of being lost in a forest that has no directions, no paths, and no landmarks contains a theme that continues to surface much later.

Those who do not like Victorian poetry will not like Canadian Victorian poetry any better; but those prepared to accept its conventions may find much to interest them. Through it they may observe a culture in the process of establishing and defining itself, assimilating a landscape that at first seems alien to it. Ontogeny repeats phylogeny: it appears to be an ordeal that each Canadian poet, perhaps each poet, undergoes individually, this grappling with the world as given. In Canada the given has not always been immediately perceived as friendly, which may have something to do with the weather. Though the angel that must be wrestled to the ground is huge, cold, and forbidding, our poets have sometimes recognized it as angel nonetheless.

The early- and middle-Victorian periods produced some oddities, but no Tennysons or even Longfellows. I have ducked Charles Heavysege's ungainly though remarkable verse drama *Saul,* which, if it is to be savoured at all, is best swallowed whole. Although I agree that its appearance in the Canada of 1857 was unexpected, I could not find an excerpt that suitably conveyed its peculiar flavour. Charles Sangster's botanical river trip of 1856 is noteworthy for its absence of gnomes, prefiguring Earle Birney on ghosts. Much more substantial, I believe, is Charles Mair, whose verse-drama *Tecumseh* (1886) demonstrates how early the Canadian imagination sought to mythologize the native Indian, an enterprise that is still being carried forward with alacrity. By 'mythologize' I do not mean 'falsify': Canadian poets, perhaps even more than American poets, have long been obsessed with the shape and inner meaning of the collision between the transplanted and the aboriginal, and by the quest for a spiritual structure that is authentic, indigenous, and accessible to them. This is a quest, and an obsession, that each generation of poets has come to anew—as anyone comparing the work of, for instance, Mair and Crawford, A.M. Klein and Douglas LePan, Al Purdy and John Newlove will quickly discover. Mair's 'The Last Bison' is an early example of the ubiquitous Canadian dying animal, as well as being almost startlingly proleptic: the sentiments, if not the form, could have come straight from the ecology movement of the 1970s and 1980s, and there is a good deal more to it than Wordsworthian sentimentality.

Isabella Valancy Crawford lived a short and obscure life, during which she nonetheless managed to produce a body of work of considerable distinction. At the time she was accused of being too masculine, no doubt because of the vigour with which she executed her narratives, which often included violent deaths of one kind or another. *Malcolm's Katie* (1884) is considered to be her most fully achieved poem, but it is best read whole. The shorter poems here included well illustrate what Smith calls her 'geographical animism'. In Crawford's world everything is alive, everything is sentient, everything has a shape that can be imaginatively comprehended.

Canada became a nation in 1867, and several poets born in the 1860s later became known as the Confederation poets. Although they were impelled partly by the desire for self-definition and partly by the somewhat ersatz national pride that political event gave rise to, their best poetry is rarely political. Rather it is carefully observed and technically accomplished lyric poetry focused chiefly on nature. Though these poets—Charles G.D. Roberts, Bliss Carman, Archibald Lampman, Wilfred Campbell, and Duncan Campbell Scott—are usually clumped together, within their convention they are quite different in tone. Roberts, who is also known for his fictional studies of wild animals, is a meditative *genre* realist; while Carman (who was, incidentally, a favourite poet of the younger Ezra Pound, which casts a new light on Pound) keeps wandering off into a rather vaporous transcendentalism. 'Low Tide on Grand Pré' is by all odds Carman's most successful poem. Lampman, in the intensity with which he regards his subject and his almost hallucinatory focus on detail, achieves in poems like 'Heat' a kind of Zen celebration of the thing itself and the loss of self. His 'The City of the End of Things' is reminiscent of Poe rather than Matthew Arnold and Keats; it is one of his best-known poems, though not characteristic. Wilfred Campbell is of interest only for his winter lake poems, which have a force and ferocity not matched by the rest of his verse. This editor has a sneaking preference for Duncan Campbell Scott. Although I recognize that the other poets are lusher and more graceful, Scott's condensed tragedies have a starkness and a moral jaggedness that evoke darkness rather than the lights and half-lights of Lampman.

This group of poets wielded considerable influence over their successors. Though none duplicated their achievement, some are worth mentioning; most notably Theodore Goodridge Roberts, who stuck with nature, and Marjorie Pickthall, who diverged into faith.

Critics in the immediate postwar years, nervous about 'modernity' and whether Canadian poetry qualified for it, tended to prefer the values we associate with short lyric poetry: noun-and-adjective accurate description, formal elegance and verbal felicity, objects in space, cosmopolitan sensibility, mythological references that are 'universal'—that is, Greek or biblical. To lean too far in this direction, however, is to downgrade or overlook entirely a strain in Canadian poetry that has been and still is very much present: the tug towards the narrative and the anecdotal, the tall tale, the kitchen-table yarn, which is also a pull in the direction of historical and local incident, vernacular speech, movement in time, and verb-and-adjective action. Many nineteenth-century writers in English, of course, wrote narrative poetry; but Canadian poets have continued to do it. Even the writers of short lyrics have shown a marked tendency to string poems together along a narrative line, as witness such recent books as Michael Ondaatje's *Billy the Kid,* Gwendolyn MacEwen's *The T.E. Lawrence Poems,* and Jay Macpherson's *The Boatman,* to name a few of many.

If the reader can be brought to indulge this view, he may not be too traumatized by my inclusion of three poets whom it has been customary to dismiss as not 'serious', although they used to be regulars in public-school readers: William Henry Drummond, Pauline Johnson, and Robert W. Service. It is true that all three contain a good deal of blood and thunder on the one hand and sentimentality and kitsch on the other. But Pauline Johnson, usually known only for such familiars as 'The Song My Paddle Sings', turns out to have been a poet of considerably more sophistication, despite her habit of dressing up in costumes and chanting in public. (Could she, by any remote possibility, be the poetic ancestor of bill bissett and The Four Horsemen?) I include one hair-raiser by Johnson about rape and murder, and one nature poem that is by no means inferior to much work of the Confederation group, just to show she can do it. Drummond, associated with saccharine favourites such as 'Leetle Bateese', also deserves re-evaluation. In view of much poetry written today, one cannot fault him for the use of dialect, which is surely only the vernacular taken to extremes. His work is filled with creepy tales, heroic episodes, and a good deal of satire—most of it directed at 'the English' as seen by the Québec *habitant*. Robert Service remains the best-known of the three, and no Canadian anthology can afford to be without him. Though he began very early to imitate himself, his tenderfoot-in-the-north is a myth of enduring vitality. The work of all three poets stems from the traditional ballad—which was oral, rhythmic, performance-oriented, and vivid, and dealt with cognate themes.

IV

I have slyly inserted my account of these three poets just before the section on E.J. Pratt, who was a narrative poet *par excellence* as well as being a poet who is both completely unique and ferociously representative, not so much of other poets as of the country he was writing about and within. There are equally good arguments for presenting him as the first of the moderns or the last of the Victorians. But he is actually a creature unto himself, a craggy original. At a time when modern poetry was heading towards the fragmentary, the discontinuous, the syncopated, Pratt wrote sustained narratives. At a time when free verse was coming in, he stuck to metrics. His poems have been called miniature epics—and 'epic' is not out of place: like the *Iliad* and the *Odyssey,* his long narrative poems present groups of men engaged in strife, overshadowed by fate-controlling powers—although, typically, Pratt does not single out any one of his men as heroes. The group itself is the hero. The enemy is usually nature in its monolithic, sinister, or unfeeling anti-human aspect. The iceberg in *The Titanic,* the Pre-Cambrian Shield in *Towards the Last Spike,* the storm in *The Roosevelt and the Antinoë,* and, more unfortunately, the torturing Indians in *Brébeuf and His Brethren* all present overwhelming obstacles against which the human spirit pits itself and wins, though sometimes only in spirit.

In addition to Pratt the twenties saw the beginnings of the modern movement in Canadian poetry, which was influenced by modernism everywhere but took its own directions. F.R. Scott, A.M. Klein, and A.J.M. Smith began publishing in Montreal; Dorothy Livesay first appeared as a young imagist. The connection of the birth of Imagism with T.E. Hulme's cross-Canada train journey, and his feeling that conventional diction was not equal to the starkness of the landscape he observed, is well known. This push towards stripped-down diction fed back into Canada through the poetry of W.W.E. Ross and Raymond Knister.

From 1930 onwards it is difficult to confine poets to any neat time slots. Many of them remain stubbornly alive, inconveniently turning out new work, defying well-meaning critical efforts to jam them into such pigeon-holes as 'thirties poet' or 'forties poet'. The story becomes like the pig in *Alice:* double it up in one place, it sticks out somewhere else. Suffice it to say that the Depression of the thirties knocked the props out from under publishing in Canada, so that some poets who ought to have been thirties poets couldn't publish until the forties. But does that make them forties poets? Some poets did manage to be thirties poets: Dorothy Livesay wrote much political poetry then; Anne Marriott's *The Wind Our Enemy* epitomizes the dustbowl Prairies; Earle Birney broke the surface then. But such diverse talents—talents that have continued to exfoliate through the decades—cannot be categorized according to period.

In the forties and fifties there was an astonishing outburst of poetic activity that, unfortunately, was not matched by a corresponding increase in readership. Earlier poets, such as Charles G.D. Roberts and Pauline Johnson, had had what used to be known as a 'public', but the modern movement took some time to build a following—especially in Canada, where puritanism and the colonial worship of imports still restricted taste. Poets were known to each other and to a small audience through such magazines as *Preview,* John Sutherland's *First Statement* and *Northern Review*, and Alan Crawley's *Contemporary Verse*; but the position of the poet in Canada in the forties was not far removed from that of the lonely, obsessive figure—the voice with no hearer—portrayed in A.M. Klein's brilliant poem 'Portrait of the Poet as Landscape'. Nevertheless, the poets continued to appear: Klein himself, whose output, though not large, was powerful and evocative; P.K. Page, who was and remains both a dazzling technician and a tranced observer who verges on mysticism; Earle Birney, with his astonishing range, deeply felt humanism, and continued vitality; Patrick Anderson, Louis Dudek, Douglas LePan, Miriam Waddington, Raymond Souster, and James Reaney, with his first inimitable primitives. In the mid-fifties Irving Layton published his first truly important books, and very quickly established the basis for a body of work, which, in exuberance of spirit, vigour of imagery, a sexuality unprecedented in Canadian poetry, and a quality Hazlitt would have called *gusto,* has not yet been surpassed. Jay Macpherson's *The Boatman* appeared in the fifties, as did Daryl Hine's remarkable *The Carnal and the Crane,* Doug Jones's crafted and resonant plainsongs in *Frost on the Sun;* first books by Eli Mandel, Anne Wilkinson, and George Johnston; and, at the end of the decade, the unique and intricate metaphysics of Margaret Avison in *Winter Sun.* A.J.M. Smith, concluding his summary in 1960, wrote: 'It is the fusion of the modern world with the archetypal patterns of myth and psychology rather than with Christianity or patriotism that gives a characteristic cosmopolitan flavour to much of the poetry of the fifties in Canada,' a flavour that he called 'complex, divided, erudite, allusive and sometimes obscure.' The classic period in Canadian poetry is always the one just before your own; and this, for me, is the age that only the usual Canadian cautiousness and dislike of hyperbole prevents me from calling golden.

V

Much has been written about the Canadian cultural 'renaissance' that took place in the sixties. This was not a creation *ex nihilo*: as we have seen, there was by 1960 already a considerable body of Canadian poetry. But something happened in the ten years between 1960 and 1970 that changed the poetic climate. What was it?

Very briefly stated, the audience available to a poet increased at an unprecedented rate, and there was a corresponding increase in the numbers of books published, the average sale, the numbers of poetry magazines, and the numbers of aspiring and actual poets. If a similar thing had happened to a population of lemmings, the reason for it would be easier to discover. Several theories have been advanced for the amoebae-in-the-petrie-dish behaviour of poetry in the sixties; all are valid, none singly suffices.

One might place the beginnings of this phenomenon in the fifties, with its coffee-house readings, which made it possible for the poet to become a public performer and persona once more. With the advent of Irving Layton, who appeared on the scene like a brightly coloured frangipani, poetry stepped out from between its hard covers and became incarnate. Whatever else his sometimes scandalized audience thought of Layton, he was hard to ignore, and so was Leonard Cohen, who followed shortly after. It was no longer necessary for the poet to shine, like A.M. Klein's poet, 'in secret. At the bottom of the sea.'

This was a general Western development, but in Canada it took an odd turn: poetry became, for a decade and partly by default, the predominant literary form in Canada. In the relative absence of novels and theatre, it was the one medium in which a newly self-aware Canadian readership could see itself reflected. Not surprisingly, the publishing houses that burgeoned in the sixties—Coach House Press, House of Anansi, Talonbooks, and Oberon—all began largely with poetry, and came to prose fiction only later.

Then there was 'cultural nationalism', variously interpreted and unevenly understood. Simply put, cultural nationalism was merely a determination on the part of writers to stay in their own country instead of moving to New York or London, and to write about what they knew and saw around them, which is only what writers everywhere have always done. But English Canada at that time felt so overshadowed by England and the States that there seemed to be something revolutionary in this stance; and, judging from the opposition it encountered, there was. In any case the movement generated much self-examination and a great deal of poetic and publishing activity until it felt it had made its point. (The most cogent embodiment of this self-scrutiny is Dennis Lee's long series of poems, 'Civil Elegies'.) Just slightly earlier, the poet's problem had been how to write at all, how to break silence, in a country as devoid of support for such an activity as Canada was then. Now the problem was how to put those two terms, 'Canada' and 'Poetry', together. It was the old problem, but in a new and more political phase.

This was not the only form of exploration generated by the sixties. In some quarters there was a shift away from the sophisticated cosmopolitanism favoured by Smith towards indigenous myth, exploration of landscape, map-making and naming of the country, and the rediscovery of history. The giant figure in this area is Al Purdy, who, like Pratt, is ruggedly unfashionable and altogether his own voice. He blends the cadences of real speech and a gangly eloquence in, typically, elegiac poems that place the human figure like a tiny dot at the intersection of geological time and astronomical space and yet manage to assert its importance.

There was also a remarkable and various amount of linguistic experiment in the sixties. On the West Coast a group of young poets—which included George Bowering, Frank Davey, and Daphne Marlatt—crystallized around the teacher Warren Tallman and the magazine *Tish*. At that time they were interested, as many such groups had been before them, in stripping poetry of what they saw as conventional rhetoric and getting down to the real image. They have since gone in many directions, but their interest in language remains. Akin to them, in Ontario, experimentalists such as bp Nichol, Joe Rosenblatt, David McFadden, and Victor Coleman were gathering around the Coach House Press. Apart from linguistic innovators there were poets who belonged to no particular group but were simply very talented: Gwen MacEwen, John Newlove, Patrick Lane, and bill bissett, for instance. Michael Ondaatje evades categorization, but his exotic imagery and violent mini-plots have gained him a reputation as one of the most vital and inventive of the younger poets.

The seventies were the sixties until 1975, and in some sense they still are, except that the rebels have become the establishment, as often happens. The younger poets represented here do not belong to any group or movement, nor do they show any signs of forming one. The breakthroughs of one age become the conventions of the next; and, in general, new poets show a tendency to move away from both linguistic experiment and political statement, towards the single-person lyric of sensibility or, as in the case of Robert Bringhurst, towards the adoption of personae, biblical and otherwise. In approach they range all the way from the condensed surrealism of Christopher Dewdney, through the fancy footwork of Peter van Toorn, to the exuberance and splatter-gun inventiveness of Pier Giorgio di Cicco, to the mordant lyricism of Marilyn Bowering and Susan Musgrave and the plangent minor-key fingering of Roo Borson. There is a renewed interest among many of them in the intricacies of rhetoric, and an emphasis on the poem as consciously crafted. None of them is like any of the others, which is an indication of the variety and energy still being generated by the writing of poetry in Canada.

VI

Until very recently it was considered mandatory to introduce any collection of Canadian poetry with some variant of the Canada-come-of-age motif: a claim that, after decades of having been provincial and inconsequential, Canadian poetry, like Canadian statesmanship or something of the sort, was finally becoming 'international' and taking its rightful place among the great. I am going to dispense with this, just as I am forgoing the usual apology for 'eclecticism'. So far as I can see, Canadian poetry is now neither more nor less 'international' than the poetries of other countries, nor is it more eclectic, eclecticism having become the order of the day. Of all the art forms, poetry—rooted as it is in the inescapably concrete, both in image and in verbal usage—is the least easily translatable from place to place as well as from language to language. Even so, Canadian poetry *is* achieving an international audience—ironically, just after a decade during which it appeared to have turned its back on the desire to do so.

Nor is it necessary any longer to conclude with the promising-beginning or threshold-of-the-future speech. Canadian poetry must now be judged by achievement; it does not need to be criticized for not being like other poetries. It is not American or English poetry *manqué* but a unique organism: spiky, tough, flexible, various, and vital. Finally, it is its own.

M.A.
1982

EDITOR'S ACKNOWLEDGEMENTS

My primary acknowledgement is to A.J.M. Smith, who edited the second *Oxford Book of Canadian Verse*. When covering once more the ground that he had covered before me I found, time after time, that he had chosen what I myself would have chosen. I had no qualms about repeating such choices, since, especially in the case of the early verse, they were often not only the best ones but the only ones possible. His thoroughness, taste, and persistence were at all times an encouragement to me.

I would not have been able to complete this task without the kind assistance of several people. Foremost among these is William Toye of Oxford University Press, who thought up the idea, twisted my arm, and acted as co-reader and consultant throughout. He has also been kind enough to choose the selections from my own work. David Staines made useful suggestions early in the process. Dennis Lee was his invaluable self: without his advice, especially about the most recent poetry, I would have been even more bewildered by choice and overwhelmed by sheer volume than I was. Ann Wilson, my editorial assistant, was indispensable. She located books obscure and otherwise, carted them through the snow and sleet, and helped me sift. Graeme Gibson did not prepare the index, but he did put up with a year's worth of obsessional behaviour. On my shoulders alone, however, rest the flaws in judgement, responsibilities for compromises, and weaknesses of intellect with which all anthologists are quite rightly credited.

M.A.

xl

THE NEW
Oxford Book
of Canadian Verse
IN ENGLISH

[*The Pleasant Life in Newfoundland*]

To the Worshipful Captaine John Mason *who did wisely and worthily
governe there divers yeeres*

The Aire in Newfoundland-land is wholesome, good;
The Fire, as sweet as any made of wood;
The Waters, very rich, both salt and fresh;
The Earth more rich, you know it is no lesse.
Where all are good, *Fire, Water, Earth, and Aire,*
What man made of these foure would not live there?

*To all those worthy Women, who have any desire to live in Newfound-Land,
specially to the modest & discreet Gentlewoman Mistris* Mason, *wife to Captaine* Mason,
who lived there divers yeeres.

Sweet Creatures, did you truely understand
The pleasant life you'd live in *Newfound-land,*
You would with *teares* desire to be brought thither:

I wish you, when you goe, faire wind, faire weather:
For if you with the passage can dispence,
When you are there, I know you'll ne'r come thence.

*To a worthy Friend, who often objects the coldnesse of the Winter in Newfound-Land,
and may serve for all those who have the like conceit.*

You say that you would live in Newfound-land,
Did not this one thing your conceit withstand;
You feare the *Winters* cold, sharp, piercing ayre.
They love it best, that have once wintered there.
Winter is there, short, wholesome, constant, cleare,
Not thicke, unwholesome, shuffling, as 'tis here.

Although in cloathes, company, buildings faire,
With England, New-found-land cannot compare:
Did some know what contentment I found there,
Alwayes enough, most times somewhat to spare,
With little paines, lesse toyle, and lesser care,
Exempt from taxings, il newes, Lawing, feare,
If cleane, and warme, no matter what you weare,
Healthy, and wealthy, if men carefull are,
With much—much more, then I will now declare,
(I say) if some wise men knew what this were,
(I doe beleeve) they'd live no other where.

1628

JOSEPH
STANSBURY

1742?–1809

To Cordelia

Believe me, Love, this vagrant life
    O'er Nova Scotia's wilds to roam,
While far from children, friends, or wife,
    Or place that I can call a home
Delights not me;—another way
My treasures, pleasures, wishes lay.

In piercing, wet, and wintry skies,
    Where man would seem in vain to toil,
I see, where'er I turn my eyes,
    Luxuriant pasture, trees and soil.
Uncharm'd I see:—another way
My fondest hopes and wishes lay.

Oh could I through the future see
    Enough to form a settled plan,
To feed my infant train and thee
    And fill the rank and style of man:
I'd cheerful be the livelong day;
Since all my wishes point that way.

2

But when I see a sordid shed
    Of birchen bark, procured with care,
Design'd to shield the aged head
    Which British mercy placed there—
'Tis too, too much: I cannot stay,
But turn with streaming eyes away.

JOSEPH
STANSBURY

Oh! how your heart would bleed to view
    Six pretty prattlers like your own,
Expos'd to every wind that blew;
    Condemn'd in such a hut to moan.
Could this be borne, Cordelia, say?
Contented in your cottage stay.

'Tis true, that in this climate rude,
    The mind resolv'd may happy be;
And may, with toil and solitude,
    Live independent and be free.
So the lone hermit yields to slow decay:
Unfriended lives—unheeded glides away.

If so far humbled that no pride remains,
    But moot indifference which way flows the stream;
Resign'd to penury, its cares and pains;
    And hope has left you like a painted dream;
Then here, Cordelia, bend your pensive way,
And close the evening of Life's wretched day.

    1784?

STANDISH
O'GRADY

1793-1841

From THE EMIGRANT

[*Winter in Lower Canada*]

Thou barren waste; unprofitable strand,
Where hemlocks brood on unproductive land,
Whose frozen air on one bleak winter's night
Can metamorphose *dark brown hares to white!*

3

Here forests crowd, unprofitable lumber,
O'er fruitless lands indefinite as number;
Where birds scarce light, and with the north winds veer
On wings of wind, and quickly disappear,
Here the rough Bear subsists his winter year,
And licks his paw and finds *no better fare*. . . .

One month we hear birds, shrill and loud and harsh,
The plaintive bittern sounding from the marsh;
The next we see the fleet-winged swallow,
The duck, the woodcock, and the ice-birds follow;
Then comes, drear clime, the lakes all stagnant grow,
And the wild wilderness is rapt in snow.

The lank Canadian eager trims his fire,
And all around their simpering stoves retire;
With fur clad friends their progenies abound,
And thus regale their buffaloes around;
Unlettered race, how few the number tells,
Their only pride a *cariole and bells!*
To mirth or mourning, thus by folly led,
To mix in pleasure or to chaunt the dead!
To seek the chapel prostrate to adore,
Or leave their fathers' coffins at the door!
Perchance they revel; still around they creep,
And talk, and smoke, and spit, and drink, and sleep!
                    .   .   .

With sanguine sash and eke with Indian's mogs,
Let Frenchmen feed on fricassees or frogs;
Brave Greenland winters, seven long months to freeze,
With naught of verdure save their Greenland trees;
Bright veiled amid the drap'ry of night,
In ice-wrought tapestry of gorgeous white,
No matter here in this sad soil who delves;
Still leave their *lower province* to themselves.
Let patriots flourish, other deeds displace,
Let adverse men new politics embrace;
Yet come it will when wisdom may control,
And one sound policy conduct the whole.

1841

OLIVER
GOLDSMITH

1794-1861

From THE RISING VILLAGE

[*The Lonely Settler*]

What noble courage must their hearts have fired,
How great the ardour which their souls inspired,
Who leaving far behind their native plain,
Have sought a home beyond the Western main;
And braved the perils of the stormy seas,
In search of wealth, of freedom, and of ease!
Oh! none can tell but they who sadly share
The bosom's anguish, and its wild despair,
What dire distress awaits the hardy bands,
That venture first on bleak and desert lands.
How great the pain, the danger, and the toil,
Which mark the first rude culture of the soil.
When, looking round, the lonely settler sees
His home amid a wilderness of trees:
How sinks his heart in those deep solitudes,
Where not a voice upon his ear intrudes;
Where solemn silence all the waste pervades,
Heightening the horror of its gloomy shades;
Save where the sturdy woodman's strokes resound,
That strew the fallen forest on the ground.
See! from their heights the lofty pines descend,
And crackling, down their pondrous lengths extend.
Soon from their boughs the curling flames arise,
Mount into air, and redden all the skies;
And where the forest once its foliage spread,
The golden corn triumphant waves its head.
  How blest, did nature's ruggedness appear
The only source of trouble or of fear;
How happy, did no hardship meet his view
No other care his anxious steps pursue;
But, while his labour gains a short repose,
And hope presents a solace for his woes,
New ills arise, new fears his peace annoy,
And other dangers all his hopes destroy.
Behold the savage tribes in wildest strain,

Approach with death and terror in their train;
No longer silence o'er the forest reigns,
No longer stillness now her power retains;
But hideous yells announce the murderous band,
Whose bloody footsteps desolate the land;
He hears them oft in sternest mood maintain,
Their right to rule the mountain and the plain;
He hears them doom the *white man's* instant death,
Shrinks from the sentence, while he gasps for breath,
Then, rousing with one effort all his might,
Darts from his hut, and saves himself by flight.
Yet, what a refuge! Here a host of foes,
On every side, his trembling steps oppose;
Here savage beasts around his cottage howl,
As through the gloomy wood they nightly prowl,
Till morning comes, and then is heard no more
The shouts of man, or beast's appalling roar;
The wandering Indian turns another way,
And brutes avoid the first approach of day.
  Yet, tho' these threat'ning dangers round him roll,
Perplex his thoughts, and agitate his soul,
By patient firmness and industrious toil,
He still retains possession of the soil;
Around his dwelling scattered huts extend,
Whilst every hut affords another friend.
And now, behold! his bold aggressors fly,
To seek their prey beneath some other sky;
Resign the haunts they can maintain no more,
And safety in far distant wilds explore.
His perils vanished, and his fears o'ercome,
Sweet hope portrays a happy peaceful home.
On every side fair prospects charm his eyes,
And future joys in every thought arise.
His humble cot, built from the neighbouring trees,
Affords protection from each chilling breeze;
His rising crops, with rich luxuriance crowned,
In waving softness shed their freshness round;
By nature nourished, by her bounty blest,
He looks to Heaven, and lulls his cares to rest.

1825

1816-1876

[*The Winter Galaxy*]

The stars are glittering in the frosty sky,
Frequent as pebbles on a broad sea-coast;
And o'er the vault the cloud-like galaxy
Has marshalled its innumerable host.
Alive all heaven seems! with wondrous glow
Tenfold refulgent every star appears,
As if some wide, celestial gale did blow,
And thrice illume the ever-kindled spheres.
Orbs, with glad orbs rejoicing, burning, beam,
Ray-crowned, with lambent lustre in their zones,
Till o'er the blue, bespangled spaces seem
Angels and great archangels on their thrones;
A host divine, whose eyes are sparkling gems,
And forms more bright than diamond diadems.

1855

[*The Dead*]

How great unto the living seem the dead!
How sacred, solemn; how heroic grown;
How vast and vague, as they obscurely tread
The shadowy confines of the dim unknown!—
For they have met the monster that we dread,
Have learned the secret not to mortal shown.
E'en as gigantic shadows on the wall
The spirit of the daunted child amaze,
So on us thoughts of the departed fall,
And with phantasma fill our gloomy gaze.
Awe and deep wonder lend the living lines,
And hope and ecstasy the borrowed beams;
While fitful fancy the full form divines,
And all is what imagination dreams.

1865

ALEXANDER
McLACHLAN

1818–1896

From THE EMIGRANT

[*Song*]

Old England is eaten by knaves,
    Yet her heart is all right at the core,
May she ne'er be the mother of slaves,
    Nor a foreign foe land on her shore.

I love my own country and race,
    Nor lightly I fled from them both,
Yet who would remain in a place
    Where there's too many spoons for the broth.

The squire's preserving his game.
    He says that God gave it to him,
And he'll banish the poor without shame,
    For touching a feather or limb.

The Justice he feels very big,
    And boasts what the law can secure,
But has two different laws in his wig,
    Which he keeps for the rich and the poor.

The Bishop he preaches and prays,
    And talks of a heavenly birth,
But somehow, for all that he says,
    He grabs a good share of the earth.

Old England is eaten by knaves,
    Yet her heart is all right at the core,
May she n'er be the mother of slaves,
    Nor a foreign foe land on her shore.

1861

[The Arrival]

ALEXANDER
McLACHLAN

Soon we entered in the woods,
O'er the trackless solitudes,
Where the spruce and cedar made
An interminable shade;
And we pick'd our way along,
Sometimes right, and sometimes wrong.
For a long and weary day
Thus we journey'd on our way;
Pick'd a path through swale and swamp,
And at ev'ning fix'd our camp
Where a cool, refreshing spring
Murmur'd like a living thing—
          .   .   .

There we laid us down to rest,
With the cold earth for our bed,
And the green boughs overhead;
And again, at break of day,
Started on our weary way,
Through morasses, over bogs,
Wading rivers, walking logs,
Scrambling over fallen trees,
Wading pond-holes to the knees;
Sometimes wand'ring from the track,
Then, to find it, turning back;
Scorning ills that would betide us,
Stout of heart, the sun to guide us.

Then there came a change of scene—
Groves of beech and maples green,
Streams that murmur'd through the glade,
Little flowers that lov'd the shade.
Lovely birds of gorgeous dye
Flitted 'mong the branches high,
Color'd like the setting sun,
But were songless, ev'ry one:
No one like the linnet grey
In our home so far away;
No one singing like the thrush
To his mate within the brush;
No one like the gentle lark,
Singing 'tween the light and dark,

Soaring from the dewy sod,
Like a herald, up to God.
Some had lovely amber wings—
Round their necks were golden rings—
Some were purple, others blue,
All were lovely, strange and new;
But, altho' surpassing fair,
Still the song was wanting there.
Then we heard the rush of pigeons,
Flocking to those lonely regions;
And anon, when all was still,
Paus'd to hear the whip-poor-will;
And we thought of the cuckoo,
But this stranger no one knew.

ALEXANDER
McLACHLAN

1861

We Live in a Rickety House

We live in a rickety house,
    In a dirty dismal street,
Where the naked hide from day,
    And thieves and drunkards meet.

And pious folks with their tracts,
    When our dens they enter in,
They point to our shirtless backs,
    As the fruits of beer and gin.

And they quote us texts to prove
    That our hearts are hard as stone,
And they feed us with the fact
    That the fault is all our own.

It will be long ere the poor
    Will learn their grog to shun
While it's raiment, food and fire,
    And religion all in one.

I wonder some pious folks   ALEXANDER
McLACHLAN
  Can look us straight in the face,
For our ignorance and crime
  Are the Church's shame and disgrace.

We live in a rickety house,
  In a dirty dismal street,
Where the naked hide from day,
  And thieves and drunkards meet.

1874

CHARLES
SANGSTER

1822–1893

From THE ST. LAWRENCE AND THE SAGUENAY

[*The Thousand Islands*]

  The bark leaps love-fraught from the land; the sea
  Lies calm before us. Many an isle is there,
  Clad with soft verdure; many a stately tree
  Uplifts its leafy branches through the air;
  The amorous current bathes the islets fair,
  As we skip, youth-like, o'er the limpid waves;
  White cloudlets speck the golden atmosphere,
  Through which the passionate sun looks down, and graves
His image on the pearls that boil from the deep caves,

  And bathe the vessel's prow. Isle after isle
  Is passed, as we glide tortuously through
  The opening vistas, that uprise and smile
  Upon us from the ever-changing view.
  Here nature, lavish of her wealth, did strew
  Her flocks of panting islets on the breast
  Of the admiring River, where they grew,
  Like shapes of Beauty, formed to give a zest
To the charmed mind, like waking Visions of the Blest.

The silver-sinewed arms of the proud Lake,   CHARLES SANGSTER
Love-wild, embrace each islet tenderly,
The zephyrs kiss the flowers when they wake
At morn, flushed with a rare simplicity;
See how they bloom around yon birchen tree,
And smile along the bank, by the sandy shore,
In lovely groups—a fair community!
The embossed rocks glitter like golden ore,
And here, the o'erarching trees form a fantastic bower.

Red walls of granite rise on either hand,
Rugged and smooth; a proud young eagle soars
Above the stately evergreens, that stand
Like watchful sentinels on these God-built towers;
And near yon beds of many coloured flowers
Browse two majestic deer, and at their side
A spotted fawn all innocently cowers;
In the rank brushwood it attempts to hide,
While the strong-antlered stag steps forth with lordly stride,

And slakes his thirst, undaunted, at the stream.
Isles of o'erwhelming beauty! surely here
The wild enthusiast might live, and dream
His life away. No Nymphic trains appear,
To charm the pale Ideal Worshipper
Of Beauty; nor Neriads from the deeps below;
Nor hideous Gnomes, to fill the breast with fear:
But crystal streams through endless landscapes flow,
And o'er the clustering Isles the softest breezes blow.

And now 'tis Night. A myriad stars have come
To cheer the earth, and sentinel the skies.
The full-orbed moon irradiates the gloom,
And fills the air with light. Each Islet lies
Immersed in shadow, soft as thy dark eyes;
Swift through the sinuous path our vessel glides,
Now hidden by the massive promontories,
Anon the bubbling silver from its sides
Spurning, like a wild bird, whose home is on the tides.

1856

From 'Sonnets Written in the Orillia Woods'

CHARLES
SANGSTER

VII

Our life is like a forest, where the sun
Glints down upon us through the throbbing leaves;
The full light rarely finds us. One by one,
Deep rooted in our souls, there springeth up
Dark groves of human passion, rich in gloom,
At first no bigger than an acorn-cup.
Hope threads the tangled labyrinth, but grieves
Till all our sins have rotted in their tomb,
And made the rich loam of each yearning heart
To bring forth fruits and flowers to new life.
We feel the dew from heaven, and there start
From some deep fountain little rills whose strife
Is drowned in music. Thus in light and shade
We live, and move, and die, through all this earthly glade.

1860

CHARLES
MAIR

1838-1927

From TECUMSEH

(i)

There was a time on this fair continent
When all things throve in spacious peacefulness.
The prosperous forests unmolested stood,
For where the stalwart oak grew there it lived
Long ages, and then died among its kind.
The hoary pines—those ancients of the earth—
Brimful of legends of the early world,
Stood thick on their own mountains unsubdued.
And all things else illumined by the sun,
Inland or by the lifted wave, had rest.
The passionate or calm pageants of the skies
No artist drew; but in the auburn west
Innumerable faces of fair cloud

Vanished in silent darkness with the day.
The prairie realm—vast ocean's paraphrase—
Rich in wild grasses numberless, and flowers
Unnamed save in mute Nature's inventory,
No civilized barbarian trenched for gain.
And all that flowed was sweet and uncorrupt
The rivers and their tributary streams,
Undammed, wound on forever, and gave up
Their lonely torrents to weird gulfs of sea,
And ocean wastes unshadowed by a sail.
And all the wild life of this western world
Knew not the fear of man; yet in those woods,
And by those plenteous streams and mighty lakes,
And on stupendous steppes of peerless plain,
And in the rocky gloom of canyons deep,
Screened by the stony ribs of mountains hoar
Which steeped their snowy peaks in purging cloud,
And down the continent where tropic suns
Warmed to her very heart the mother earth,
And in the congeal'd north where silence self
Ached with intensity of stubborn frost,
There lived a soul more wild than barbarous;
A tameless soul—the sunburnt savage free—
Free, and untainted by the greed of gain:
Great Nature's man content with Nature's food.

(ii)

LEFROY. I love you better than I love my race;
And could I mass my fondness for my friends,
Augment it with my love of noble brutes,
Tap every spring of reverence and respect,
And all affections bright and beautiful—
Still would my love for you outweigh them all.
IENA. Speak not of love! Speak of the Long-Knife's hate!
Oh, it is pitiful to creep in fear
O'er lands where once our fathers stept in pride!
The Long-Knife strengthens, whilst our race decays,
And falls before him as our forests fall.
First comes his pioneer, the bee, and soon
The mast which plumped the wild deer fats his swine.
His cattle pasture where the bison fed;

His flowers, his very weeds, displace our own—
Aggressive as himself. All, all thrust back!
Destruction follows us, and swift decay.
Oh, I have lain for hours upon the grass,
And gazed into the tenderest blue of heaven—
Cleansed as with dew, so limpid, pure and sweet—
All flecked with silver packs of standing cloud
Most beautiful! But watch them narrowly!
Those clouds will sheer small fleeces from their sides,
Which, melting in our sight as in a dream,
Will vanish all like phantoms in the sky.
So melts our heedless race! Some weaned away,
And wedded to rough-handed pioneers,
Who, fierce as wolves in hatred of our kind,
Yet from their shrill and acid women turn,
Prizing our maidens for their gentleness.
Some by outlandish fevers die, and some—
Caught in the white man's toils and vices mean—
Court death, and find it in the trader's cup.
And all are driven from their heritage,
Far from our fathers' seats and sepulchres,
And girdled with the growing glooms of war;
Resting a moment here, a moment there,
Whilst ever through our plains and forest realms
Bursts the pale spoiler, armed, with eager quest,
And ruinous lust of land. I think of all—
And own Tecumseh right. 'Tis he alone
Can stem this tide of sorrows dark and deep;
So must I bend my feeble will to his,
And, for my people's welfare, banish love.

1886

Song from 'The Last Bison'

Hear me, ye smokeless skies and grass-green earth,
  Since by your sufferance still I breathe and live!
Through you fond Nature gave me birth,
  And food and freedom—all she had to give.
Enough! I grew, and with my kindred ranged
Their realm stupendous, changeless and unchanged,

Save by the toll of nations primitive,
Who throve on us, and loved our life-stream's roar,
And lived beside its wave, and camped upon its shore.

They loved us, and they wasted not. They slew,
    With pious hand, but for their daily need;
Not wantonly, but as the due
    Of stern necessity which Life doth breed.
Yea, even as earth gave us herbage meet,
So yielded we, in turn, our substance sweet
        To quit the claims of hunger, not of greed.
So stood it with us that what either did
Could not be on the earth foregone, nor Heaven forbid.

And, so, companioned in the blameless strife
    Enjoined upon all creatures, small and great,
Our ways were venial, and our life
    Ended in fair fulfilment of our fate.
No gold to them by sordid hands was passed;
No greedy herdsman housed us from the blast;
        Ours was the liberty of regions rife
In winter's snow, in summer's fruits and flowers—
Ours were the virgin prairies, and their rapture ours!

So fared it with us both; yea, thus it stood
    In all our wanderings from place to place,
Until the red man mixed his blood
    With paler currents. Then arose a race—
The reckless hunters of the plains—who vied
In wanton slaughter for the tongue and hide,
        To satisfy vain ends and longings base.
This grew; and yet we flourished, and our name
Prospered until the pale destroyer's concourse came.

Then fell a double terror on the plains,
    The swift inspreading of destruction dire—
Strange men, who ravaged our domains
    On every hand, and ringed us round with fire;
Pale enemies, who slew with equal mirth
The harmless or the hurtful things of earth,
        In dead fruition of their mad desire:
The ministers of mischief and of might,
Who yearn for havoc as the world's supreme delight.

So waned the myriads which had waxed before
   When subject to the simple needs of men.
As yields to eating seas the shore,
   So yielded our vast multitude, and then—
It scattered! Meagre bands, in wild dismay,
Were parted and, for shelter, fled away
      To barren wastes, to mountain gorge and glen.
A respite brief from stern pursuit and care,
For still the spoiler sought, and still he slew us there.

CHARLES
MAIR

Hear me, thou grass-green earth, ye smokeless skies,
   Since by your sufferance still I breathe and live!
The charity which man denies
   Ye still would tender to the fugitive!
I feel your mercy in my veins—at length
My heart revives, and strengthens with your strength—
      Too late, too late, the courage ye would give!
Naught can avail these wounds, this failing breath,
This frame which feels, at last, the wily touch of death.

Here must the last of all his kindred fall;
   Yet, midst these gathering shadows, ere I die—
Responsive to an inward call,
   My spirit fain would rise and prophesy.
I see our spoilers build their cities great
Upon our plains—I see their rich estate:
      The centuries in dim procession fly!
Long ages roll, and then at length is bared
The time when they who spared not are no longer spared.

Once more my vision sweeps the prairies wide,
   But now no peopled cities greet the sight;
All perished, now, their pomp and pride:
   In solitude the wild wind takes delight.
Naught but the vacant wilderness is seen,
And grassy mounds, where cities once had been.
      The earth smiles as of yore, the skies are bright,
Wild cattle graze and bellow on the plain,
And savage nations roam o'er native wilds again!

1901

ISABELLA
VALANCY
CRAWFORD

1850-1887

A Battle

Slowly the Moon her banderoles of light
Unfurls upon the sky; her fingers drip
Pale, silvery tides; her armoured warriors
Leave Day's bright tents of azure and of gold,
Wherein they hid them, and in silence flock
Upon the solemn battlefield of Night
To try great issues with the blind old king,
The Titan Darkness, who great Pharoah fought
With groping hands, and conquered for a span.

The starry hosts with silver lances prick
The scarlet fringes of the tents of Day,
And turn their crystal shields upon their breasts,
And point their radiant lances, and so wait
The stirring of the giant in his caves.

The solitary hills send long, sad sighs
As the blind Titan grasps their locks of pine
And trembling larch to drag him toward the sky,
That his wild-seeking hands may clutch the Moon
From her war-chariot, scythed and wheeled with light,
Crush bright-mailed stars, and so, a sightless king,
Reign in black desolation! Low-set vales
Weep under the black hollow of his foot.
While sobs the sea beneath his lashing hair
Of rolling mists, which, strong as iron cords,
Twine round tall masts and drag them to the reefs.

Swifter rolls up Astarte's light-scythed car;
Dense rise the jewelled lances, groves of light;
Red flouts Mars' banner in the voiceless war
(The mightiest combat is the tongueless one);
The silvery dartings of the lances prick
His fingers from the mountains, catch his locks
And toss them in black fragments to the winds,
Pierce the vast hollow of his misty foot,

Level their diamond tips against his breast, ISABELLA
VALANCY
CRAWFORD
And force him down to lair within his pit
And thro' its chinks thrust down his groping hands
To quicken Hell with horror—for the strength
That is not of the Heavens is of Hell.

1874

The Camp of Souls

My white canoe, like the silvery air
   O'er the River of Death that darkly rolls
When the moons of the world are round and fair,
   I paddle back from the 'Camp of Souls'.
When the wishton-wish in the low swamp grieves
Come the dark plumes of red 'Singing Leaves'.

Two hundred times have the moons of spring
   Rolled over the bright bay's azure breath
Since they decked me with plumes of an eagle's wing,
   And painted my face with the 'paint of death',
And from their pipes o'er my corpse there broke
The solemn rings of the blue 'last smoke'.

Two hundred times have the wintry moons
   Wrapped the dead earth in a blanket white;
Two hundred times have the wild sky loons
   Shrieked in the flush of the golden light
Of the first sweet dawn, when the summer weaves
Her dusky wigwam of perfect leaves.

Two hundred moons of the falling leaf
   Since they laid my bow in my dead right hand
And chanted above me the 'song of grief'
   As I took my way to the spirit land;
Yet when the swallow the blue air cleaves
Come the dark plumes of red 'Singing Leaves'.

White are the wigwams in that far camp,
   And the star-eyed deer on the plains are found;
No bitter marshes or tangled swamp
   In the Manitou's happy hunting-ground!

And the moon of summer forever rolls
Above the red men in their 'Camp of Souls'.

ISABELLA
VALANCY
CRAWFORD

Blue are its lakes as the wild dove's breast,
    And their murmurs soft as her gentle note;
As the calm, large stars in the deep sky rest,
    The yellow lilies upon them float;
And canoes, like flakes of the silvery snow,
Thro' the tall, rustling rice-beds come and go.

Green are its forests; no warrior wind
    Rushes on war trail the dusk grove through,
With leaf-scalps of tall trees mourning behind;
    But South Wind, heart friend of Great Manitou,
When ferns and leaves with cool dews are wet,
Blows flowery breaths from his red calumet.

Never upon them the white frosts lie,
    Nor glow their green boughs with the 'paint of death';
Manitou smiles in the crystal sky,
    Close breathing above them His life-strong breath;
And He speaks no more in fierce thunder sound,
So near is His happy hunting-ground.

Yet often I love, in my white canoe,
    To come to the forests and camps of earth:
'Twas there death's black arrow pierced me through;
    'Twas there my red-browed mother gave me birth;
There I, in the light of a young man's dawn,
Won the lily heart of dusk 'Springing Fawn'.

And love is a cord woven out of life,
    And dyed in the red of the living heart;
And time is the hunter's rusty knife,
    That cannot cut the red strands apart:
And I sail from the spirit shore to scan
Where the weaving of that strong cord began.

But I may not come with a giftless hand,
    So richly I pile, in my white canoe,
Flowers that bloom in the spirit land,
    Immortal smiles of Great Manitou.
When I paddle back to the shores of earth
I scatter them over the white man's hearth.

20

For love is the breath of the soul set free;
    So I cross the river that darkly rolls,
That my spirit may whisper soft to thee
    Of *thine* who wait in the 'Camp of Souls'.
When the bright day laughs, or the wan night grieves,
Come the dusky plumes of red 'Singing Leaves'.

ISABELLA
VALANCY
CRAWFORD

1880

The Dark Stag

A startled stag, the blue-grey Night,
    Leaps down beyond black pines.
Behind—a length of yellow light—
    The hunter's arrow shines:
His moccasins are stained with red,
    He bends upon his knee,
From covering peaks his shafts are sped,
The blue mists plume his mighty head,—
    Well may the swift Night flee!

The pale, pale Moon, a snow-white doe,
    Bounds by his dappled flank:
They beat the stars down as they go,
    Like wood-bells growing rank.
The winds lift dewlaps from the ground,
    Leap from the quaking reeds;
Their hoarse bays shake the forests round,
With keen cries on the track they bound,—
    Swift, swift the dark stag speeds!

Away! his white doe, far behind,
    Lies wounded on the plain;
Yells at his flank the nimblest wind,
    His large tears fall in rain;
Like lily-pads, small clouds grow white
    About his darkling way;
From his bald nest upon the height
The red-eyed eagle sees his flight;
He falters, turns, the antlered Night,—
    The dark stag stands at bay!

His feet are in the waves of space;
　　His antlers broad and dun
He lowers he turns his velvet face
　　To front the hunter, Sun;
He stamps the lilied clouds, and high
　　His branches fill the west.
The lean stork sails across the sky,
The shy loon shrieks to see him die,
　　The winds leap at his breast.

Roar the rent lakes as thro' the wave
　　Their silver warriors plunge,
As vaults from core of crystal cave
　　The strong, fierce muskallunge;
Red torches of the sumach glare,
　　Fall's council-fires are lit;
The bittern, squaw-like, scolds the air;
The wild duck splashes loudly where
　　The rustling rice-spears knit.

Shaft after shaft the red Sun speeds:
　　Rent the stag's dappled side,
His breast, fanged by the shrill winds, bleeds,
　　He staggers on the tide;
He feels the hungry waves of space
　　Rush at him high and blue;
Their white spray smites his dusky face,
Swifter the Sun's fierce arrows race
　　And pierce his stout heart thro'.

His antlers fall; once more he spurns
　　The hoarse hounds of the day;
His blood upon the crisp blue burns,
　　Reddens the mounting spray;
His branches smite the wave—with cries
　　The loud winds pause and flag—
He sinks in space—red glow the skies,
The brown earth crimsons as he dies,
　　The strong and dusky stag.

1883

Said the Canoe

ISABELLA
VALANCY
CRAWFORD

My masters twain made me a bed
Of pine-boughs resinous, and cedar;
Of moss, a soft and gentle breeder
Of dreams of rest; and me they spread
With furry skins and, laughing, said:
'Now she shall lay her polished sides
As queens do rest, or dainty brides,
Our slender lady of the tides!'

My masters twain their camp-soul lit;
Streamed incense from the hissing cones;
Large crimson flashes grew and whirled;
Thin golden nerves of sly light curled
Round the dun camp; and rose faint zones,
Half way about each grim bole knit,
Like a shy child that would bedeck
With its soft clasp a Brave's red neck,
Yet sees the rough shield on his breast,
The awful plumes shake on his crest,
And, fearful, drops his timid face,
Nor dares complete the sweet embrace.

Into the hollow hearts of brakes—
Yet warm from sides of does and stags
Passed to the crisp, dark river-flags—
Sinuous, red as copper-snakes,
Sharp-headed serpents, made of light,
Glided and hid themselves in night.

My masters twain the slaughtered deer
Hung on forked boughs with thongs of leather:
Bound were his stiff, slim feet together,
His eyes like dead stars cold and drear.
The wandering firelight drew near
And laid its wide palm, red and anxious,
On the sharp splendour of his branches,
On the white foam grown hard and sere
  On flank and shoulder.
Death—hard as breast of granite boulder—
  Under his lashes
Peered thro' his eyes at his life's grey ashes.

My masters twain sang songs that wove—
As they burnished hunting-blade and rifle—
A golden thread with a cobweb trifle,
Loud of the chase and low of love:
'O Love! art thou a silver fish,
Shy of the line and shy of gaffing,
Which we do follow, fierce, yet laughing,
Casting at thee the light-winged wish?
And at the last shall we bring thee up
From the crystal darkness, under the cup
   Of lily folden
   On broad leaves golden?

'O Love! art thou a silver deer
With feet as swift as wing of swallow,
While we with rushing arrows follow?
And at the last shall we draw near
And o'er thy velvet neck cast thongs
Woven of roses, stars and songs—
   New chains all moulden
   Of rare gems olden?'

They hung the slaughtered fish like swords
   On saplings slender; like scimitars,
   Bright, and ruddied from new-dead wars,
Blazed in the light the scaly hordes.

They piled up boughs beneath the trees,
Of cedar web and green fir tassel.
   Low did the pointed pine tops rustle,
The camp-fire blushed to the tender breeze.

The hounds laid dewlaps on the ground
   With needles of pine, sweet, soft and rusty,
   Dreamed of the dead stag stout and lusty;
A bat by the red flames wove its round.

The darkness built its wigwam walls
   Close round the camp, and at its curtain
   Pressed shapes, thin, woven and uncertain
As white locks of tall waterfalls.

1884

The Log Jam

Dere's a beeg jam up de reever, w'ere rapide is runnin' fas',
  An' de log we cut las' winter is takin' it all de room;
So boss of de gang is swearin', for not'ing at all can pass
  An' float away down de current till somebody break de boom.

'Here's for de man will tak' de job, holiday for a week
  Extra monee w'en pay day come, an' ten dollar suit of clothes.
'T is n't so hard work run de log, if only you do it quick—
  W'ere's de man of de gang den is ready to say, "Here goes?" '

Dere was de job for a feller, handy an' young an' smart,
  Willin' to tak' hees chances, willin' to risk hees life.
'Cos many a t'ing is safer, dan tryin' de boom to start,
  For if de log wance ketch you, dey're cuttin' you lak a knife.

Aleck Lachance he lissen, an' answer heem right away
  'Marie Louise dat's leevin' off on de shore close by
She's sayin' de word was mak' me mos' happies' man to-day
  An' if you ax de reason I'm ready to go, dat's w'y.'

Pierre Delorme he's spikin' den, an' O! but he's lookin' glad.
  'Dis morning de sam' girl tole me, she mus' say to me,
    "Good-bye Pierre."
So no wan can stop me goin', for I feel I was comin' mad
  An' wedder I see to-morrow, dat's not'ing, for I don't care.'

Aleck Lachance was steady, he's bully boy all aroun',
  Always sendin' de monee to hees moder away below,
Now an' den savin' a leetle for buyin' de house an' groun',
  An' never done t'inkin', t'inkin' of Marie Louise Lebeau.

Pierre was a half-breed feller, we call heem de grand Nor' Wes'—
  Dat is de place he's leevin' w'en he work for de Compagnie,
Dey say he's marry de squaw dere, never min' about all de res'—
  An' affer he get hees monee, he's de boy for de jamboree!

W.H.
DRUMMOND

Ev'ry wan start off cheerin' w'en dey pass on de log out dere
  Jompin' about lak monkey, Aleck an' Pierre Delorme.
Workin' de sam' as twenty, an' runnin' off ev'ryw'ere,
  An' busy on all de places, lak beaver before de storm.

Den we hear some wan shoutin', an' dere was dat crazy girl,
  Marie Louise, on de hillside, cryin' an' raisin' row.
Could n't do not'ing worser! mos' foolish t'ing on de worl'
  For Pierre Delorme an' Aleck wasn't workin' upon de scow.

Bote of dem turn aroun' dere w'en girl is commencin' cry,
  Lak woman I wance remember, got los' on de bush t'ree day,
'Look how de log is movin'! I'm seein' it wit' ma eye,
  Come back out of all dem danger!' an' den she was faint away.

Ten year I been reever driver, an' mebbe know somet'ing too,
  An' dere was n't a man don't watch for de minute dem log she
    go;
But never a word from de boss dere, stannin' wit' all hees crew,
  So how she can see dem movin' don't ax me, for I dunno.

Hitch dem all up togeder, t'ousan' horse crazy mad—
  Only a couple of feller for han'le dem ev'ry wan,
Scare dem wit' t'onder, an' lightning, an' den't is n't half so bad
  As log runnin' down de rapide, affer de boom she's gone.

See dem nex' day on de basin, you t'ink dey was t'roo de fight
  Cut wit' de sword an' bullet, lyin' along de shore
You'd pity de log, I'm sure, an' say 't was terrible sight
  But man goin' t'roo de sam' t'ing, you'd pity dat man some
    more.

An' Pierre w'en he see dem goin' an' log jompin' up an' down
  De sign of de cross he's makin' an' drive on de water dere,
He know it's all up hees chances an' he rader be goin' drown
  Dan ketch by de rollin' timber, an' dat's how he go, poor
    Pierre.

Aleck's red shirt is blazin' off w'ere we hear de log
  Crackin' away an' bangin', sam' as a honder gun,
Lak' sun on de morning tryin' to peep t'roo de reever fog—
  But Aleck's red shirt is redder dan ever I see de sun.

26

An' w'en dey're tryin' wake her: Marie Louise Lebeau,
  On her neck dey fin' a locket, she's kipin' so nice an' warm,
An' dey're tolin' de funny story, de funnies' I dunno—
  For de face, Baptême! dey see dere, was de half-breed Pierre
    Delorme!

1897

CHARLES
  G.D.
ROBERTS
<hr>
860-1943

Tantramar Revisited

Summers and summers have come, and gone with the flight of
  the swallow;
Sunshine and thunder have been, storm, and winter, and frost;
Many and many a sorrow has all but died from remembrance,
Many a dream of joy fall'n in the shadow of pain.
Hands of chance and change have marred, or moulded, or broken,
Busy with spirit or flesh, all I most have adored;
Even the bosom of Earth is strewn with heavier shadows,—
Only in these green hills, aslant to the sea, no change!
Here where the road that has climbed from the inland valleys and
  woodlands,
Dips from the hill-tops down, straight to the base of the hills,—
Here, from my vantage-ground, I can see the scattering houses,
Stained with time, set warm in orchards, meadows, and wheat,
Dotting the broad bright slopes outspread to southward and
  eastward,
Wind-swept all day long, blown by the south-east wind.

Skirting the sunbright uplands stretches a riband of meadow,
Shorn of the labouring grass, bulwarked well from the sea,
Fenced on its seaward border with long clay dykes from the
  turbid
Surge and flow of the tides vexing the Westmoreland shores.
Yonder, toward the left, lie broad the Westmoreland marshes,—
Miles on miles they extend, level, and grassy, and dim,
Clear from the long red sweep of flats to the sky in the distance,

Save for the outlying heights, green-rampired Cumberland Point;
Miles on miles outrolled, and the river-channels divide them,—
Miles on miles of green, barred by the hurtling gusts.

Miles on miles beyond the tawny bay is Minudie.
There are the low blue hills; villages gleam at their feet.
Nearer a white sail shines across the water, and nearer
Still are the slim, grey masts of fishing boats dry on the flats.
Ah, how well I remember those wide red flats, above tidemark
Pale with scurf of the salt, seamed and baked in the sun!
Well I remember the piles of blocks and ropes, and the net-reels
Wound with the beaded nets, dripping and dark from the sea!
Now at this season the nets are unwound; they hang from the
   rafters
Over the fresh-stowed hay in upland barns, and the wind
Blows all day through the chinks, with the streaks of sunlight,
   and sways them
Softly at will; or they lie heaped in the gloom of a loft.

Now at this season the reels are empty and idle; I see them
Over the lines of the dykes, over the gossiping grass.
Now at this season they swing in the long strong wind, thro' the
   lonesome
Golden afternoon, shunned by the foraging gulls.
Near about sunset the crane will journey homeward above them;
Round them, under the moon, all the calm night long,
Winnowing soft grey wings of marsh-owls wander and wander,
Now to the broad, lit marsh, now to the dusk of the dike.
Soon, thro' their dew-wet frames, in the live keen freshness of
   morning,
Out of the teeth of the dawn blows back the awakening wind.
Then, as the blue day mounts, and the low-shot shafts of the
   sunlight
Glance from the tide to the shore, gossamers jewelled with dew
Sparkle and wave, where late sea-spoiling fathoms of driftnet
Myriad-meshed, uploomed sombrely over the land.

Well I remember it all. The salt, raw scent of the margin;
While, with men at the windlass, groaned each reel, and the net,
Surging in ponderous lengths, uprose and coiled in its station;
Then each man to his home,—well I remember it all!

Yet, as I sit and watch, this present peace of the landscape,—
Stranded boats, these reels empty and idle, the hush,
One grey hawk slow-wheeling above yon cluster of haystacks,—
More than the old-time stir this stillness welcomes me home.
Ah, the old-time stir, how once it stung me with rapture,—
Old-time sweetness, the winds freighted with honey and salt!
Yet will I stay my steps and not go down to the marshland,—
Muse and recall far off, rather remember than see,—
Lest on too close sight I miss the darling illusion,
Spy at their task even here the hands of chance and change.

1886

The Potato Harvest

A high bare field, brown from the plough, and borne
   Aslant from sunset; amber wastes of sky
   Washing the ridge; a clamour of crows that fly
In from the wide flats where the spent tides mourn
To yon their rocking roosts in pines wind-torn;
   A line of grey snake-fence, that zigzags by
   A pond, and cattle; from the homestead nigh
The long deep summonings of the supper horn.

Black on the ridge, against that lonely flush,
   A cart, and stoop-necked oxen; ranged beside
   Some barrels; and the day-worn harvest-folk,
Here emptying their baskets, jar the hush
   With hollow thunders. Down the dusk hillside
   Lumbers the wain; and day fades out like smoke.

1886

The Pea-Fields

CHARLES
G.D.
ROBERTS

These are the fields of light, and laughing air,
    And yellow butterflies, and foraging bees,
    And whitish, wayward blossoms winged as these,
And pale green tangles like a seamaid's hair.
Pale, pale the blue, but pure beyond compare,
    And pale the sparkle of the far-off seas,
    A-shimmer like these fluttering slopes of peas,
And pale the open landscape everywhere.

From fence to fence a perfumed breath exhales
    O'er the bright pallor of the well-loved fields,—
My fields of Tantramar in summer-time;
    And, scorning the poor feed their pasture yields,
Up from the bushy lots the cattle climb,
    To gaze with longing through the grey, mossed rails.

1893

The Mowing

This is the voice of high midsummer's heat.
    The rasping vibrant clamour soars and shrills
    O'er all the meadowy range of shadeless hills,
As if a host of giant cicadæ beat
The cymbals of their wings with tireless feet,
    Or brazen grasshoppers with triumphing note
    From the long swath proclaimed the fate that smote
The clover and timothy-tops and meadowsweet.

The crying knives glide on; the green swath lies.
    And all noon long the sun, with chemic ray,
    Seals up each cordial essence in its cell,
That in the dusky stalls, some winter's day,
    The spirit of June, here prisoned by his spell,
    May cheer the herds with pasture memories.

1893

The Herring Weir

CHARLES
G.D.
ROBERTS

Back to the green deeps of the outer bay
   The red and amber currents glide and cringe,
   Diminishing behind a luminous fringe
Of cream-white surf and wandering wraiths of spray.
Stealthily, in the old reluctant way,
   The red flats are uncovered, mile on mile,
   To glitter in the sun a golden while.
Far down the flats, a phantom sharply grey,

The herring weir emerges, quick with spoil.
   Slowly the tide forsakes it. Then draws near,
Descending from the farm-house on the height,
A cart, with gaping tubs. The oxen toil
   Sombrely o'er the level to the weir,
   And drag a long black trail across the light.

1893

The Skater

My glad feet shod with the glittering steel
I was the god of the wingèd heel.

The hills in the far white sky were lost;
The world lay still in the wide white frost;

And the woods hung hushed in their long white dream
By the ghostly, glimmering, ice-blue stream.

Here was a pathway, smooth like glass,
Where I and the wandering wind might pass

To the far-off palaces, drifted deep,
Where Winter's retinue rests in sleep.

I followed the lure, I fled like a bird,
Till the startled hollows awoke and heard

A spinning whisper, a sibilant twang,
As the stroke of the steel on the tense ice rang;

And the wandering wind was left behind
As faster, faster I followed my mind;

Till the blood sang high in my eager brain,
And the joy of my flight was almost pain.

Then I stayed the rush of my eager speed
And silently went as a drifting seed,—

Slowly, furtively, till my eyes
Grew big with the awe of a dim surmise,

And the hair of my neck began to creep
At hearing the wilderness talk in sleep.

Shapes in the fir-gloom drifted near.
In the deep of my heart I heard my fear.

And I turned and fled, like a soul pursued,
From the white, inviolate solitude.

1901

Heat

From plains that reel to southward, dim,
    The road runs by me white and bare;
Up the steep hill it seems to swim
    Beyond, and melt into the glare.
Upward half-way, or it may be
    Nearer the summit, slowly steals
A hay-cart, moving dustily
    With idly clacking wheels.

By his cart's side the wagoner
    Is slouching slowly at his ease,
Half-hidden in the windless blur
    Of white dust puffing to his knees.
This wagon on the height above,
    From sky to sky on either hand,
Is the sole thing that seems to move
    In all the heat-held land.

Beyond me in the fields the sun
    Soaks in the grass and hath his will;
I count the marguerites one by one;
    Even the buttercups are still.
On the brook yonder not a breath
    Disturbs the spider or the midge.
The water-bugs draw close beneath
    The cool gloom of the bridge.

Where the far elm-tree shadows flood
    Dark patches in the burning grass,
The cows, each with their peaceful cud,
    Lie waiting for the heat to pass.
From somewhere on the slope near by
    Into the pale depth of the noon
A wandering thrush slides leisurely
    His thin revolving tune.

In intervals of dreams I hear
    The cricket from the droughty ground;
The grasshoppers spin into mine ear
    A small innumerable sound.
I lift mine eyes sometimes to gaze:
    The burning sky-line blinds my sight:
The woods far off are blue with haze:
    The hills are drenched in light.

And yet to me not this or that
    Is always sharp or always sweet;
In the sloped shadow of my hat
    I lean at rest, and drain the heat;
Nay more, I think some blessèd power
    Hath brought me wandering idly here:
In the full furnace of this hour
    My thoughts grow keen and clear.

1888

In November

With loitering step and quiet eye,
Beneath the low November sky,
I wandered in the woods, and found
A clearing, where the broken ground
Was scattered with black stumps and briers,
And the old wreck of forest fires.
It was a bleak and sandy spot,
And, all about, the vacant plot
Was peopled and inhabited
By scores of mulleins long since dead.
A silent and forsaken brood
In that mute opening of the wood,
So shrivelled and so thin they were,
So grey, so haggard, and austere,
Not plants at all they seemed to me,
But rather some spare company
Of hermit folk, who long ago,
Wandering in bodies to and fro,
Had chanced upon this lonely way,
And rested thus, till death one day
Surprised them at their compline prayer,
And left them standing lifeless there.

There was no sound about the wood ARCHIBALD
LAMPMAN
Save the wind's secret stir. I stood
Among the mullein-stalks as still
As if myself had grown to be
One of their sombre company,
A body without wish or will.
And as I stood, quite suddenly,
Down from a furrow in the sky
The sun shone out a little space
Across that silent sober place,
Over the sand heaps and brown sod,
The mulleins and dead goldenrod,
And passed beyond the thickets grey,
And lit the fallen leaves that lay,
Level and deep within the wood,
A rustling yellow multitude.

And all around me the thin light,
So sere, so melancholy bright,
Fell like the half-reflected gleam
Or shadow of some former dream;
A moment's golden reverie
Poured out on every plant and tree
A semblance of weird joy, or less,
A sort of spectral happiness;
And I, too, standing idly there,
With muffled hands in the chill air,
Felt the warm glow about my feet,
And shuddering betwixt cold and heat,
Drew my thoughts closer, like a cloak,
While something in my blood awoke,
A nameless and unnatural cheer,
A pleasure secret and austere.

1895

The City of the End of Things

Beside the pounding cataracts
Of midnight streams unknown to us
'Tis builded in the leafless tracts
And valleys huge of Tartarus.

Lurid and lofty and vast it seems;
It hath no rounded name that rings,
But I have heard it called in dreams
The City of the End of Things.

Its roofs and iron towers have grown
None knoweth how high within the night,
But in its murky streets far down
A flaming terrible and bright
Shakes all the stalking shadows there,
Across the walls, across the floors,
And shifts upon the upper air
From out a thousand furnace doors;
And all the while an awful sound
Keeps roaring on continually,
And crashes in the ceaseless round
Of a gigantic harmony.
Through its grim depths re-echoing
And all its weary height of walls,
With measured roar and iron ring,
The inhuman music lifts and falls.
Where no thing rests and no man is,
And only fire and night hold sway;
The beat, the thunder and the hiss
Cease not, and change not, night nor day.
And moving at unheard commands,
The abysses and vast fires between,
Flit figures that with clanking hands
Obey a hideous routine;
They are not flesh, they are not bone,
They see not with the human eye,
And from their iron lips is blown
A dreadful and monotonous cry;
And whoso of our mortal race
Should find that city unaware,
Lean Death would smite him face to face,
And blanch him with its venomed air:
Or caught by the terrific spell,
Each thread of memory snapt and cut,
His soul would shrivel and its shell
Go rattling like an empty nut.

It was not always so, but once,

In days that no man thinks upon, ARCHIBALD
LAMPMAN
Fair voices echoed from its stones,
The light above it leaped and shone:
Once there were multitudes of men,
That built that city in their pride,
Until its might was made, and then
They withered age by age and died.
But now of that prodigious race,
Three only in an iron tower,
Set like carved idols face to face,
Remain the masters of its power;
And at the city gate a fourth,
Gigantic and with dreadful eyes,
Sits looking toward the lightless north,
Beyond the reach of memories;
Fast rooted to the lurid floor,
A bulk that never moves a jot,
In his pale body dwells no more,
Or mind or soul,—an idiot!
But sometime in the end those three
Shall perish and their hands be still,
And with the master's touch shall flee
Their incommunicable skill.
A stillness absolute as death
Along the slacking wheels shall lie,
And, flagging at a single breath,
The fires that moulder out and die.
The roar shall vanish at its height,
And over that tremendous town
The silence of eternal night
Shall gather close and settle down.
All its grim grandeur, tower and hall,
Shall be abandoned utterly,
And into rust and dust shall fall
From century to century;
Nor ever living thing shall grow,
Nor trunk of tree, nor blade of grass;
No drop shall fall, no wind shall blow,
Nor sound of any foot shall pass:
Alone of its accusèd state,
One thing the hand of Time shall spare,
For the grim Idiot at the gate
Is deathless and eternal there.

1895

Winter Evening

ARCHIBALD
LAMPMAN

To-night the very horses springing by
Toss gold from whitened nostrils. In a dream
The streets that narrow to the westward gleam
Like rows of golden palaces; and high
From all the crowded chimneys tower and die
A thousand aureoles. Down in the west
The brimming plains beneath the sunset rest,
One burning sea of gold. Soon, soon shall fly
The glorious vision, and the hours shall feel
A mightier master; soon from height to height,
With silence and the sharp unpitying stars,
Stern creeping frosts, and winds that touch like steel,
Out of the depth beyond the eastern bars,
Glittering and still shall come the awful night.

1899

A Thunderstorm

A moment the wild swallows like a flight
Of withered gust-caught leaves, serenely high,
Toss in the windrack up the muttering sky.
The leaves hang still. Above the weird twilight,
The hurrying centres of the storm unite
And spreading with huge trunk and rolling fringe,
Each wheeled upon its own tremendous hinge,
Tower darkening on. And now from heaven's height,
With the long roar of elm trees swept and swayed,
And pelted waters, on the vanished plain
Plunges the blast. Behind the wild white flash
That splits abroad the pealing thunder-crash,
Over bleared fields and gardens disarrayed,
Column on column comes the drenching rain.

1899

To a Millionaire

ARCHIBALD
LAMPMAN

The world in gloom and splendour passes by,
And thou in the midst of it with brows that gleam,
A creature of that old distorted dream
That makes the sound of life an evil cry.
Good men perform just deeds, and brave men die,
And win not honour such as gold can give,
While the vain multitudes plod on, and live,
And serve the curse that pins them down: But I
Think only of the unnumbered broken hearts,
The hunger and the mortal strife for bread,
Old age and youth alike mistaught, misfed,
By want and rags and homelessness made vile,
The griefs and hates, and all the meaner parts
That balance thy one grim misgotten pile.

1900

WILFRED
CAMPBELL

1858–1918

Indian Summer

Along the line of smoky hills
    The crimson forest stands,
And all the day the blue-jay calls
    Throughout the autumn lands.

Now by the brook the maple leans
    With all his glory spread,
And all the sumachs on the hills
    Have turned their green to red.

Now by great marshes wrapt in mist,
    Or past some river's mouth,
Throughout the long, still autumn day
    Wild birds are flying south.

1888

The Winter Lakes

WILFRED
CAMPBELL

Out in a world of death far to the northward lying,
    Under the sun and the moon, under the dusk and the day;
Under the glimmer of stars and the purple of sunsets dying,
    Wan and waste and white, stretch the great lakes away.

Never a bud of spring, never a laugh of summer,
    Never a dream of love, never a song of bird;
But only the silence and white, the shores that grow chiller and
    dumber,
    Wherever the ice winds sob, and the griefs of winter are heard.

Crags that are black and wet out of the grey lake looming,
    Under the sunset's flush and the pallid, faint glimmer of dawn;
Shadowy, ghost-like shores, where midnight surfs are booming
    Thunders of wintry woe over the spaces wan.

Lands that loom like spectres, whited regions of winter,
    Wastes of desolate woods, deserts of water and shore:
A world of winter and death, within these regions who enter,
    Lost to summer and life, go to return no more.

Moons that glimmer above, waters that lie white under,
    Miles and miles of lake far out under the night;
Foaming crests of waves, surfs that shoreward thunder,
    Shadowy shapes that flee, haunting the spaces white.

Lonely hidden bays, moon-lit, ice-rimmed, winding,
    Fringed by forests and crags, haunted by shadowy shores;
Hushed from the outward strife, where the mighty surf is
    grinding
    Death and hate on the rocks, as sandward and landward it
    roars.

1889

How One Winter Came in the Lake Region

WILFRED
CAMPBELL

For weeks and weeks the autumn world stood still,
   Clothed in the shadow of a smoky haze;
The fields were dead, the wind had lost its will,
And all the lands were hushed by wood and hill,
   In those grey, withered days.

Behind a mist the blear sun rose and set,
   At night the moon would nestle in a cloud;
The fisherman, a ghost, did cast his net;
The lake its shores forgot to chafe and fret,
   And hushed its caverns loud.

Far in the smoky woods the birds were mute,
   Save that from blackened tree a jay would scream,
Or far in swamps the lizard's lonesome lute
Would pipe in thirst, or by some gnarlèd root
   The tree-toad trilled his dream.

From day to day still hushed the season's mood,
   The streams stayed in their runnels shrunk and dry;
Suns rose aghast by wave and shore and wood,
And all the world, with ominous silence, stood
   In weird expectancy:

When one strange night the sun like blood went down,
   Flooding the heavens in a ruddy hue;
Red grew the lake, the sere fields parched and brown,
Red grew the marshes where the creeks stole down,
   But never a wind-breath blew.

That night I felt the winter in my veins,
   A joyous tremor of the icy glow;
And woke to hear the north's wild vibrant strains,
While far and wide, by withered woods and plains,
   Fast fell the driving snow.

1893

Morning on the Shore

WILFRED
CAMPBELL

The lake is blue with morning; and the sky
  Sweet, clear, and burnished as an orient pearl.
  High in its vastness, scream and skim and whirl
White gull-flocks where the gleaming beaches die
  Into dim distance, where great marshes lie.
  Far in ashore the woods are warm with dreams,
  The dew-wet road in sunny sunlight gleams,
The sweet, cool earth, the clear blue heaven on high.

Across the morn a carolling school-boy goes,
Filling the world with youth to heaven's stair;
  Some chattering squirrel answers from his tree:
But down beyond the headland, where ice-floes
Are great in winter, pleading in mute prayer.
  A dead, drowned face stares up immutably.

1893

BLISS
CARMAN

1861-1929

Low Tide on Grand Pré

The sun goes down, and over all
  These barren reaches by the tide
Such unelusive glories fall,
  I almost dream they yet will bide
  Until the coming of the tide.

And yet I know that not for us,
  By any ecstasy of dream,
He lingers to keep luminous
  A little while the grievous stream,
  Which frets, uncomforted of dream—

A grievous stream, that to and fro
  Athrough the fields of Acadie
Goes wandering, as if to know
  Why one beloved face should be
  So long from home and Acadie.

Was it a year or lives ago
    We took the grasses in our hands,
And caught the summer flying low
    Over the waving meadow lands,
    And held it there between our hands?

The while the river at our feet—
    A drowsy inland meadow stream—
At set of sun the after-heat
    Made running gold, and in the gleam
    We freed our birch upon the stream.

There down along the elms at dusk
    We lifted dripping blade to drift,
Through twilight scented fine like musk,
    Where night and gloom awhile uplift,
    Nor sunder soul and soul adrift.

And that we took into our hands
    Spirit of life or subtler thing—
Breathed on us there, and loosed the bands
    Of death, and taught us, whispering,
    The secret of some wonder-thing.

Then all your face grew light, and seemed
    To hold the shadow of the sun;
The evening faltered, and I deemed
    That time was ripe, and years had done
    Their wheeling underneath the sun.

So all desire and all regret,
    And fear and memory, were naught;
One to remember or forget
    The keen delight our hands had caught;
    Morrow and yesterday were naught.

The night has fallen, and the tide . . .
    Now and again comes drifting home,
Across these aching barrens wide,
    A sigh like driven wind or foam:
    In grief the flood is bursting home.

1893

BLISS
CARMAN

Lord of My Heart's Elation

BLISS
CARMAN

Lord of my heart's elation,
Spirit of things unseen,
Be thou my aspiration
Consuming and serene!

Bear up, bear out, bear onward
This mortal soul alone,
To selfhood or oblivion,
Incredibly thine own,—

As the foamheads are loosened
And blown along the sea,
Or sink and merge forever
In that which bids them be.

I, too, must climb in wonder,
Uplift at thy command,—
Be one with my frail fellows
Beneath the wind's strong hand,

A fleet and shadowy column
Of dust or mountain rain,
To walk the earth a moment
And be dissolved again.

Be thou my exaltation
Or fortitude of mien,
Lord of the world's elation,
Thou breath of things unseen!

1903

Morning in the Hills

BLISS
CARMAN

How quiet is the morning in the hills!
The stealthy shadows of the summer clouds
Trail through the cañon, and the mountain stream
Sounds his sonorous music far below
In the deep-wooded wind-enchanted clove.

Hemlock and aspen, chestnut, beech, and fir
Go tiering down from storm-worn crest and ledge,
While in the hollows of the dark ravine
See the red road emerge, then disappear
Towards the wide plain and fertile valley lands.

My forest cabin half-way up the glen
Is solitary, save for one wise thrush,
The sound of falling water, and the wind
Mysteriously conversing with the leaves.

Here I abide unvisited by doubt,
Dreaming of far-off turmoil and despair,
The race of men and love and fleeting time,
What life may be, or beauty, caught and held
For a brief moment at eternal poise.

What impulse now shall quicken and make live
This outward semblance and this inward self?
One breath of being fills the bubble world,
Colored and frail, with fleeting change on change.

Surely some God contrived so fair a thing
In the vast leisure of uncounted days,
And touched in with the breath of living joy,
Wondrous and fair and wise! It must be so.

1912

The Unnamed Lake

It sleeps among the thousand hills
　　Where no man ever trod,
And only nature's music fills
　　The silences of God.

Great mountains tower above its shore,
　　Green rushes fringe its brim,
And o'er its breast for evermore
　　The wanton breezes skim.

Dark clouds that intercept the sun
　　Go there in Spring to weep,
And there, when Autumn days are done,
　　White mists lie down to sleep.

Sunrise and sunset crown with gold
　　The peaks of ageless stone,
Where winds have thundered from of old
　　And storms have set their throne.

No echoes of the world afar
　　Disturb it night or day,
But sun and shadow, moon and star
　　Pass and repass for aye.

'Twas in the grey of early dawn
　　When first the lake we spied,
And fragments of a cloud were drawn
　　Half down the mountain side.

Along the shore a heron flew,
　　And from a speck on high
That hovered in the deepening blue,
　　We heard the fish-hawk's cry.

Among the cloud-capt solitudes,
    No sound the silence broke,
Save when, in whispers down the woods,
    The guardian mountains spoke.

Through tangled brush and dewy brake,
    Returning whence we came,
We passed in silence, and the lake
    We left without a name.

1897

DUNCAN
CAMPBELL
SCOTT

1862–1947

At the Cedars

You had two girls—Baptiste—
One is Virginie—
Hold hard—Baptiste!
Listen to me.

The whole drive was jammed
In that bend at the Cedars,
The rapids were dammed
With the logs tight rammed
And crammed; you might know
The Devil had clinched them below.

We worked three days—not a budge,
'She's as tight as a wedge, on the ledge,'
Says our foreman;
'Mon Dieu! boys, look here,
We must get this thing clear.'
He cursed at the men
And we went for it then;
With our cant-dogs arow,
We just gave he-yo-ho;
When she gave a big shove
From above.

The gang yelled and tore
For the shore,
The logs gave a grind
Like a wolf's jaws behind,
And as quick as a flash,
With a shove and a crash,
They were down in a mash,
But I and ten more,
All but Isaàc Dufour,
Were ashore.

He leaped on a log in the front of the rush,
And shot out from the bind
While the jam roared behind;
As he floated along
He balanced his pole
And tossed us a song.
But just as we cheered,
Up darted a log from the bottom,
Leaped thirty feet square and fair,
And came down on his own.

He went up like a block
With the shock,
And when he was there
In the air,
Kissed his hand
To the land;
When he dropped
My heart stopped,
For the first logs had caught him
And crushed him;
When he rose in his place
There was blood on his face.

There were some girls, Baptiste,
Picking berries on the hillside,
Where the river curls, Baptiste,
You know—on the still side
One was down by the water,
She saw Isaàc
Fall back.

She did not scream, Baptiste,
She launched her canoe;
It did seem, Baptiste,
That she wanted to die too,
For before you could think
The birch cracked like a shell
In that rush of hell,
And I saw them both sink—

Baptiste!—
He had two girls,
One is Virginie,
What God calls the other
Is not known to me.

1893

The Forsaken

I

Once in the winter
Out on a lake
In the heart of the north-land,
Far from the Fort
And far from the hunters,
A Chippewa woman
With her sick baby,
Crouched in the last hours
Of a great storm.
Frozen and hungry,
She fished through the ice
With a line of the twisted
Bark of the cedar,
And a rabbit-bone hook
Polished and barbed;
Fished with the bare hook
All through the wild day,
Fished and caught nothing;
While the young chieftain
Tugged at her breasts,
Or slept in the lacings

Of the warm *tikanagan*.
All the lake-surface
Streamed with the hissing
Of millions of iceflakes
Hurled by the wind;
Behind her the round
Of a lonely island
Roared like a fire
With the voice of the storm
In the deeps of the cedars.
Valiant, unshaken,
She took of her own flesh,
Baited the fish-hook
Drew in a gray-trout,
Drew in his fellows,
Heaped them beside her,
Dead in the snow.
Valiant, unshaken,
She faced the long distance,
Wolf-haunted and lonely,
Sure of her goal
And the life of her dear one:
Tramped for two days,
On the third in the morning,
Saw the strong bulk
Of the Fort by the river,
Saw the wood-smoke
Hang soft in the spruces,
Heard the keen yelp
Of the ravenous huskies
Fighting for whitefish:
Then she had rest.

II
Years and years after,
When she was old and withered,
When her son was an old man
And his children filled with vigour,
They came in their northern tour on the verge of winter,
To an island in a lonely lake.
There one night they camped, and on the morrow
Gathered their kettles and birch-bark

Their rabbit-skin robes and their mink-traps,
Launched their canoes and slunk away through the islands,
Left her alone forever,
Without a word of farewell,
Because she was old and useless,
Like a paddle broken and warped,
Or a pole that was splintered.
Then, without a sigh,
Valiant, unshaken,
She smoothed her dark locks under her kerchief,
Composed her shawl in state,
Then folded her hands ridged with sinews and corded with veins,
Folded them across her breasts spent with the nourishing of
    children,
Gazed at the sky past the tops of the cedars,
Saw two spangled nights arise out of the twilight,
Saw two days go by filled with the tranquil sunshine,
Saw, without pain, or dread, or even a moment of longing:
Then on the third great night there came thronging and thronging
Millions of snowflakes out of a windless cloud;
They covered her close with a beautiful crystal shroud,
Covered her deep and silent.
But in the frost of the dawn,
Up from the life below,
Rose a column of breath
Through a tiny cleft in the snow,
Fragile, delicately drawn,
Wavering with its own weakness,
In the wilderness a sign of the spirit,
Persisting still in the sight of the sun
Till day was done.
Then all light was gathered up by the hand of God and hid in His
    breast,
Then there was born a silence deeper than silence,
Then she had rest.

1905

On the Way to the Mission

D.C.
SCOTT

They dogged him all one afternoon,
Through the bright snow,
Two whitemen servants of greed;
He knew that they were there,
But he turned not his head;
He was an Indian trapper;
He planted his snow-shoes firmly,
He dragged the long toboggan
Without rest.

The three figures drifted
Like shadows in the mind of a seer;
The snow-shoes were whisperers
On the threshold of awe;
The toboggan made the sound of wings,
A wood-pigeon sloping to her nest.

The Indian's face was calm.
He strode with the sorrow of fore-knowledge,
But his eyes were jewels of content
Set in circles of peace.

They would have shot him;
But momently in the deep forest,
They saw something flit by his side:
Their hearts stopped with fear.
Then the moon rose.
They would have left him to the spirit,
But they saw the long toboggan
Rounded well with furs,
With many a silver fox-skin,
With the pelts of mink and of otter.
They were the servants of greed;
When the moon grew brighter
And the spruces were dark with sleep,
They shot him.
When he fell on a shield of moonlight
One of his arms clung to his burden;
The snow was not melted:
The spirit passed away.

Then the servants of greed
Tore off the cover to count their gains;
They shuddered away into the shadows,
Hearing each the loud heart of the other.
Silence was born.

There in the tender moonlight,
    As sweet as they were in life,
Glimmered the ivory features,
    Of the Indian's wife.

In the manner of Montagnais women
    Her hair was rolled with braid;
Under her waxen fingers
    A crucifix was laid.

He was drawing her down to the Mission,
    To bury her there in spring,
When the bloodroot comes and the windflower
    To silver everything.

But as a gift of plunder
    Side by side were they laid,
The moon went on to her setting
    And covered them with shade.

1905

At Gull Lake: August, 1810

Gull Lake set in the rolling prairie—
Still there are reeds on the shore,
As of old the poplars shimmer
As summer passes;
Winter freezes the shallow lake to the core;
Storm passes,
Heat parches the sedges and grasses,
Night comes with moon-glimmer,
Dawn with the morning-star;
All proceeds in the flow of Time
As a hundred years ago.

Then two camps were pitched on the shore,
The clustered teepees
Of Tabashaw Chief of the Saulteaux.
And on a knoll tufted with poplars
Two grey tents of a trader—
Nairne of the Orkneys.
Before his tents under the shade of the poplars
Sat Keejigo, third of the wives
Of Tabashaw Chief of the Saulteaux;
Clad in the skins of antelopes
Broidered with porcupine quills
Coloured with vivid dyes,
Vermilion here and there
In the roots of her hair,
A half-moon of powder-blue
On her brow, her cheeks
Scored with light ochre streaks.
Keejigo daughter of Launay
The Normandy hunter
And Oshawan of the Saulteaux,
Troubled by fugitive visions
In the smoke of the camp-fires,
In the close dark of the teepee,
Flutterings of colour
Along the flow of the prairies,
Spangles of flower tints
Caught in the wonder of dawn,
Dreams of sounds unheard—
The echoes of echo,
Star she was named for
Keejigo, star of the morning,
Voices of storm—
Wind-rush and lightning,—
The beauty of terror;
The twilight moon
Coloured like a prairie lily,
The round moon of pure snow,
The beauty of peace;
Premonitions of love and of beauty
Vague as shadows cast by a shadow.
Now she had found her hero,
And offered her body and spirit
With abject unreasoning passion,

As Earth abandons herself
To the sun and the thrust of the lightning.
Quiet were all the leaves of the poplars,
Breathless the air under their shadow,
As Keejigo spoke of these things to her heart
In the beautiful speech of the Saulteaux.

D.C.
SCOTT

> *The flower lives on the prairie,*
> *The wind in the sky,*
> *I am here my beloved;*
> *The wind and the flower.*

> *The crane hides in the sand-hills,*
> *Where does the wolverine hide?*
> *I am here my beloved,*
> *Heart's-blood on the feathers,*
> *The foot caught in the trap.*

> *Take the flower in your hand,*
> *The wind in your nostrils;*
> *I am here my beloved;*
> *Release the captive,*
> *Heal the wound under the feathers.*

A storm-cloud was marching
Vast on the prairie,
Scored with livid ropes of hail,
Quick with nervous vines of lightning—
Twice had Nairne turned her away
Afraid of the venom of Tabashaw,
Twice had the Chief fired at his tents
And now when two bullets
Whistled above the encampment
He yelled, 'Drive this bitch to her master.'

Keejigo went down a path by the lake;
Thick at the tangled edges,
The reeds and the sedges
Were grey as ashes
Against the death-black water;
The lightning scored with double flashes
The dark lake-mirror and loud
Came the instant thunder.

Her lips still moved to the words of her music,
'Release the captive,
Heal the wound under the feathers.'

At the top of the bank
The old wives caught her and cast her down
Where Tabashaw crouched by his camp-fire.
He snatched a live brand from the embers,
Seared her cheeks,
Blinded her eyes,
Destroyed her beauty with fire,
Screaming, 'Take that face to your lover.'
Keejigo held her face to the fury
And made no sound.
The old wives dragged her away
And threw her over the bank
Like a dead dog.

Then burst the storm—
The Indians' screams and the howls of the dogs
Lost in the crash of hail
That smashed the sedges and reeds,
Stripped the poplars of leaves,
Tore and blazed onwards,
Wasting itself with riot and tumult—
Supreme in the beauty of terror.

The setting sun struck the retreating cloud
With a rainbow, not an arc but a column
Built with the glory of seven metals;
Beyond in the purple deeps of the vortex
Fell the quivering vines of the lightning.
The wind withdrew the veil from the shrine of the moon,
She rose changing her dusky shade for the glow
Of the prairie lily, till free of all blemish of colour
She came to her zenith without a cloud or a star,
A lovely perfection, snow-pure in the heaven of midnight.
After the beauty of terror the beauty of peace.

But Keejigo came no more to the camps of her people;
Only the midnight moon knew where she felt her way,
Only the leaves of autumn, the snows of winter
Knew where she lay.

En Route

D.C.
SCOTT

The train has stopped for no apparent reason
In the wilds;
A frozen lake is level and fretted over
With rippled wind lines;
The sun is burning in the South; the season
Is winter trembling at a touch of spring.
A little hill with birches and a ring
Of cedars—all so still, so pure with snow—
It seems a tiny landscape in the moon.
Long wisps of shadow from the naked birches
Lie on the white in lines of cobweb-grey;
From the cedar roots the snow has shrunk away,
One almost hears it tinkle as it thaws.
Traces there are of wild things in the snow—
Partridge at play, tracks of the foxes' paws
That broke a path to sun them in the trees.
They're going fast where all impressions go
On a frail substance—images like these,
Vagaries the unconscious mind receives
From nowhere, and lets go to nothingness
With the lost flush of last year's autumn leaves.

1935

Ojistoh

I am Ojistoh, I am she, the wife
Of him whose name breathes bravery and life
And courage to the tribe that calls him chief.
I am Ojistoh, his white star, and he
Is land, and lake, and sky—and soul to me.

Ah! but they hated him, those Huron braves,
Him who had flung their warriors into graves,
Him who had crushed them underneath his heel,
Whose arm was iron, and whose heart was steel
To all—save me, Ojistoh, chosen wife
Of my great Mohawk, white star of his life.

Ah! but they hated him, and councilled long
With subtle witchcraft how to work him wrong;
How to avenge their dead, and strike him where
His pride was highest, and his fame most fair.
Their hearts grew weak as women at his name:
They dared no war-path since my Mohawk came
With ashen bow, and flinten arrow-head
To pierce their craven bodies; but their dead
Must be avenged. Avenged? They dared not walk
In day and meet his deadly tomahawk;
They dared not face his fearless scalping knife;
So Niyoh!*—then they thought of me, his wife.

O! evil, evil face of them they sent
With evil Huron speech: 'Would I consent
To take of wealth? be queen of all their tribe?
Have wampum ermine?' Back I flung the bribe
Into their teeth, and said, 'While I have life
Know this—Ojistoh is the Mohawk's wife.'

Wah! how we struggled! But their arms were strong.
They flung me on their pony's back, with thong

* God, in the Mohawk language.

Round ankle, wrist, and shoulder. Then upleapt
The one I hated most: his eye he swept
Over my misery, and sneering said,
'Thus, fair Ojistoh, we avenge our dead.'

PAULINE
JOHNSON

And we two rode, rode as a sea wind-chased,
I, bound with buckskin to his hated waist,
He, sneering, laughing, jeering, while he lashed
The horse to foam, as on and on we dashed.
Plunging through creek and river, bush and trail,
On, on we galloped like a northern gale.
At last, his distant Huron fires aflame
We saw, and nearer, nearer still we came.

I, bound behind him in the captive's place,
Scarcely could see the outline of his face.
I smiled, and laid my cheek against his back:
'Loose thou my hands,' I said. 'This pace let slack.
Forget we now that thou and I are foes.
I like thee well, and wish to clasp thee close;
I like the courage of thine eye and brow;
I like thee better than my Mohawk now.'

He cut the cords; we ceased our maddened haste
I wound my arms about his tawny waist;
My hand crept up the buckskin of his belt;
His knife hilt in my burning palm I felt;
One hand caressed his cheek, the other drew
The weapon softly—'I love you, love you,'
I whispered, 'love you as my life.'
And—buried in his back his scalping knife.

Ha! how I rode, rode as a sea wind-chased,
Mad with sudden freedom, mad with haste,
Back to my Mohawk and my home. I lashed
That horse to foam, as on and on I dashed.
Plunging thro' creek and river, bush and trail,
On, on I galloped like a northern gale.
And then my distant Mohawk's fires aflame
I saw, as nearer, nearer still I came,
My hands all wet, stained with a life's red dye,
But pure my soul, pure as those stars on high—
'My Mohawk's pure white star, Ojistoh, still am I.'

1912

Marshlands

PAULINE
JOHNSON

A thin wet sky, that yellows at the rim,
And meets with sun-lost lip the marsh's brim.

The pools low lying, dank with moss and mould,
Glint through their mildews like large cups of gold.

Among the wild rice in the still lagoon,
In monotone the lizard shrills his tune.

The wild goose, homing, seeks a sheltering,
Where rushes grow, and oozing lichens cling.

Late cranes with heavy wing, and lazy flight,
Sail up the silence with the nearing night.

And like a spirit, swathed in some soft veil,
Steals twilight and its shadows o'er the swale.

Hushed lie the sedges, and the vapours creep,
Thick, grey and humid, while the marshes sleep.

1912

In Flanders Fields

In Flanders fields the poppies blow
Between the crosses, row on row,
    That mark our place; and in the sky
    The larks, still bravely singing, fly
Scarce heard amid the guns below.

We are the Dead. Short days ago
We lived, felt dawn, saw sunset glow,
    Loved and were loved, and now we lie
        In Flanders fields.

Take up our quarrel with the foe:
To you from failing hands we throw
    The torch; be yours to hold it high.
    If ye break faith with us who die
We shall not sleep, though poppies grow
        In Flanders fields.

1915

ROBERT
SERVICE

1874–1958

The Cremation of Sam McGee

> There are strange things done in the midnight sun
>   By the men who moil for gold;
> The Arctic trails have their secret tales
>   That would make your blood run cold;
> The Northern Lights have seen queer sights,
>   But the queerest they ever did see
> Was that night on the marge of Lake Lebarge
>   I cremated Sam McGee.

Now Sam McGee was from Tennessee, where the cotton blooms and blows.
Why he left his home in the South to roam 'round the Pole, God only knows.
He was always cold, but the land of gold seemed to hold him like a spell;
Though he'd often say in his homely way that 'he'd sooner live in hell.'

On a Christmas Day we were mushing our way over the Dawson trail.
Talk of your cold! through the parka's fold it stabbed like a driven nail.
If our eyes we'd close, then the lashes froze till sometimes we couldn't see;
It wasn't much fun, but the only one to whimper was Sam McGee.

And that very night, as we lay packed tight in our robes beneath the snow,
And the dogs were fed, and the stars o'erhead were dancing heel and toe,
He turned to me, and 'Cap', says he, 'I'll cash in this trip, I guess;
And if I do, I'm asking that you won't refuse my last request.'

Well, he seemed so low that I couldn't say no; then he says with a sort of moan:
'It's the cursed cold, and it's got right hold till I'm chilled clean through to the bone.

Yet 'tain't being dead—it's my awful dread of the icy grave that
  pains;
So I want you to swear that, foul or fair, you'll cremate my last
  remains.'

A pal's last need is a thing to heed, so I swore I would not fail;
And we started on at the streak of dawn; but God! he looked
  ghastly pale.
He crouched on the sleigh, and he raved all day of his home in
  Tennessee;
And before nightfall a corpse was all that was left of Sam McGee.

There wasn't a breath in that land of death, and I hurried,
  horror-driven,
With a corpse half hid that I couldn't get rid, because of a promise
  given;
It was lashed to the sleigh, and it seemed to say: 'You may tax
  your brawn and brains,
But you promised true, and it's up to you to cremate those last
  remains.'

Now a promise made is a debt unpaid, and the trail has its own
  stern code.
In the days to come, though my lips were dumb, in my heart how
  I cursed that load.
In the long, long night, by the lone firelight, while the huskies,
  round in a ring,
Howled out their woes to the homeless snows—O God! how I
  loathed the thing.

And every day that quiet clay seemed to heavy and heavier grow;
And on I went, though the dogs were spent and the grub was
  getting low;
The trail was bad, and I felt half mad, but I swore I would not
  give in;
And I'd often sing to the hateful thing, and it hearkened with a
  grin.

Till I came to the marge of Lake Lebarge, and a derelict there lay;
It was jammed in the ice, but I saw in a trice it was called the
  'Alice May'.
And I looked at it, and I thought a bit, and I looked at my frozen
  chum;

Then 'Here', said I, with a sudden cry, 'is my cre-ma-tor-eum.'

Some planks I tore from the cabin floor, and I lit the boiler fire;
Some coal I found that was lying around, and I heaped the fuel
   higher;
The flames just soared, and the furnace roared—such a blaze you
   seldom see;
And I burrowed a hole in the glowing coal, and I stuffed in Sam
   McGee.

Then I made a hike, for I didn't like to hear him sizzle so;
And the heavens scowled, and the huskies howled, and the wind
   began to blow.
It was icy cold, but the hot sweat rolled down my cheeks, and I
   don't know why;
And the greasy smoke in an inky cloak went streaking down the
   sky.

I do not know how long in the snow I wrestled with grisly fear;
But the stars came out and they danced about ere again I ventured
   near;
I was sick with dread, but I bravely said: 'I'll just take a peep
   inside.
I guess he's cooked, and it's time I looked'; . . . then the door I
   opened wide.

And there sat Sam, looking cool and calm, in the heart of the
   furnace roar;
And he wore a smile you could see a mile, and he said: 'Please
   close that door.
It's fine in here, but I greatly fear you'll let in the cold and
   storm—
Since I left Plumtree, down in Tennessee, it's the first time I've
   been warm.'

> There are strange things done in the midnight sun
>   By the men who moil for gold;
> The Arctic trails have their secret tales
>   That would make your blood run cold;
> The Northern Lights have seen queer sights,
>   But the queerest they ever did see
> Was that night on the marge of Lake Lebarge
>   I cremated Sam McGee.   1907

THEODORE
GOODRIDGE
ROBERTS
1877-1953

The Blue Heron

In a green place lanced through
With amber and gold and blue—
A place of water and weeds,
And roses pinker than dawn
And ranks of lush young reeds
And grasses straightly withdrawn
   From graven ripples of sands,
   The still blue heron stands.

   Smoke-blue he is, and grey
   As embers of yesterday.
   Still he is as death;
   Like stone or shadow of stone
   Without a pulse or breath;
   Motionless and alone
   There 'midst the lily-stems—
   But his eyes are alive like gems.

   Still as a shadow; still
   Grey feather and yellow bill,
   Still as an image made
   Of mist and smoke half hid
   By windless sunshine and shade
   Save when a yellow lid
   Slides and is gone like a breath . . .
   Death-still—and sudden as death!

1926

E. J.
PRATT

1882-1964

The Shark

He seemed to know the harbour,
So leisurely he swam;
His fin,
Like a piece of sheet-iron,
Three-cornered,
And with knife-edge,
Stirred not a bubble
As it moved
With its base-line on the water.

His body was tubular
And tapered
And smoke-blue,
And as he passed the wharf
He turned,
And snapped at a flat-fish
That was dead and floating.
And I saw the flash of a white throat,
And a double row of white teeth,
And eyes of metallic grey,
Hard and narrow and slit.

Then out of the harbour,
With that three-cornered fin
Shearing without a bubble the water
Lithely,
Leisurely,
He swam—
That strange fish,
Tubular, tapered, smoke-blue,
Part vulture, part wolf,
Part neither—for his blood was cold.

1923

From THE TITANIC

E.J.
PRATT

[*The Final Moments*]

The fo'c'sle had gone under the creep
Of the water. Though without a wind, a lop
Was forming on the wells now fathoms deep.
The seventy feet—the boat deck's normal drop—
Was down to ten. Rising, falling, and waiting,
Rising again, the swell that edged and curled
Around the second bridge, over the top
Of the air-shafts, backed, resurged and whirled
Into the stokehold through the fiddley grating.

Under the final strain the two wire guys
Of the forward funnel tugged and broke at the eyes:
With buckled plates the stack leaned, fell and smashed
The starboard wing of the flying bridge, went through
The lower, then tilting at the davits crashed
Over, driving a wave aboard that drew
Back to the sea some fifty sailors and
The captain with the last of the bridge command.

Out on the water was the same display
Of fear and self-control as on the deck—
Challenge and hesitation and delay,
The quick return, the will to save, the race
Of snapping oars to put the realm of space
Between the half-filled lifeboats and the wreck.
The swimmers whom the waters did not take
With their instant death-chill struck out for the wake
Of the nearer boats, gained on them, hailed
The steersmen and were saved: the weaker failed
And fagged and sank. A man clutched at the rim
Of a gunwale, and a woman's jewelled fist
Struck at his face: two others seized his wrist,
As he released his hold, and gathering him
Over the side, they staunched the cut from the ring.
And there were many deeds envisaging
Volitions where self-preservation fought
Its red primordial struggle with the 'ought',
In those high moments when the gambler tossed
Upon the chance and uncomplaining lost.

Aboard the ship, whatever hope of dawn
Gleamed from the *Carpathia*'s riding lights was gone,
For every knot was matched by each degree
Of list. The stern was lifted bodily
When the bow had sunk three hundred feet, and set
Against the horizon stars in silhouette
Were the blade curves of the screws, hump of the rudder.
The downward pull and after buoyancy
Held her a minute poised but for a shudder
That caught her frame as with the upward stroke
Of the sea a boiler or a bulkhead broke.

Climbing the ladders, gripping shroud and stay,
Storm-rail, ringbolt or fairlead, every place
That might befriend the clutch of hand or brace
Of foot, the fourteen hundred made their way
To the heights of the aft decks, crowding the inches
Around the docking bridge and cargo winches.
And now that last salt tonic which had kept
The valour of the heart alive—the bows
Of the immortal seven that had swept
The strings to outplay, outdie their orders, ceased.
Five minutes more, the angle had increased
From eighty on to ninety when the rows
Of deck and port-hole lights went out, flashed back
A brilliant second and again went black.
Another bulkhead crashed, then following
The passage of the engines as they tore
From their foundations, taking everything
Clean through the bows from 'midships with a roar
Which drowned all cries upon the deck and shook
The watchers in the boats, the liner took
Her thousand fathoms journey to her grave.

.   .   .

And out there in the starlight, with no trace
Upon it of its deed but the last wave
From the *Titanic* fretting at its base,
Silent, composed, ringed by its icy broods,
The grey shape with the palaeolithic face
Was still the master of the longitudes.

1935

Silences

E.J.
PRATT

There is no silence upon the earth or under the earth like the
    silence under the sea;
No cries announcing birth,
No sounds declaring death.
There is silence when the milt is laid on the spawn in the weeds
    and fungus of the rock-clefts;
And silence in the growth and struggle for life.
The bonitoes pounce upon the mackerel,
And are themselves caught by the barracudas,
The sharks kill the barracudas
And the great molluscs rend the sharks,
And all noiselessly—
Though swift be the action and final the conflict,
The drama is silent.

There is no fury upon the earth like the fury under the sea.
For growl and cough and snarl are the tokens of spendthrifts who
    know not the ultimate economy of rage.
Moreover, the pace of the blood is too fast.
But under the waves the blood is sluggard and has the same
    temperature as that of the sea.

There is something pre-reptilian about a silent kill.

Two men may end their hostilities just with their battlecries.
'The devil take you,' says one.
'I'll see you in hell first,' says the other.
And these introductory salutes followed by a hail of gutturals and
    sibilants are often the beginning of friendship, for who would
    not prefer to be lustily damned than to be half-heartedly
    blessed?
No one need fear oaths that are properly enunciated, for they
    belong to the inheritance of just men made perfect, and, for
    all we know, of such may be the Kingdom of Heaven.
But let silent hate be put away for it feeds upon the heart of the
    hater.
Today I watched two pairs of eyes. One pair was black and the
    other grey. And while the owners thereof, for the space of
    five seconds, walked past each other, the grey snapped at the
    black and the black riddled the grey.
One looked to say—'The cat,'
And the other—'The cur.'

But no words were spoken;
Not so much as a hiss or a murmur came through the perfect
  enamel of the teeth; not so much as a gesture of enmity.
If the right upper lip curled over the canine, it went unnoticed.
The lashes veiled the eyes not for an instant in the passing.
And as between the two in respect to candour of intention or
  eternity of wish, there was no choice, for the stare was mutual
  and absolute.
A word would have dulled the exquisite edge of the feeling,
An oath would have flawed the crystallization of the hate.
For only such culture could grow in a climate of silence,—
Away back before the emergence of fur or feather, back to the
  unvocal sea and down deep where the darkness spills its wash
  on the threshold of light, where the lids never close upon the
  eyes, where the inhabitants slay in silence and are as silently
  slain.

1937

From BRÉBEUF AND HIS BRETHREN

[*The Martyrdom of Brébeuf and Lalemant, 16 March 1649*]

XII

No doubt in the mind of Brébeuf that this was the last
Journey—three miles over the snow. He knew
That the margins as thin as they were by which he escaped
From death through the eighteen years of his mission toil
Did not belong to this chapter: not by his pen
Would this be told. He knew his place in the line,
For the blaze of the trail that was cut on the bark by Jogues
Shone still. He had heard the story as told by writ
And word of survivors—of how a captive slave
Of the hunters, the skin of his thighs cracked with the frost,
He would steal from the tents to the birches, make a rough cross
From two branches, set it in snow and on the peel
Inscribe his vows and dedicate to the Name
In 'litanies of love' what fragments were left
From the wrack of his flesh; of his escape from the tribes;
Of his journey to France where he knocked at the door of the
  College
Of Rennes, was gathered in as a mendicant friar,

Nameless, unknown, till he gave for proof to the priest
His scarred credentials of faith, the nail-less hands
And withered arms—the signs of the Mohawk fury.
Nor yet was the story finished—he had come again
Back to his mission to get the second death.
And the comrades of Jogues—Goupil, Eustache and Couture,
Had been stripped and made to run the double files
And take the blows—one hundred clubs to each line—
And this as the prelude to torture, leisured, minute,
Where thorns on the quick, scallop shells to the joints of the
      thumbs,
Provided the sport for children and squaws till the end.
And adding salt to the blood of Brébeuf was the thought
Of Daniel—was it months or a week ago?
So far, so near, it seemed in time, so close
In leagues—just over there to the south it was
He faced the arrows and died in front of his church.

But winding into the greater artery
Of thought that bore upon the coming passion
Were little tributaries of wayward wish
And reminiscence. Paris with its vespers
Was folded in the mind of Lalemant,
And the soft Gothic lights and traceries
Were shading down the ridges of his vows.
But two years past at Bourges he had walked the cloisters,
Companioned by Saint Augustine and Francis,
And wrapped in quiet holy mists. Brébeuf,
His mind a moment throwing back the curtain
Of eighteen years, could see the orchard lands,
The *cidreries,* the peasants at the Fairs,
The undulating miles of wheat and barley,
Gardens and pastures rolling like a sea
From Lisieux to Le Havre. Just now the surf
Was pounding on the limestone Norman beaches
And on the reefs of Calvados. Had dawn
This very day not flung her surplices
Around the headlands and with golden fire
Consumed the silken argosies that made
For Rouen from the estuary of the Seine?
A moment only for that veil to lift—
A moment only for those bells to die
That rang their matins at Condé-sur-Vire.

71

By noon St. Ignace! The arrival there
The signal for the battle-cries of triumph,
The gauntlet of the clubs. The stakes were set
And the ordeal of Jogues was re-enacted
Upon the priests—even with wilder fury,
For here at last was trapped their greatest victim,
Echon. The Iroquois had waited long
For this event. Their hatred for the Hurons
Fused with their hatred for the French and priests
Was to be vented on this sacrifice,
And to that camp had come apostate Hurons,
United with their foes in common hate
To settle up their reckoning with *Echon.*

.   .   .

Now three o'clock, and capping the height of the passion,
Confusing the sacraments under the pines of the forest,
Under the incense of balsam, under the smoke
Of the pitch, was offered the rite of the font. On the head,
The breast, the loins and the legs, the boiling water!
While the mocking paraphrase of the symbols was hurled
At their faces like shards of flint from the arrow heads—
'We baptize thee with water . . .
That thou mayest be led
To Heaven . . .
To that end we do anoint thee.
We treat thee as a friend: we are the cause
Of thy happiness; we are thy priests; the more
Thou sufferest, the more thy God will reward thee,
So give us thanks for our kind offices.'

The fury of taunt was followed by fury of blow.
Why did not the flesh of Brébeuf cringe to the scourge,
Respond to the heat, for rarely the Iroquois found
A victim that would not cry out in such pain—yet here
The fire was on the wrong fuel. Whenever he spoke,
It was to rally the soul of his friend whose turn
Was to come through the night while the eyes were uplifted
    in prayer,
Imploring the Lady of Sorrows, the mother of Christ,
As pain brimmed over the cup and the will was called
To stand the test of the coals. And sometimes the speech
Of Brébeuf struck out, thundering reproof to his foes,
Half-rebuke, half-defiance, giving them roar for roar.

Was it because the chancel became the arena,
Brébeuf a lion at bay, not a lamb on the altar,
As if the might of a Roman were joined to the cause
Of Judaea? Speech they could stop for they girdled his lips,
But never a moan could they get. Where was the source
Of his strength, the home of his courage that topped the best
Of their braves and even out-fabled the lore of their legends?
In the bunch of his shoulders which often had carried a load
Extorting the envy of guides at an Ottawa portage?
The heat of the hatchets was finding a path to that source.
In the thews of his thighs which had mastered the trails of the
    Neutrals?
They would gash and beribbon those muscles. Was it the blood?
They would draw it fresh from its fountain. Was it the heart?
They dug for it, fought for the scraps in the way of the wolves.
But not in these was the valour or stamina lodged;
Nor in the symbol of Richelieu's robes or the seals
Of Mazarin's charters, nor in the stir of the *lilies*
Upon the Imperial folds; nor yet in the words
Loyola wrote on a table of lava-stone
In the cave of Manresa—not in these the source—
But in the sound of invisible trumpets blowing
Around two slabs of board, right-angled, hammered
By Roman nails and hung on a Jewish hill.

The wheel had come full circle with the visions
In France of Brébeuf poured through the mould of St. Ignace.
Lalemant died in the morning at nine, in the flame
Of the pitch belts. Flushed with the sight of the bodies, the foes
Gathered their clans and moved back to the north and west
To join in the fight against the tribes of the Petuns.
There was nothing now that could stem the Iroquois blast.
However undaunted the souls of the priests who were left,
However fierce the sporadic counter attacks
Of the Hurons striking in roving bands from the ambush,
Or smashing out at their foes in garrison raids,
The villages fell before a blizzard of axes
And arrows and spears, and then were put to the torch.

The days were dark at the fort and heavier grew
The burdens on Ragueneau's shoulders. Decision was his.
No word from the east could arrive in time to shape
The step he must take. To and fro—from altar to hill,

From hill to altar, he walked and prayed and watched.   E.J.
PRATT
As governing priest of the Mission he felt the pride
Of his Order whipping his pulse, for was not St. Ignace
The highest test of the Faith? And all that torture
And death could do to the body was done. The Will
And the Cause in their triumph survived.
   Loyola's mountains,
Sublime at their summits, were scaled to the uttermost peak.
Ragueneau, the Shepherd, now looked on a battered fold.
In a whirlwind of fire St. Jean, like St. Joseph, crashed
Under the Iroquois impact. Firm at his post,
Garnier suffered the fate of Daniel. And now
Chabanel, last in the roll of the martyrs, entrapped
On his knees in the woods met death at apostate hands.

The drama was drawing close to its end. It fell
To Ragueneau's lot to perform a final rite—
To offer the fort in sacrificial fire!
He applied the torch himself. *'Inside an hour,'*
He wrote, *'we saw the fruit of ten years' labour*
Ascend in smoke,—then looked our last at the fields,
Put altar-vessels and food on a raft of logs,
And made our way to the island of St. Joseph.'
But even from there was the old tale retold—
Of hunger and the search for roots and acorns;
Of cold and persecution unto death
By the Iroquois; of Jesuit will and courage
As the shepherd-priest with Chaumonot led back
The remnant of a nation to Quebec.

1940

The Truant

E.J.
PRATT

'What have you there?' the great Panjandrum said
To the Master of the Revels who had led
A bucking truant with a stiff backbone
Close to the foot of the Almighty's throne.
'Right Reverend, most adored,
And forcibly acknowledged Lord
By the keen logic of your two-edged sword!
This creature has presumed to classify
Himself—a biped, rational, six feet high
And two feet wide; weighs fourteen stone;
Is guilty of a multitude of sins.
He has abjured his choric origins,
And like an undomesticated slattern,
Walks with tangential step unknown
Within the weave of the atomic pattern.
He has developed concepts, grins
Obscenely at your Royal bulletins,
Possesses what he calls a will
Which challenges your power to kill.'

'What is his pedigree?'

'The base is guaranteed, your Majesty—
Calcium, carbon, phosphorus, vapour
And other fundamentals spun
From the umbilicus of the sun,
And yet he says he will not caper
Around your throne, nor toe the rules
For the ballet of the fiery molecules.'
'His concepts and denials—scrap them, burn them—
To the chemists with them promptly.'
                              'Sire,
The stuff is not amenable to fire.
Nothing but their own kind can overturn them.
The chemists have sent back the same old story—
"With our extreme gelatinous apology,
We beg to inform your Imperial Majesty,
Unto whom be dominion and power and glory,
There still remains that strange precipitate
Which has the quality to resist
Our oldest and most trusted catalyst.

It is a substance we cannot cremate
By temperatures known to our Laboratory." '

And the great Panjandrum's face grew dark—
'I'll put those chemists to their annual purge,
And I myself shall be the thaumaturge
To find the nature of this fellow's spark.
Come, bring him nearer by yon halter rope:
I'll analyse him with the cosmoscope.'

Pulled forward with his neck awry,
The little fellow six feet short,
Aware he was about to die,
Committed grave contempt of court
By answering with a flinchless stare
The Awful Presence seated there.

The ALL HIGH swore until his face was black.
He called him a coprophagite,
A genus *homo*, egomaniac,
Third cousin to the family of worms,
A sporozoan from the ooze of night,
Spawn of a spavined troglodyte:
He swore by all the catalogue of terms
Known since the slang of carboniferous Time.
He said that he could trace him back
To pollywogs and earwigs in the slime.
And in his shrillest tenor he began
Reciting his indictment of the man,
Until he closed upon this capital crime—
'You are accused of singing out of key
(A foul unmitigated dissonance),
Of shuffling in the measures of the dance,
Then walking out with that defiant, free
Toss of your head, banging the doors,
Leaving a stench upon the jacinth floors.
You have fallen like a curse
On the mechanics of my Universe.

'Herewith I measure out your penalty—
Hearken while you hear, look while you see:
I send you now upon your homeward route
Where you shall find

Humiliation for your pride of mind.
I shall make deaf the ear, and dim the eye,
Put palsy in your touch, make mute
Your speech, intoxicate your cells and dry
Your blood and marrow, shoot
Arthritic needles through your cartilage,
And having parched you with old age,
I'll pass you wormwise through the mire;
And when your rebel will
Is mouldered, all desire
Shrivelled, all your concepts broken,
Backward in dust I'll blow you till
You join my spiral festival of fire.
Go, Master of the Revels—I have spoken.'

And the little genus *homo*, six feet high,
Standing erect, countered with this reply—
'You dumb insouciant invertebrate,
You rule a lower than a feudal state—
A realm of flunkey decimals that run,
Return; return and run; again return,
Each group around its little sun,
And every sun a satellite.
There they go by day and night,
Nothing to do but run and burn,
Taking turn and turn about,
Light-year in and light-year out,
Dancing, dancing in quadrillions,
Never leaving their pavilions.

'Your astronomical conceit
Of bulk and power is anserine.
Your ignorance so thick,
You did not know your own arithmetic.
We flung the graphs about your flying feet;
We measured your diameter—
Merely a line
Of zeros prefaced by an integer.
Before we came
You had no name.

You did not know direction or your pace;
We taught you all you ever knew

Of motion, time and space.
We healed you of your vertigo
And put you in our kindergarten show,
Perambulated you through prisms, drew
Your mileage through the Milky Way,
Lassoed your comets when they ran astray,
Yoked Leo, Taurus, and your team of Bears
To pull our kiddy cars of inverse squares.

'Boast not about your harmony,
Your perfect curves, your rings
Of *pure and endless light*—'Twas we
Who pinned upon your Seraphim their wings,
And when your brassy heavens rang
With joy that morning while the planets sang
Their choruses of archangelic lore,
'Twas we who ordered the notes upon their score
Out of our winds and strings.
Yes! all your shapely forms
Are ours—parabolas of silver light,
Those blueprints of your spiral stairs
From nadir depth to zenith height,
Coronas, rainbows after storms,
Auroras on your eastern tapestries
And constellations over western seas.

'And when, one day, grown conscious of your age,
While pondering an eolith,
We turned a human page
And blotted out a cosmic myth
With all its baby symbols to explain
The sunlight in Apollo's eyes,
Our rising pulses and the birth of pain,
Fear, and that fern-and-fungus breath
Stalking our nostrils to our caves of death—
That day we learned how to anatomize
Your body, calibrate your size
And set a mirror up before your face
To show you what you really were—a rain
Of dull Lucretian atoms crowding space,
A series of concentric waves which any fool
Might make by dropping stones within a pool,

Or an exploding bomb forever in flight
Bursting like hell through Chaos and Old Night.

E.J.
PRATT

'You oldest of the hierarchs
Composed of electronic sparks,
We grant you speed,
We grant you power, and fire
That ends in ash, but we concede
To you no pain nor joy nor love nor hate,
No final tableau of desire,
No causes won or lost, no free
Adventure at the outposts—only
The degradation of your energy
When at some late
Slow number of your dance your sergeant-major Fate
Will catch you blind and groping and will send
You reeling on that long and lonely
Lockstep of your wave-lengths towards your end.

'We who have met
With stubborn calm the dawn's hot fusillades;
Who have seen the forehead sweat
Under the tug of pulleys on the joints,
Under the liquidating tally
Of the cat-and-truncheon bastinades;
Who have taught our souls to rally
To mountain horns and the sea's rockets
When the needle ran demented through the points;
We who have learned to clench
Our fists and raise our lightless sockets
To morning skies after the midnight raids,
Yet cocked our ears to bugles on the barricades,
And in cathedral rubble found a way to quench
A dying thirst within a Galilean valley—
No! by the Rood, we will not join your ballet.'

1943

The Pre-Cambrian Shield

(i)
On the North Shore a reptile lay asleep—
A hybrid that the myths might have conceived,
But not delivered, as progenitor
Of crawling, gliding things upon the earth.
She lay snug in the folds of a huge boa
Whose tail had covered Labrador and swished
Atlantic tides, whose body coiled itself
Around the Hudson Bay, then curled up north
Through Manitoba and Saskatchewan
To Great Slave Lake. In continental reach
The neck went past the Great Bear Lake until
Its head was hidden in the Arctic Seas.
This folded reptile was asleep or dead:
So motionless, she seemed stone dead—just seemed:
She was too old for death, too old for life,
For as if jealous of all living forms
She had lain there before bivalves began
To catacomb their shells on western mountains.
Somewhere within this life-death zone she sprawled,
Torpid upon a rock-and-mineral mattress.
Ice-ages had passed by and over her,
But these, for all their motion, had but sheared
Her spotty carboniferous hair or made
Her ridges stand out like the spikes of molochs.
Her back grown stronger every million years,
She had shed water by the longer rivers
To Hudson Bay and by the shorter streams
To the great basins to the south, had filled
Them up, would keep them filled until the end
Of Time.

(ii)
DYNAMITE ON THE NORTH SHORE

The lizard was in sanguinary mood.
She had been waked again: she felt her sleep
Had lasted a few seconds of her time.
The insects had come back—the ants, if ants

They were—dragging *those* trees, *those* logs athwart
Her levels, driving in *those* spikes; and how
The long grey snakes unknown within her region
Wormed from the east, unstriped, sunning themselves
Uncoiled upon the logs and then moved on,
Growing each day, ever keeping abreast!
She watched them, waiting for a bloody moment,
Until the borers halted at a spot,
The most invulnerable of her whole column,
Drove in that iron, wrenched it in the holes,
Hitting, digging, twisting. Why that spot?
Not this the former itch. That sharp proboscis
Was out for more than self-sufficing blood
About the cuticle: 'twas out for business
In the deep layers and the arteries.
And this consistent punching at her belly
With fire and thunder slapped her like an insult,
As with the blasts the caches of her broods
Broke—nickel, copper, silver and fool's gold,
Burst from their immemorial dormitories
To sprawl indecent in the light of day.
Another warning—this time different.

Westward above her webs she had a trap—
A thing called muskeg, easy on the eyes
Stung with the dust of gravel. Cotton grass,
Its white spires blending with the orchids,
Peeked through green table-cloths of sphagnum moss.
Carnivorous bladder-wort studded the acres,
Passing the water-fleas through their digestion.
Sweet-gale and sundew edged the dwarf black spruce;
And herds of cariboo had left their hoof-marks,
Betraying visual solidity,
But like the thousands of the pitcher plants,
Their downward-pointing hairs alluring insects,
Deceptive—and the men were moving west!
Now was her time. She took three engines, sank them
With seven tracks down through the hidden lake
To the rock bed, then over them she spread
A counterpane of leather-leaf and slime.
A warning, that was all for now. 'Twas sleep
She wanted, sleep, for drowsing was her pastime
And waiting through eternities of seasons.

As for intruders bred for skeletons—
Some day perhaps when ice began to move,
Or some convulsion ran fires through her tombs,
She might stir in her sleep and far below
The reach of steel and blast of dynamite,
She'd claim their bones as her possessive right
And wrap them cold in her pre-Cambrian folds.

1952

MARJORIE PICKTHALL

1883–1922

Père Lalement

I lift the Lord on high,
Under the murmuring hemlock boughs, and see
The small birds of the forest lingering by
And making melody.
These are mine acolytes and these my choir,
And this mine altar in the cool green shade,
Where the wild soft-eyed does draw nigh
Wondering, as in the byre
Of Bethlehem the oxen heard Thy cry
And saw Thee, unafraid.

My boatmen sit apart,
Wolf-eyed, wolf-sinewed, stiller than the trees.
Help me, O Lord, for very slow of heart
And hard of faith are these.
Cruel are they, yet Thy children. Foul are they,
Yet wert Thou born to save them utterly.
Then make me as I pray
Just to their hates, kind to their sorrows, wise
After their speech, and strong before their free
Indomitable eyes.

Do the French lilies reign
Over Mont Royal and Stadacona still?
Up the St. Lawrence comes the spring again,

Crowning each southward hill MARJORIE
And blossoming pool with beauty, while I roam
Far from the perilous folds that are my home,
There where we built St. Ignace for our needs,
Shaped the rough roof tree, turned the first sweet sod,
St. Ignace and St. Louis, little beads
On the rosary of God.

Pines shall Thy pillars be,
Fairer than those Sidonian cedars brought
By Hiram out of Tyre, and each birch-tree
Shines like a holy thought.
But come no worshippers; shall I confess,
St. Francis-like, the birds of the wilderness?
O, with Thy love my lonely head uphold.
A wandering shepherd I, who hath no sheep;
A wandering soul, who hath no scrip, nor gold,
Nor anywhere to sleep.

My hour of rest is done;
On the smooth ripple lifts the long canoe;
The hemlocks murmur sadly as the sun
Slants his dim arrows through.
Whither I go I know not, nor the way,
Dark with strange passions, vexed with heathen charms,
Holding I know not what of life or death;
Only be Thou beside me day by day,
Thy rod my guide and comfort, underneath
Thy everlasting arms.

1913

Quiet

MARJORIE
PICKTHALL

Come not the earliest petal here, but only
Wind, cloud, and star,
Lovely and far,
Make it less lonely.

Few are the feet that seek her here, but sleeping
Thoughts sweet as flowers
Linger for hours,
Things winged, yet weeping.

Here in the immortal empire of the grasses,
Time, like one wrong
Note in a song,
With their bloom, passes.

1922

Two Souls

A Letter from Père Jogues

Most reverend Father, I have borne all wrong,
Agonies, griefs, revengements. Yet not I,
But rather He Who knew and loved us long,
And came at last to die.
In my maimed hands ye see Him, in my face
His poor abiding place,

'Lo, they will hear My voice and understand;
Go, seek My wandering sheep,' the Shepherd saith,
So, o'er the world I sought them, hand in hand
With the dark brother of our Order, Death.
Under the shadow of his bitterest rod,
Behold, two souls for God!

Like the reed-feeding swans that cannot choose
But hear the voice of summer, in swift flight
Up from Three Rivers came the long canoes
Through calm of day and night,
I in the foremost, Coupil and Couture,
Whose fiery crowns are sure.

Sweet shines the summer over Normandy,   MARJORIE
And bright on Arles among her blossoming vines,   PICKTHALL
But O, more sweet than any land or sea
The northern summer shines.
Each night a silvered dream to cast away,
Each golden dream a day—

So we went on, and our dark Hurons smiled,
Singing the child-songs of the woodpecker,
Through clear green glooms and amber bars enisled
Of tamarack and fir.
Till one cried, 'Lo, a shadow and a dread
Steals from the isles ahead!'

Death laid a sudden silence on his lips.
In tumult of torn waters at the side.
Crashing, he fell, and all our little ships
Shook on that reddening tide.
Then the blue noon was torn with steel and flame,
And the Five Nations came.

1925

KENNETH
LESLIE

1892-1974

Halibut Cove Harvest

The kettle sang the boy to a half-sleep;
and the stir, stir of the kettle's lid
drummed a new age
into the boy's day-dream.
His mind strove with the mind of steam
and conquered it
and pressed it down and shaped it
to the panting giant
whose breath lies heavy on the world.

This is a song of harvest;
the weather thickens with a harsh wind

on this salt-seared coast;
offshore a trawler, smoke-smearing the horizon,
reaps the sea.

Here on the beach
in the cove of the handliner
rain flattens the ungathered dulse
and no cheek reddens to the rain.
From the knock-kneed landing
a faltering path is lost among the rocks
to a door that is closed with a nail.
Seams widen and the paint falls off in curling flakes
from the brave, the bold so little time ago,
the dory high and dry,
anchored in hungry grass.

This is the song of harvest:
the belching trawler raping the sea,
the cobweb ghosts against the window
watching the wilderness uproot the doorsill with a weed.

1938

Sonnet

The silver herring throbbed thick in my seine,
silver of life, life's silver sheen of glory;
my hands, cut with the cold, hurt with the pain
of hauling the net, pulled the heavy dory,
heavy with life, low in the water, deep
plunged to the gunwale's lips in the stress of rowing,
the pulse of rowing that puts the world to sleep,
world within world endlessly ebbing, flowing.
At length you stood on the landing and you cried,
with quick low cries you timed me stroke on stroke
as I steadily won my way with the fulling tide
and crossed the threshold where the last wave broke
and coasted over the step of water and threw
straight through the air my mooring line to you.

1938

W.W.E.
ROSS

1894-1966

The Diver

I would like to dive
Down
Into this still pool
Where the rocks at the bottom are safely deep,

Into the green
Of the water seen from within,
A strange light
Streaming past my eyes—

Things hostile;
You cannot stay here, they seem to say;
The rocks, slime-covered, the undulating
Fronds of weeds—

And drift slowly
Among the cooler zones;
Then, upward turning,
Break from the green glimmer

Into the light,
White and ordinary of the day,
And the mild air,
With the breeze and the comfortable shore.

1968

If Ice

If
ice shall melt
if
thinly the fresh
cold clear   water
running   shall make
grooves in the sides
of the ice;
if life return
after death
or depart not at death,
then shall buds
burst into   May-
leafing, the blooms of May
appear like stars
on the brown dry
forest-bed.

1968

The Snake Trying

The snake trying
to escape the pursuing stick,
with sudden curvings of thin
long body. How beautiful

and graceful are his shapes!
He glides through the water away
from the stroke. O let him go
over the water

into the reeds to hide
without hurt. Small and green
he is harmless even to children.
Along the sand

he lay until observed
and chased away, and now
he vanishes in the ripples
among the green slim reeds.   1968

RAYMOND
KNISTER

1899-1932

Boy Remembers in the Field

What if the sun comes out
And the new furrows do not look smeared?

This is April, and the sumach candles
Have guttered long ago.
The crows in the twisted apple limbs
Are as moveless and dark.

Drops on the wires, cold cheeks,
The mist, the long snorts, silence . . .
The horses will steam when the sun comes;
Crows, go, shrieking.

Another bird now; sweet . . .
Pitiful life, useless,
Innocently creeping
On a useless planet
Again.

If any voice called, I would hear?
It has been the same before.
Soil glistens, the furrow rolls, sleet shifts, brightens.

1942

Nell

RAYMOND
KNISTER

Nellie Rakerfield
Came from an estate in Scotland,
Two years old, and won a championship.
It was not her fault that her foals
Were few, and mostly died or were runted.
She worked every day when she raised them,
Never was tired of dragging her
Nineteen hundred pounds
About the farm and the roads, with
Great loads behind it.
She never kicked, bit, nor crowded
In the stall,
Was always ready at a chirp
And seemed to have forgotten delicate care.

But the day they hitched her
To the corpse of her six-months-old colt,
She tried to run away, half way to the bush.
She never seemed quite so willing, afterward.
But the colt was too heavy.

1949

February's Forgotten Mitts

Shep lies long-bodied upon the auburn grass—
It has been dried in the glance of the sudden sun.
As you pass he wrinkles a sideward eye to the astounding blue of
    heaven.
Half a mile away the year's first cackling of hens, aroused from
    the cold.
The boughs of the elm and the maple wait, expectant.
The fields and roads rejoice in slithering mud over the frost.
Somewhere a well-clear, golden echo of children's voices crying
    and calling.
After dinner Pete looks around for his mitts.
He has lost them about the barn this morning:
Spring has flung forward an unringed hand.

1949

F. R.
SCOTT

b. 1899

The Canadian Authors Meet

Expansive puppets percolate self-unction
Beneath a portrait of the Prince of Wales.
Miss Crochet's muse has somehow failed to function,
Yet she's a poetess. Beaming, she sails

From group to chattering group, with such a dear
Victorian saintliness, as is her fashion,
Greeting the other unknowns with a cheer—
Virgins of sixty who still write of passion.

The air is heavy with Canadian topics,
And Carman, Lampman, Roberts, Campbell, Scott,
Are measured for their faith and philanthropics,
Their zeal for God and King, their earnest thought.

The cakes are sweet, but sweeter is the feeling
That one is mixing with the *literati*;
It warms the old, and melts the most congealing.
Really, it is a most delightful party.

Shall we go round the mulberry bush, or shall
We gather at the river, or shall we
Appoint a poet Laureate this Fall,
Or shall we have another cup of tea?

O Canada, O Canada, Oh can
A day go by without new authors springing
To paint the native maple, and to plan
More ways to set the selfsame welkin ringing?

1927

Brébeuf and his Brethren

When Lalemant and de Brébeuf, brave souls,
Were dying by the slow and dreadful coals
Their brother Jesuits in France and Spain
Were burning heretics with equal pain.
For both the human torture made a feast:
Then is priest savage, or Red Indian priest?

1941

W.L.M.K.

How shall we speak of Canada,
Mackenzie King dead?
The Mother's boy in the lonely room
With his dog, his medium and his ruins?

He blunted us.

We had no shape
Because he never took sides,
And no sides
Because he never allowed them to take shape.

He skillfully avoided what was wrong
Without saying what was right,
And never let his on the one hand
Know what his on the other hand was doing.

The height of his ambition
Was to pile a Parliamentary Committee on a Royal Commission,
To have 'conscription if necessary
But not necessarily conscription',
To let Parliament decide—
Later.

Postpone, postpone, abstain.

Only one thread was certain:
After World War I
Business as usual,

After World War II
Orderly decontrol.
Always he led us back to where we were before.

F.R.
SCOTT

He seemed to be in the centre
Because we had no centre,
No vision
To pierce the smoke-screen of his politics.

Truly he will be remembered
Wherever men honour ingenuity,
Ambiguity, inactivity, and political longevity.

Let us raise up a temple
To the cult of mediocrity,
Do nothing by halves
Which can be done by quarters.

1954

Lakeshore

The lake is sharp along the shore
Trimming the bevelled edge of land
To level curves; the fretted sands
Go slanting down through liquid air
Till stones below shift here and there
Floating upon their broken sky
All netted by the prism wave
And rippled where the currents are.

I stare through windows at this cave
Where fish, like planes, slow-motioned, fly.
Poised in a still of gravity
The narrow minnow, flicking fin,
Hangs in a paler, ochre sun,
His doorways open everywhere.

And I am a tall frond that waves
Its head below its rooted feet
Seeking the light that draws it down

To forest floors beyond its reach
Vivid with gloom and eerie dreams.

F.R.
SCOTT

The water's deepest colonnades
Contract the blood, and to this home
That stirs the dark amphibian
With me the naked swimmers come
Drawn to their prehistoric womb.

They too are liquid as they fall
Like tumbled water loosed above
Until they lie, diagonal,
Within the cool and sheltered grove
Stroked by the fingertips of love.

Silent, our sport is drowned in fact
Too virginal for speech or sound
And each is personal and laned
Along his private aqueduct.

Too soon the tether of the lungs
Is taut and straining, and we rise
Upon our undeveloped wings
Toward the prison of our ground
A secret anguish in our thighs
And mermaids in our memories.

This is our talent, to have grown
Upright in posture, false-erect,
A landed gentry, circumspect,
Tied to a horizontal soil
The floor and ceiling of the soul;
Striving, with cold and fishy care
To make an ocean of the air.

Sometimes, upon a crowded street,
I feel the sudden rain come down
And in the old, magnetic sound
I hear the opening of a gate
That loosens all the seven seas.
Watching the whole creation drown
I muse, alone, on Ararat.

1954

Laurentian Shield

F.R.
SCOTT

Hidden in wonder and snow, or sudden with summer,
This land stares at the sun in a huge silence
Endlessly repeating something we cannot hear.
Inarticulate, arctic,
Not written on by history, empty as paper,
It leans away from the world with songs in its lakes
Older than love, and lost in the miles.

This waiting is wanting.
It will choose its language
When it has chosen its technic,
A tongue to shape the vowels of its productivity.

A language of flesh and of roses.

Now there are pre-words,
Cabin syllables,
Nouns of settlement
Slowly forming, with steel syntax,
The long sentence of its exploitation.

The first cry was the hunter, hungry for fur,
And the digger for gold, nomad, no-man, a particle;
Then the bold commands of monopoly, big with machines,
Carving its kingdoms out of the public wealth;
And now the drone of the plane, scouting the ice,
Fills all the emptiness with neighbourhood
And links our future over the vanished pole.

But a deeper note is sounding, heard in the mines,
The scattered camps and the mills, a language of life,
And what will be written in the full culture of occupation
Will come, presently, tomorrow,
From millions whose hands can turn this rock into children.

1954

Night Club

F.R.
SCOTT

The girls, brighter than wine, are clothed and naked.
They pose in abandon by the pools of their laughter.
One man is with them, but all, all are invited
To the short-term ceremony—and something after.

Certainly it is bogus, it is tawdry, and beauty
Is bottled and sold for profit, yet cannot be hidden.
Even the clap-trap adolescent vulgarity
Reminds us of banquets to which we long to be bidden.

It is a hard game, living on third-rate levels,
Getting our love through the eyes, our power through drink,
While inside we nurse the fading image of something
Of which the mind too soon even ceases to think.

1964

ROBERT
FINCH

b. 1900

Last Visit

The place we could never enter hides away still
While the sea below keeps watch through the pines on the hill,
But the once forbidding gate hangs by a hinge
And the winding road to the house has a weedy fringe.
No one goes up any more now the house has gone.
Not a single stone is left on another stone.
Where siren windows gave you the sea in their glasses
The wind smooths out a coverlet of grasses
And yellow daisies dance a flaming wreath
Remembering those that crowned the absent hearth.
Instead of a poem alive with joy and sorrow
The day is always a day with no tomorrow
Yet look to the sea as when yesterday was there
And nothing has changed except what brought us here.

1966

Silverthorn Bush

ROBERT
FINCH

I am a dispossessed Ontario wood
That took the circling weather as my crown,
Now noise makes havoc of my whispered mood
And enterprise has laughed my towers down.

Is there a poem where I blossom still?
Do paintings keep my solitude secure?
Somewhere remote adventure must distil
Part of its fragrance from an air so pure.

I am the springing memory of my past
In vagabond and child who held me dear,
Theirs is the surest witness that I last
In buds of mine that I no longer bear.

If you can overtake their truant youth
Ask them to flash my secret on your sight,
They heard my pensive river spill its truth
And felt my hidden fibres tug the light.

The riddle is how disappearance puts
A dusty end to a green revery
Yet leaves me nourished by so many roots
That I shall never cease ceasing to be.

1966

A.J.M.
SMITH

1902–1980

The Lonely Land

Cedar and jagged fir
uplift sharp barbs
against the gray
and cloud-piled sky;
and in the bay
blown spume and windrift
and thin, bitter spray
snap
at the whirling sky;
and the pine trees
lean one way.

A wild duck calls
to her mate,
and the ragged
and passionate tones
stagger and fall,
and recover,
and stagger and fall,
on these stones—
are lost
in the lapping of water
on smooth, flat stones.
This is a beauty
of dissonance,
this resonance
of stony strand,
this smoky cry
curled over a black pine
like a broken
and wind-battered branch
when the wind
bends the tops of the pines
and curdles the sky
from the north.

This is the beauty

of strength
broken by strength
and still strong.

1936

The Common Man

I
Somewhere his number must have been betrayed,
Caught in the dazzle that the goldfish made
Or lost in the gas of the first mock raid.

A jittery clerk with a slippery pen
Condemned him to limbo, a headless hen
Gyrating about in a bloodstained pen.

He lived by luck and a sense of touch.
These were his two gifts and they were not too much.
One was a black patch and the other a crutch.

He lived at last on scraps of a food card
Chewed up and torn and found in the yard
Beside a corpse the death ray only charred.

II
To survive, at first an escapist's whim,
Became with time, as his trim grew slim,
Less a point of honour than a duty grim.

He was the only man in the world
Not registered. He was a node, a furled
Forgotten flag, a still point still unwhirled.

His function was to stand outside.
At first he thought this helped him when he tried
To tell who told the truth, who plainly lied.

He was the unseen watcher standing there
By the sweating statue in Parliament Square,
The one who could not care and had to care.

III

His job was to listen in on the queues,
To decode the official releases, and fuse
The cheers on parade with the jeers in the mews.

The diminishing pressure of hands
Gave him a valuable clue. Mourning bands
Were not worn, but he noticed that sands

Were much sought after for building castles on.
(The castles might crumble but not burn down.
Incendiaries fizzle in sand and soon are done.)

The dead were not mentioned, though each was planted.
Even the stricken areas were not haunted.
The dead, being of spirit, were not wanted.

IV

At last his 'amour-propre' became 'the public weal':
He was the common man, Platonic and ideal,
Mercurial and elusive, yet alive and real.

He was the public good, the target one
At whom each sugar-coated poison-spraying gun
Was levelled. Whatever was done was done

To him. He was the ear communiqués
Addressed, the simple mind for which the maze
Of policy was clarified. His praise

Was what the leaders said was their reward.
To pierce his heart the patriotic sword
Was dipped in ink and gall and flourished hard.

V

He fell, of course. An abstract man
Who ended much as he began—
An exile in a universal plan.

Not to let the leaders down became his mission.
To ascertain their will was his obsession.
His hope, somehow to wangle their permission

To speak and be himself and have a name,
And shake abstraction's disembodied shame,
And play, not overlook, the murderous game. . . .

A.J.M.
SMITH

He boils a soiled shard of his purloined card
And bends where the lamplight ends over the hard
Significant puzzle. The ignorant policeman walks the yard.

1954

The Dead

The dead
Stare out of empty sockets
In the blank faces of loudspeakers;
    Their red
Fingerless stumps paw at the web
Of the mind stretched out on newspapers.

    Father
Finds the comfortable funnies
Not so funny and not comfortable;
    Rather
Against his will he takes the dead
Into his usual organ of deep thought,

    The pit
Of his stomach; there he becomes
Aware of the dead; there he feels sad.
    At night
The stories of bombings and legends
Of ack-ack trouble his bowels.

    The dead
Walk in his sleep. He cries out, ah!
There is a kind of fighting in his guts.
    His bed
Creaks with the ceaseless tread
Of the shiftless dead.

    They come
With no accusing look; their eyes

Are drained of any light but pity's;
   His doom
Is this, there is not any spark
Of fellowship in these dead eyes.

   He lives,
Indeed, but might as well be dead
As these anonymous statistics,
   Whose loves
Were just as kind as his, whose lives
Were precious, being irreplaceable.

1954

Resurrection of Arp

On the third day rose Arp
out of the black sleeve of the tomb;
he could see like a cat in the dark,
but the light left him dumb.

He stood up to testify,
and his tongue wouldn't work
in the old groove; he had to try
other tongues, including the Scandinavian.

The saints were all well pleased;
his periods rattled and rolled;
heresies scattered like ninepins;
all the tickets were sold.

When they turned down the gas
everybody could see there was
a halo of tongues of pale fire
licking the grease off his hair,

and a white bird
fluttered away in the rafters;
people heard
the breaking of a mysterious wind (laughter).

He spoke another language
majestic beautiful wild

holy superlative believable
and undefiled

by any comprehensible
syllable
to provoke dissent
or found a schism. . . .

After the gratifyingly large
number of converts had been given receipts
the meeting adjourned to the social hall
for sexual intercourse (dancing) and eats.

Arp talked to the reporters:
on the whole, was glad to have cheated the tomb,
though the angels had been 'extremely courteous',
and death, after all, was only 'another room'.

1954

RONALD
EVERSON

b. 1903

One-night Expensive Hotel
(Trying to reverse Baudelaire's DOUBLE ROOM)

Evening outdoors is only a larger lobby
cluttered with voices and faces. Shadowy.
On-off street signs are splashing me with blood.

I rush back into the lobby. Decades of faces
struggle in noisy heaps on chairs and rug.
I slit one heap. New faces press against me.

Forced to my room, I hear loud voices
locked in the mirror, the bed, the dresser drawers.
Blood streams from a lampbulb overhead.

I tell a dictaphone memos, sales orders

for a long time, slowly tidying the room,
stopping the blood. Soon I shall risk the bed,
wriggling down among mute faces of bone.

1958

Injured Maple

Lightning scratched our sugar maple, blood
poisoning it   This evening in myriads
samaras swelling from twigs litter the ground

                    and heaved roots mound
on bedrock our quilt of grass

Writhed branches will scatter saplings to murder the lawn

The injured maple knows nothing about a population explosion
It is impossible for me to believe that the maple thinks

Yet why does the insensate sick wood, chilled
by lightning, suddenly increase her seeds?

My body is injured by years   I have no child
                    I suspect the maple
is somehow sly as Lot's chaste daughters at incest wild
                    or Macbeth murdering for high-plumed sons

I stand here fearful at dusk under the primitive active tree

1963

Pauper Woodland

RONALD
EVERSON

Settlers abandoned our county long ago
leaving cellar caves and piled stone mounds
  grassy serpents of Early Man

  Their jonquils bloomed
and under lilacs lily of the valley

  Monied with silence
we lived for five years in that wilderness

Autumns a small invasion of wanderers returned
  to squatter homes
  some even from summer jobs
Smoke signals waved good morning out of valleys

We visited around Jem Sofer's cabin
a mansion of hardwood planks prone on each other
was papered indoors with ladies for extra warming

  Sofer was Indian
  my woodland mentor
He splinted and healed the broken leg of a bobcat

A bear had scratched oak bark one night
away beyond my reach Another morning
  moose prints many yards apart
  where the night runner passed our home

November we found a stranger cutting wood
as the scrub darkened to forest All around him
yellow sawdust lit the frozen ground
and at the centre of radiance the man's red smile

1969

Stranded in My Ontario

RONALD
EVERSON

Madame Maynard of the hard pebble
       beach eight thousand years old
       above glacial lake Scugog

My husband died fallen in that stone quarry
       pointing her flint finger
at a bruise of shadows where hawks swoop
over the chasm for any continuing stir

The old woman motionless by my hardtop car
and her lopsided home sandblasted granite grey

She has been stranded for decades in my Ontario
       down from her mind-glittering origins
       in French Canada

       Daynight swoops year after year
above the quarry of her last-stand stone beach
Daynight swoops in grooves along her forehead
       along her sweet cheeks
       and dear fractured mouth

       I have seen her slowly stiffen with age,
a drumlin too hard-up for travelling farther

Madame Maynard has been ground down to a grey pebble
       of strong Breton dignity

1969

EARLE
BIRNEY

b. 1904

Anglosaxon Street

Dawn drizzle ended   dampness steams from
blotching brick and   blank plasterwaste
Faded housepatterns   hoary and finicky
unfold stuttering   stick like a phonograph

Here is a ghetto   gotten for goyim
O with care denuded   of nigger and kike
No coonsmell rankles   reeks only cellarrot
Ottar of carexhaust   catcorpse and cookinggrease
Imperial hearts   heave in this haven
Cracks across windows   are welded with slogans
There'll Always Be An England   enhances geraniums
and V's for Victory   vanquish the housefly

Ho! with climbing sun   march the bleached beldames
festooned with shopping bags   farded flatarched
bigthewed Saxonwives   stepping over buttrivers
waddling back wienerladen   to suckle smallfry

Hoy! with sunslope   shrieking over hydrants
flood from learninghall   the lean fingerlings
Nordic nobblecheeked   not all clean of nose
leaping Commandowise   into leprous lanes

What! after whistleblow!   spewed from wheelboat
after daylight doughtiness   dire handplay
in sewertrench or sandpit   come Saxonthegns
Junebrown Jutekings   jawslack for meat

Sit after supper   on smeared doorsteps
not humbly swearing   hatedeeds on Huns
profiteers politicians   pacifists Jews

Then by twobit magic   to muse in movie
unlock picturehoard   or lope to alehall
soaking bleakly   in beer skittleless

Home again to hotbox   and humid husbandhood
in slumbertrough adding   sleepily to Anglekin
Alongside in lanenooks   carling and leman
caterwaul and clip   careless of Saxonry
with moonglow and haste   and a higher heartbeat

Slumbers now slumtrack   unstinks cooling
waiting brief for milkmaid   mornstar and worldrise

1942

David

EARLE
BIRNEY

I

David and I that summer cut trails on the Survey,
All week in the valley for wages, in air that was steeped
In the wail of mosquitoes, but over the sunalive week-ends
We climbed, to get from the ruck of the camp, the surly

Poker, the wrangling, the snoring under the fetid
Tents, and because we had joy in our lengthening coltish
Muscles, and mountains for David were made to see over,
Stairs from the valleys and steps to the sun's retreats.

II

Our first was Mount Gleam. We hiked in the long afternoon
To a curling lake and lost the lure of the faceted
Cone in the swell of its sprawling shoulders. Past
The inlet we grilled our bacon, the strips festooned

On a poplar prong, in the hurrying slant of the sunset.
Then the two of us rolled in the blanket while round us the cold
Pines thrust at the stars. The dawn was a floating
Of mists till we reached to the slopes above timber, and won

To snow like fire in the sunlight. The peak was upthrust
Like a fist in a frozen ocean of rock that swirled
Into valleys the moon could be rolled in. Remotely unfurling
Eastward the alien prairie glittered. Down through the dusty

Skree on the west we descended, and David showed me
How to use the give of shale for giant incredible
Strides. I remember, before the larches' edge,
That I jumped a long green surf of juniper flowing

Away from the wind, and landed in gentian and saxifrage
Spilled on the moss. Then the darkening firs
And the sudden whirring of water that knifed down a fern-hidden
Cliff and splashed unseen into mist in the shadows.

III

One Sunday on Rampart's arête a rainsquall caught us,
And passed, and we clung by our blueing fingers and bootnails
An endless hour in the sun, not daring to move
Till the ice had steamed from the slate. And David taught me

How time on a knife-edge can pass with the guessing of
    fragments
Remembered from poets, the naming of strata beside one,
And matching of stories from schooldays. . . . We crawled astride
The peak to feast on the marching ranges flagged

By the fading shreds of the shattered stormcloud. Lingering
There it was David who spied to the south, remote,
And unmapped, a sunlit spire on Sawback, an overhang
Crooked like a talon. David named it the Finger.

That day we chanced on the skull and the splayed white ribs
Of a mountain goat underneath a cliff-face, caught
On a rock. Around were the silken feathers of hawks.
And that was the first I knew that a goat could slip.

IV

And then Inglismaldie. Now I remember only
The long ascent of the lonely valley, the live
Pine spirally scarred by lightning, the slicing pipe
Of invisible pika, and great prints, by the lowest

Snow, of a grizzly. There it was too that David
Taught me to read the scroll of coral in limestone
And the beetle-seal in the shale of ghostly trilobites,
Letters delivered to man from the Cambrian waves.

V

On Sundance we tried from the col and the going was hard.
The air howled from our feet to the smudged rocks
And the papery lake below. At an outthrust we baulked
Till David clung with his left to a dint in the scarp,

Lobbed the iceaxe over the rocky lip,
Slipped from his holds and hung by the quivering pick,
Twisted his long legs up into space and kicked
To the crest. Then grinning, he reached with his freckled wrist

And drew me up after. We set a new time for that climb.
That day returning we found a robin gyrating
In grass, wing-broken. I caught it to tame but David
Took and killed it, and said, 'Could you teach it to fly?'

VI

In August, the second attempt, we ascended The Fortress.
By the forks of the Spray we caught five trout and fried them
Over a balsam fire. The woods were alive
With the vaulting of mule-deer and drenched with clouds all the
    morning,

Till we burst at noon to the flashing and floating round
Of the peaks. Coming down we picked in our hats the bright
And sunhot raspberries, eating them under a mighty
Spruce, while a marten moving like quicksilver scouted us.

VII

But always we talked of the Finger on Sawback, unknown
And hooked, till the first afternoon in September we slogged
Through the musky woods, past a swamp that quivered with
    frog-song,
And camped by a bottle-green lake. But under the cold

Breath of the glacier sleep would not come, the moon-light
Etching the Finger. We rose and trod past the feathery
Larch, while the stars went out, and the quiet heather
Flushed, and the skyline pulsed with the surging bloom

Of incredible dawn in the Rockies. David spotted
Bighorns across the moraine and sent them leaping
With yodels the ramparts redoubled and rolled to the peaks,
And the peaks to the sun. The ice in the morning thaw

Was a gurgling world of crystal and cold blue chasms,
And seracs that shone like frozen saltgreen waves.
At the base of the Finger we tried once and failed. Then David
Edged to the west and discovered the chimney; the last

Hundred feet we fought the rock and shouldered and kneed
Our way for an hour and made it. Unroping we formed
A cairn on the rotting tip. Then I turned to look north
At the glistening wedge of giant Assiniboine, heedless

Of handhold. And one foot gave. I swayed and shouted.
David turned sharp and reached out his arm and steadied me,
Turning again with a grin and his lips ready
To jest. But the strain crumbled his foothold. Without

A gasp he was gone. I froze to the sound of grating
Edge-nails and fingers, the slither of stones, the lone
Second of silence, the nightmare thud. Then only
The wind and the muted beat of unknowing cascades.

VIII
Somehow I worked down the fifty impossible feet
To the ledge, calling and getting no answer but echoes
Released in the cirque, and trying not to reflect
What an answer would mean. He lay still, with his lean

Young face upturned and strangely unmarred, but his legs
Splayed beneath him, beside the final drop,
Six hundred feet sheer to the ice. My throat stopped
When I reached him, for he was alive. He opened his gray

Straight eyes and brokenly murmured 'over . . . over'.
And I, feeling beneath him a cruel fang
Of the ledge thrust in his back, but not understanding,
Mumbled stupidly, 'Best not to move,' and spoke

Of his pain. But he said, 'I can't move. . . . If only I felt
Some pain.' Then my shame stung the tears to my eyes
As I crouched, and I cursed myself, but he cried,
Louder, 'No, Bobbie! Don't ever blame yourself.

I didn't test my foothold.' He shut the lids
Of his eyes to the stare of the sky, while I moistened his lips
From our water flask and tearing my shirt into strips
I swabbed the shredded hands. But the blood slid

From his side and stained the stone and the thirsting lichens,
And yet I dared not lift him up from the gore
Of the rock. Then he whispered, 'Bob, I want to go over!'
This time I knew what he meant and I grasped for a lie

And said, 'I'll be back here by midnight with ropes
And men from the camp and we'll cradle you out.' But I knew

That the day and the night must pass and the cold dews
Of another morning before such men unknowing

The ways of mountains could win to the chimney's top.
And then, how long? And he knew . . . and the hell of hours
After that, if he lived till we came, roping him out.
But I curled beside him and whispered, 'The bleeding will stop.

You can last.' He said only, 'Perhaps. . . . For what? A
   wheelchair,
Bob?' His eyes brightening with fever upbraided me.
I could not look at him more and said, 'Then I'll stay
With you.' But he did not speak, for the clouding fever.

I lay dazed and stared at the long valley,
The glistening hair of a creek on the rug stretched
By the firs, while the sun leaned round and flooded the ledge,
The moss, and David still as a broken doll.

I hunched to my knees to leave, but he called and his voice
Now was sharpened with fear. 'For Christ's sake push me over!
If I could move. . . . Or die. . . .' The sweat ran from his
   forehead,
But only his eyes moved. A hawk was buoying

Blackly its wings over the wrinkled ice.
The purr of a waterfall rose and sank with the wind.
Above us climbed the last joint of the Finger
Beckoning bleakly the wide indifferent sky.

Even then in the sun it grew cold lying there. . . . And I knew
He had tested his holds. It was I who had not. . . . I looked
At the blood on the ledge, and the far valley. I looked
At last in his eyes. He breathed, 'I'd do it for you, Bob.'

IX
I will not remember how nor why I could twist
Up the wind-devilled peak, and down through the chimney's
   empty
Horror, and over the traverse alone. I remember
Only the pounding fear I would stumble on It

When I came to the grave-cold maw of the bergschrund . . . EARLE
BIRNEY
   reeling
Over the sun-cankered snowbridge, shying the caves
In the névé . . . the fear, and the need to make sure It was there
On the ice, the running and falling and running, leaping

Of gaping greenthroated crevasses, alone and pursued
By the Finger's lengthening shadow. At last through the fanged
And blinding seracs I slid to the milky wrangling
Falls at the glacier's snout, through the rocks piled huge

On the humped moraine, and into the spectral larches,
Alone. By the glooming lake I sank and chilled
My mouth but I could not rest and stumbled still
To the valley, losing my way in the ragged marsh.

I was glad of the mire that covered the stains, on my ripped
Boots, of his blood, but panic was on me, the reek
Of the bog, the purple glimmer of toadstools obscene
In the twilight. I staggered clear to a firewaste, tripped

And fell with a shriek on my shoulder. It somehow eased
My heart to know I was hurt, but I did not faint
And I could not stop while over me hung the range
Of the Sawback. In blackness I searched for the trail by the creek

And found it . . . My feet squelched a slug and horror
Rose again in my nostrils. I hurled myself
Down the path. In the woods behind some animal yelped.
Then I saw the glimmer of tents and babbled my story.

I said that he fell straight to the ice where they found him,
And none but the sun and incurious clouds have lingered
Around the marks of that day on the ledge of the Finger,
That day, the last of my youth, on the last of our mountains.

1942

Slug in Woods

EARLE
BIRNEY

For eyes he waves greentipped
taut horns of slime   They dipped
hours back   across a reef
a salmonberry leaf
then strained to grope past fin
of spruce   Now eyes suck in
as through the hemlock butts
of his day's ledge there cuts
a vixen chipmunk   Stilled
is he—green mucus chilled
or blotched and soapy stone
pinguid in moss   alone
Hours on   he will resume
his silver scrawl   illume
his palimpsest   emboss
his diver's line across
that waving green illim-
itable seafloor   Slim
young jay his sudden shark
The wrecks he skirts are dark
and fungussed firlogs   whom
spirea sprays emplume
encoral   Dew his shell
while mounting boles foretell
of isles in dappled air
fathoms above his care
Azygous muted life
himself his viscid wife
foodward he noses cold beneath his sea
So spends a summer's jasper century

1942

Bushed

EARLE
BIRNEY

He invented a rainbow but lightning struck it
shattered it into the lake-lap of a mountain
so big his mind slowed when he looked at it

Yet he built a shack on the shore
learned to roast porcupine belly and
wore the quills on his hatband

At first he was out with the dawn
whether it yellowed bright as wood-columbine
or was only a fuzzed moth in a flannel of storm
But he found the mountain was clearly alive
sent messages whizzing down every hot morning
boomed proclamations at noon and spread out
a white guard of goat
before falling asleep on its feet at sundown

When he tried his eyes on the lake   ospreys
would fall like valkyries
choosing the cut-throat
He took then to waiting
till the night smoke rose from the boil of the sunset

But the moon carved unknown totems
out of the lakeshore
owls in the beardusky woods derided him
moosehorned cedars circled his swamps and tossed
their antlers up to the stars
then he knew   though the mountain slept   the winds
were shaping its peak to an arrowhead
poised

And now he could only
bar himself in and wait
for the great flint to come singing into his heart

1952

Can. Lit.

(or *them able leave her ever*)

since we'd always sky about
when we had eagles they flew out
leaving no shadow bigger than wren's
to trouble even our broodiest hens

too busy bridging loneliness
to be alone
we hacked in railway ties
what Emily etched in bone

we French & English never lost
our civil war
endure it still
a bloody civil bore

the wounded sirened off
no Whitman wanted
it's only by our lack of ghosts
we're haunted

1962

The Bear on the Delhi Road

Unreal   tall as a myth
by the road the Himalayan bear
is beating the brilliant air
with his crooked arms
About him two men   bare
spindly as locusts   leap

One pulls on a ring
in the great soft nose   His mate
flicks   flicks with a stick
up at the rolling eyes

They have not led him here
down from the fabulous hills

to this bald alien plain
and the clamorous world   to kill
but simply to teach him to dance

They are peaceful both   these spare
men of Kashmir   and the bear
alive is their living   too
If   far on the Delhi way
around him galvanic they dance
it is merely to wear   wear
from his shaggy body the tranced
wish forever to stay
only an ambling bear
four-footed in berries

It is no more joyous for them
in this hot dust to prance
out of reach of the praying claws
sharpened to paw for ants
in the shadows of deodars
It is not easy to free
myth from reality
or rear this fellow up
to lurch   lurch with them
in the tranced dancing of men

1962

EARLE
BIRNEY

My Love Is Young

my love is young & i am old
she'll need a new man soon
but still we wake to clip and talk
to laugh as one
to eat and walk
beneath our five-year moon

good moon   good sun
that we do love
i pray the world believe me
& never tell me when it's time
that i'm to die
or she's to leave me

Toronto 1978

Dazzle

Light looks from a dazzled leaf,
Stares like a small sun,
Glitters, and in the breeze
Leaps to another leaf.

Light speaks and the morning answers,
The surest answer from the tree,
Up, up, up, up and all open,
But the flight and the song breaking free
Of the branch answer, answer also,
And the brightest answer is the eye—

Light blazes from the car windshield,
Prints tendrils on the shimmering wall,
Twinkles in the flower cup . . .
Up, up, up, up
Answer the vine and the grassblade,
The squirrel and the ball out of sight,
Answer all the shapes broken up
Into shimmer and shadow. Light

Comes to the eye from the answer,
Not direct from the fiery core—
From the kindled pebble under the sprinkler
To the glittering eye
That answers with so much seen
And the blinded 'Why?'

Light plays with the chorus of the living
While the dead hurry down
Earthward to lift to the dazzle
Any answering form.

1957

Cold

DOROTHY
ROBERTS

My grandparents lived to a great age in the cold—
O cruel preservative, the hard day beginning
With night and zero and the firewood
Numbing the fingers. God could have been in the flame
Responsive among the birch sticks, roaring
Up through the comforting pipes, and served all day
From the frosted woodpile, the continuing flame
As the sun almost let go of the bitter world.

But for them He stayed in the cold,
In the outer absolutes of cold among the fiery orbits,
And gave them the white breath and the blood pumping
Through hard activity stringing out the muscles
Into great age. They lived in cold
And were seasoned by it and preached it
And knew that it blazed
In the burning bush of antiquity
With starry flowers.

1957

JOHN
GLASSCO

1909–1981

Quebec Farmhouse

Admire the face of plastered stone,
    The roof descending like a song
        Over the washed and anointed walls,
    Over the house that hugs the earth
    Like a feudal souvenir: oh see
The sweet submissive fortress of itself
        That the landscape owns!

    And inside is the night, the airless dark
        Of the race so conquered it has made
        Perpetual conquest of itself,
    Upon desertion's ruin piling

The inward desert of surrender, JOHN
GLASSCO
Drawing in all its powers, puffing its soul,
    Raising its arms to God.

This is the closed, enclosing house
    That set its flinty face against
    The rebel children dowered with speech
To break it open, to make it live
And flower in the cathedral beauty
Of a pure heaven of Canadian blue—
    The larks so maimed

They still must hark and hurry back
    To the paradisal place of gray,
    The clash of keys, the click of beads,
The sisters walking leglessly,
While under the wealth and weight of stone
All the bright demons of forbidden joy
    Shriek on, year after year.

1971

The Entailed Farm

A footpath would have been enough.
The muddy mile of side-road has no purpose
Save as it serves for others to link up
Crossroads marked on the map with a nameless cross
By way of these choked and heartless fields of paintbrush
And the mute, sealed house,

Where the spring's tooth, stripping shingles, scaling
Beam and clapboard, probes for the rot below
Porch and pediment and blind bow-window,
And the wooden trunk with the coloured cardboard lining
Lies where it fell when the wall of the flying wing
Fell down ten years ago;

Where the stone wall is a haven for snake and squirrel, JOHN GLASSCO
The steepled dovecote for phoebe and willow-wren,
And the falling field-gates, trigged by an earthen swell,
Open on a wild where nothing is raised or penned,
On rusty acres of witch-grass and wild sorrel
Where the field-birds cry and contend.

You, tourist, salesman, family out for a picnic,
Who saw the bearded man that walked like a bear,
His pair of water-pails slung from a wooden neckyoke,
Slipping in by the woodshed—Come away,
That naked door is proof against all knocking!
Standing and knocking there,

You might as well expect time's gate to open
On the living past, the garden bloom again,
The house stand upright, hay-barn's swayback coping
Stiffen, and see as in a fretted frame
Men in the meadow and a small boy whooping
The red oxen down that orchard lane,

Or revive the slow strong greed of the coffined farmer
Who cleared, stumped, fenced, rotating sinew and sweat,
Beating the ploughshare into an honest dollar,
Who living and dying planned to cheat time's night
Through the same white-bearded boy—who is hiding somewhere
Now, till you're out of sight,

And have left him alone: alone with the grief or anger
Or whatever it is that flickers but will not die
In the dull brain of the victim turned avenger,
At war with a shadow, in flight from passers-by,
From us—who are free from all but the hint of attainder,
Who can meet a stranger's eye

With a good face, can answer a question, give a reason,
For whom the world's fields and fences stand up plain,
Nor dazzle in sunlight or crumble behind the rain:
From us, with our hearts but lightly tinged with poison,
Who composed our quarrel early and in good season
Buried the hatchet in our father's brain.

1971

One Last Word

JOHN
GLASSCO

For M. McC.

Now that I have your hand, let me persuade you
The means are more important than the end,
Ends being only an excuse for action,
For adventures sought for their own sake alone,
Pictures along the way, feelings
Released in love: so, acting out our dreams
We justify movement by giving it a purpose
(Who can be still forever?)
This is the rationale of travel
And the formula of lovers.

Dearest, it is not for the amusement of certain tissues,
Nor for whatever may thread our loins like a vein
                              of miraculous water
That now (under the music) I speak your name—
But for the journey we shall take together
Through a transfigured landscape
Of beasts and birds and people
Where everything is new.
                      Listen,
The embarkation for Cythera
Is eternal because it ends nowhere:
No port for those tasselled sails! And for our love
No outcome,
Only the modesty
The perfection
Of the flight or death of a bird.

1971

122

RALPH
GUSTAFSON

b. 1909

Columbus Reaches Juana, 1492

Letter of Guacanagari the Indian to his nephew, 1562

We fled from the sight inland and that night
We put our seed into the wombs of our women
So that we would live. The great curves
Of the shining cloth were white and rose
Dry out of the horizons of the sea. My solution
Was: the winds of the sun are many, they
Were between us. The ships were habitations
Many huts high with levels and blinding metal
Between, the heights not coming though they rode
The swell that crashed to us. Coverings
Such as we could not imagine. We waited, the grass
Not moving though the parrots screamed in the silence
And fell silent at the three thunders. The women
Were beyond at the huts. We commanded
The thunder in our ears. My armpits
Wet and I could smell fear. I watched.
The godhood of the sails in my mind
Became less: man's waste marked the hulls.
The sun shone. They came at noon. I thought of Naa
And her soft breasts. My length was nothing
And tight against me. The shark cut
The shadow and was not afraid. When they came
It was amidst blades lifted on the sea. We moved
Back. The birds rose and were without purpose.
I saw that they were encased. Whether they had
Hair all over, I could not tell. I was sorry
To give up the banner of many colours they carried above them.
It was torn. Many hands had not cared for it.

I write as it was.

These men are not gods.

Jesus be with you.

1966 (rev. 1982)

Mothy Monologue

RALPH
GUSTAFSON

Matthew VI, 19

The moth flew a bee-line,
The flame beckoned but there was
A globe around it. The moth acted
Drunk after. My heart went
Out.

That Phnom-Penh child
Bombed in the stairway looks like roasted
Meat—except for the arms and legs.

Moths don't fly bee-lines.

This one did. All the way back
To Moscow.

The cellar stairs all
Are lined with human meat.

This,
In times of truce . . .

My heart goes out.

At least all the little children
Are dead reasonably.

Insurgent
Howitzers are within killing
Distance of the kindergarten . . .

So what's new?

Well, let's see,
The Khmer-Rouge should exempt those
Not near burial details.
The smell crosses the Pacific.

Of course,
Hanoi is absolutely right.
So is Saigon.

My heart goes out.

Then again, the world's population
Is explosive. A village a day
Is born in India.

For infant mortality,
Thank God.

The globe is where I study.
Guerillas prevent my seeing
Angkor Wat. I have been down
The Chao Phya River, though,
Where the poor are happy—or seem happy—
Pounding laundry on the bank stones,
And jumping in the river, the kids.
Maybe we better leave Thailand
Alone. The hovel coming next
Sports a TV aerial . . . . I'm drifting
Down the river on a sugar boat.
I travel this way, my own
Sweet way. I don't like
Guided tours . . . .

To return to my study:

Eastward, the world is rich with oil.
They are jacking Israel from the sands of time.

I better sign off.

I smell
Something burning.

1977

Wednesday at North Hatley

RALPH
GUSTAFSON

It snows on this place
And a gentleness obtains.
The garden fills with white,
Last summer's hedgerow
Bears a burden and birds
Are scarce. The grosbeak
Fights for seeds, the squirrel
Walks his slender wire.
There is a victory;
The heart endures, the house
Achieves its warmth and where
He needs to, man in woollen
Mitts, in muffler, without
A deathwish, northern, walks.
Except he stop at drifts
He cannot hear this snow,
The wind has fallen, and where
The lake awaits, the road
Is his. Softly the snow
Falls. Chance is against him.
But softly the snow falls.

1977

Heirloom

My father bequeathed me no wide estates;
No keys and ledgers were my heritage;
Only some holy books with *yahrzeit* dates
Writ mournfully upon a blank front page—

Books of the Baal Shem Tov, and of his wonders;
Pamphlets upon the devil and his crew;
Prayers against road demons, witches, thunders;
And sundry other tomes for a good Jew.

Beautiful: though no pictures on them, save
The scorpion crawling on a printed track;
The Virgin floating on a scriptural wave,
Square letters twinkling in the Zodiac.

The snuff left on this page, now brown and old,
The tallow stains of midnight liturgy—
These are my coat of arms, and these unfold
My noble lineage, my proud ancestry!

And my tears, too, have stained this heirloomed ground,
When reading in these treatises some weird
Miracle, I turned a leaf and found
A white hair fallen from my father's beard.

1940

The Break-up

They suck and whisper it in mercury,
the thermometers. It is shouted red
from all the Aprils hanging on the walls.
In the dockyard stalls
the stevedores, their hooks rusty, wonder; the
wintering sailors in the taverns bet.

A week, and it will crack! Here's money that
a fortnight sees the floes, the smokestacks red!
Outside *The Anchor's* glass, St. Lawrence lies
rigid and white and wise,
nor ripple and dip, but fathom-frozen flat.
There are no hammers will break that granite lid.

But it will come! Some dead of night with boom
to wake the wagering city, it will break,
will crack, will melt its muscle-bound tides
and raise from their iced tomb
the pyramided fish, the unlockered ships,
and last year's blue and bloated suicides.

1948

Indian Reservation: Caughnawaga

Where are the braves, the faces like autumn fruit,
who stared at the child from the coloured frontispiece?
And the monosyllabic chief who spoke with his throat?
Where are the tribes, the feathered bestiaries?—
Rank Aesop's animals erect and red,
with fur on their names to make all live things kin'—
Chief Running Deer, Black Bear, Old Buffalo Head?

Childhood, that wished me Indian, hoped that
one afterschool I'd leave the classroom chalk,
the varnish smell, the watered dust of the street,
to join the clean outdoors and the Iroquois track.
Childhood; but always,—as on a calendar,—
there stood that chief, with arms akimbo, waiting
the runaway mascot paddling to his shore.

With what strange moccasin stealth that scene is changed!
With French names, without paint, in overalls,
their bronze, like their nobility expunged,—
the men. Beneath their alimentary shawls
sit like black tents their squaws; while for the tourist's
brown pennies scattered at the old church door,
the ragged papooses jump, and bite the dust.

Their past is sold in a shop: the beaded shoes,
the sweetgrass basket, the curio Indian,
burnt wood and gaudy cloth and inch-canoes—
trophies and scalpings for a traveller's den.
Sometimes, it's true, they dance, but for a bribe;
after a deal don the bedraggled feather
and welcome a white mayor to the tribe.

This is a grassy ghetto, and no home.
And these are fauna in a museum kept.
The better hunters have prevailed. The game,
losing its blood, now makes these grounds its crypt.
The animals pale, the shine of the fur is lost,
bleached are their living bones. About them watch
as through a mist, the pious prosperous ghosts.

1948

A.M.
KLEIN

Portrait of the Poet as Landscape

I
Not an editorial-writer, bereaved with bartlett,
mourns him, the shelved Lycidas.
No actress squeezes a glycerine tear for him.
The radio broadcast lets his passing pass.
And with the police, no record. Nobody, it appears,
either under his real name or his alias,
missed him enough to report.

It is possible that he is dead, and not discovered.
It is possible that he can be found some place
in a narrow closet, like the corpse in a detective story,
standing, his eyes staring, and ready to fall on his face.
It is also possible that he is alive
and amnesiac, or mad, or in retired disgrace,
or beyond recognition lost in love.

We are sure only that from our real society
he has disappeared; he simply does not count,
except in the pullulation of vital statistics—
somebody's vote, perhaps, an anonymous taunt

of the Gallup poll, a dot in a government table—
but not felt, and certainly far from eminent—
in a shouting mob, somebody's sigh.

A.M.
KLEIN

O, he who unrolled our culture from his scroll—
the prince's quote, the rostrum-rounding roar—
who under one name made articulate
heaven, and under another the seven-circled air,
is, if he is at all, a number, an x,
a Mr. Smith in a hotel register,—
incognito, lost, lacunal.

II
The truth is he's not dead, but only ignored—
like the mirroring lenses forgotten on a brow
that shine with the guilt of their unnoticed world.
The truth is he lives among neighbours, who, though they will
     allow
him a passable fellow, think him eccentric, not solid,
a type that one can forgive, and for that matter, forgo.

Himself he has his moods, just like a poet.
Sometimes, depressed to nadir, he will think all lost,
will see himself as throwback, relict, freak,
his mother's miscarriage, his great-grandfather's ghost,
and he will curse his quintuplet senses, and their tutors
in whom he put, as he should not have put, his trust.

Then he will remember his travels over that body—
the torso verb, the beautiful face of the noun,
and all those shaped and warm auxiliaries!
A first love it was, the recognition of his own.
Dear limbs adverbial, complexion of adjective,
dimple and dip of conjugation!

And then remember how this made a change in him
affecting for always the glow and growth of his being;
how suddenly was aware of the air, like shaken tinfoil,
of the patents of nature, the shock of belated seeing,
the lonelinesses peering from the eyes of crowds;
the integers of thought; the cube-roots of feeling.

Thus, zoomed to zenith, sometimes he hopes again,

and sees himself as a character, with a rehearsed role:
the Count of Monte Cristo, come for his revenges;
the unsuspected heir, with papers; the risen soul;
or the chloroformed prince awaking from his flowers;
or—deflated again—the convict on parole.

III
He is alone; yet not completely alone.
Pins on a map of a colour similar to his,
each city has one, sometimes more than one;
here, caretakers of art, in colleges;
in offices, there, with arm-bands, and green-shaded;
and there, pounding their catalogued beats in libraries,—

everywhere menial, a shadow's shadow.
And always for their egos—their outmoded art.
Thus, having lost the bevel in the ear,
they know neither up nor down, mistake the part
for the whole, curl themselves in a comma,
talk technics, make a colon their eyes. They distort—

such is the pain of their frustration—truth
to something convolute and cerebral.
How they do fear the slap of the flat of the platitude!
Now Pavlov's victims, their mouths water at bell,
the platter empty.
                    See they set twenty-one jewels
into their watches; the time they do not tell!

Some, patagonian in their own esteem,
and longing for the multiplying word,
join party and wear pins, now have a message,
an ear, and the convention-hall's regard.
Upon the knees of ventriloquists, they own,
of their dandled brightness, only the paint and board.

And some go mystical, and some go mad.
One stares at a mirror all day long, as if
to recognize himself; another courts
angels,—for here he does not fear rebuff;
and a third, alone, and sick with sex, and rapt,
doodles him symbols convex and concave.

O schizoid solitudes! O purities
curdling upon themselves! Who live for themselves,
or for each other, but for nobody else;
desire affection, private and public loves;
are friendly, and then quarrel and surmise
the secret perversions of each other's lives.

IV

He suspects that something has happened, a law
been passed, a nightmare ordered. Set apart,
he finds himself, with special haircut and dress,
as on a reservation. Introvert.
He does not understand this; sad conjecture
muscles and palls thrombotic on his heart.

He thinks an impostor, having studied his personal biography,
his gestures, his moods, now has come forward to pose
in the shivering vacuums his absence leaves.
Wigged with his laurel, that other, and faked with his face,
he pats the heads of his children, pecks his wife,
and is at home, and slippered, in his house.

So he guesses at the impertinent silhouette
that talks to his phone-piece and slits open his mail.
Is it the local tycoon who for a hobby
plays poet, he so epical in steel?
The orator, making a pause? Or is that man
he who blows his flash of brass in the jittering hall?

Or is he cuckolded by the troubadour
rich and successful out of celluloid?
Or by the don who unrhymes atoms? Or
the chemist death built up? Pride, lost impostor'd pride,
it is another, another, whoever he is,
who rides where he should ride.

V

Fame, the adrenalin: to be talked about;
to be a verb; to be introduced as *The:*
to smile with endorsement from slick paper; make
caprices anecdotal; to nod to the world; to see
one's name like a song upon the marquees played;
to be forgotten with embarrassment; to be—
to be.

It has its attractions, but is not the thing;
nor is it the ape mimesis who speaks from the tree
ancestral; nor the merkin joy . . .
Rather it is stark infelicity
which stirs him from his sleep, undressed, asleep
to walk upon roofs and window-sills and defy
the gape of gravity.

VI
Therefore he seeds illusions. Look, he is
the nth Adam taking a green inventory
in world but scarcely uttered, naming, praising,
the flowering fiats in the meadow, the
syllabled fur, stars aspirate, the pollen
whose sweet collision sounds eternally.
For to praise

the world—he, solitary man—is breath
to him. Until it has been praised, that part
has not been. Item by exciting item—
air to his lungs, and pressured blood to his heart.—
they are pulsated, and breathed, until they map,
not the world's, but his own body's chart!

And now in imagination he has climbed
another planet, the better to look
with single camera view upon this earth—
its total scope, and each afflated tick,
its talk, its trick, its tracklessness—and this,
this he would like to write down in a book!

To find a new function for the *déclassé* craft
archaic like the fletcher's; to make a new thing;
to say the word that will become sixth sense;
perhaps by necessity and indirection bring
new forms to life, anonymously, new creeds—
O, somehow pay back the daily larcenies of the lung!

These are not mean ambitions. It is already something
merely to entertain them. Meanwhile, he
makes of his status as zero a rich garland,
a halo of his anonymity,
and lives alone, and in his secret shines
1948   like phosphorus. At the bottom of the sea.

Green Rain

I remember long veils of green rain
Feathered like the shawl of my grandmother—
Green from the half-green of the spring trees
Waving in the valley.

I remember the road
Like the one which leads to my grandmother's house,
A warm house, with green carpets,
Geraniums, a trilling canary
And shining horse-hair chairs;
And the silence, full of the rain's falling
Was like my grandmother's parlour
Alive with herself and her voice, rising and falling—
Rain and wind intermingled.

I remember on that day
I was thinking only of my love
And of my love's house.
But now I remember the day
As I remember my grandmother.
I remember the rain as the feathery fringe of her shawl.

1932

Without Benefit of Tape

The real poems are being written in outports
on backwoods farms
in passageways where pantries still exist
or where geraniums
nail light to the window
while out of the window boy in the flying field
is pulled to heaven on the keel of a kite.

Stories breed in the north: DOROTHY
LIVESAY
men with snow in their mouths
trample and shake at the bit
kneading the woman down under blankets of snow
icing her breath, her eyes.

The living speech is shouted out
by men and women leaving railway lines
to trundle home, pack-sacked
just company for deer or bear—

   Hallooed
across the counter, in a corner store
it booms upon the river's shore:
on midnight roads where hikers flag you down
speech echoes from the canyon's wall
   resonant
   indubitable.

1967

Waking in the Dark

Whenever I see him
in mind's eye
I see him light-haired and laughing
running in a green field

But day comes
radio is turned on
newspaper is insinuated
under the door
and there   between comic strips
ads   and girdled girls
black words mushroom:

It's going to take a hundred years DOROTHY
LIVESAY
          the experts say
to finish this genocide
a hundred years to annihilate a people
to bitter the ricefields with blood
dry Delta's water into salt—
a hundred years
                    so our grandchildren growing up
                    and their children
will be humans who feel no pity
                    for the green earth
and who look upon procreation
                    with indifference

When I see my grandchild running
in a game of football
his helmet is empty
in his right arm
he carries his head.

1969

The Uninvited

Always a third one's there
where any two are walking out
along a river-bank   so mirror-still
sheathed in sheets
of sky   pillows of cloud—
their footprints crunch the hardening earth
their eyes delight in trees   stripped clean
winter-prepared
with only the rose-hips red
and the plump fingers of sumach

And always between the two
(scuffing the leaves, laughing
and fingers locked)
goes a third lover   his or hers

who walked this way with one or other   once
flung back the head   snapped branches of dark pine
in armfuls   before snowfall

DOROTHY
LIVESAY

> I walk beside you
> trace
> a shadow's shade
> skating on silver
> hear
> another voice
> singing under ice

1969

The Children's Letters

They are my secret food
consumed in the most hushed corners
of my room
when no one's looking
I hold them up to sunlight
at the window
to see aright
to hear behind the spindly words
a child's tentative
                    first footsteps
a small voice stuttering
                    at the sky
'bird . . . bird . . .'

Whether these be
my children or my grandchildren
they're ghostly visitors
food of a solitary kind—
they leap on shafts of sunlight
through the mind's
shutters.

1971

Spain

DOROTHY
LIVESAY

When the bare branch responds to leaf and light
Remember them: it is for this they fight.
It is for haze-swept hills and the green thrust
Of pine, that they lie choked with battle dust.

You who hold beauty at your finger-tips
Hold it because the splintering gunshot rips
Between your comrades' eyes; hold it across
Their bodies' barricade of blood and loss.

You who live quietly in sunlit space
Reading The Herald after morning grace
Can count peace dear, when it has driven
Your sons to struggle for this grim, new heaven.

MALCOLM
LOWRY

1909-1957

Christ Walks in This Infernal District Too

Beneath the Malebolge lies Hastings Street,
The province of the pimp upon his beat,
Where each in his little world of drugs or crime
Moves helplessly or, hopeful, begs a dime
Wherewith to purchase half a pint of piss—
Although he will be cheated, even in this.
I hope, although I doubt it, God knows
This place where chancres blossom like the rose,
For on each face is such a hard despair
That nothing like a grief could enter there.
And on this scene from all excuse exempt
The mountains gaze in absolute contempt,
Yet this is also Canada, my friend,
Yours to absolve of ruin, or make an end.

1963

For Under the Volcano

MALCOLM
LOWRY

A dead lemon like a cowled old woman crouching in the cold.
A white pylon of salt and the flies
taxiing on the orange table, rain, rain, a scraping peon
and a scraping pen writing bowed words.
War. And the broken necked streetcars outside
and a sudden broken thought of a girl's face in Hoboken
a tilted turtle dying slowly on the stoop
of the sea-food restaurant, blood
lacing its mouth and the white floor—
ready for the ternedos tomorrow.
There will be no morrow, tomorrow is over.
Clover and the smell of fircones and the deep grass,
and turkey mole sauce and England
suddenly, a thought of home, but then
the mariachis, discordant, for the beaked bird
of maguey is on the wing, the waiter bears
a flowing black dish of emotion,
the peon's face is a mass of corruption.
We discard the horripilation of the weather
in this ghastly land of the half-buried man
where we live with Canute, the sundial and the red snapper,
the leper, the creeper, together in the green tower,
and play at sunset on the mundial flute and guitar
the song, the song of the eternal waiting of Canute,
the wrong of my waiting, the flute of my weeping,
betrothed to the puking vacuum and the unfleshible root
and the rain on the train outside creeping, creeping,
only emptiness now in my soul sleeping
where once strutted tigers lemonade scruffy green lepers
liquors pears scrubbed peppers and stuffed Leopardis;
and the sound of the train and the rain on the brain . . .
So far from barn and field and little lane—
this pyre of Bierce and springboard of Hart Crane!
Death so far away from home and wife
I fear. And prayed for my sick life—

'A corpse should be transported by express,' said the Consul
mysteriously, waking up suddenly.

1963

Xochitepec

MALCOLM
LOWRY

Those animals that follow us in dream
Are swallowed by the dawn, but what of those
Which hunt us, snuff, stalk us out in life, close
In upon it, belly-down, haunt our scheme
Of building, with shapes of delirium,
Symbols of death, heraldic, and shadows,
Glowering?—Just before we left Tlalpám
Our cats lay quivering under the maguey;
A meaning had slunk, and now died, with them.
The boy slung them half stiff down the ravine,
Which now we entered, and whose name is hell.
But still our last night had its animal:
The puppy, in the cabaret, obscene,
Looping-the-loop and soiling all the floor,
And fastening itself to that horror
Of our last night: while the very last day
As I sat bowed, frozen over mescal,
They dragged two kicking fawns through the hotel
And slit their throats, behind the barroom door. . . .

1963

The Lighthouse Invites the Storm

The lighthouse invites the storm and lights it.
Driven by tempest the tall freighter heels
Under the crag where the fiery seabird wheels,
And lightning of spume over rocks ignites it.
Oh, birds of the darkness of winter whose flights it
Importunes with frost, when ice congeals
On wings bonded for flight by zero's seals,
What good spirit undulates you still like kites that
Children are guardians of in cold blue? . . .

1963

1910–1961

Lens

I
The poet's daily chore
Is my long duty;
To keep and cherish my good lens
For love and war
And wasps about the lilies
And mutiny within.

My woman's eye is weak
And veiled with milk;
My working eye is muscled
With a curious tension,
Stretched and open
As the eyes of children;
Trusting in its vision
Even should it see
The holy holy spirit gambol
Counterheadwise,
Lithe and warm as any animal.

My woman's iris circles
A blind pupil;
The poet's eye is crystal,
Polished to accept the negative,
The contradictions in a proof
And the accidental
Candour of the shadows;
The shutter, oiled and smooth
Clicks on the grace of heroes
Or on some bestial act
When lit with radiance
The afterwords the actors speak
Give depths to violence,

Or if the bull is great
And the matador
And the sword
Itself the metaphor.

II
In my dark room the years
Lie in solution,
Develop film by film.
Slow at first and dim
Their shadows bite
On the fine white pulp of paper.

An early snap of fire
Licking the arms of air
I hold against the light, compare
The details with a prehistoric view
Of land and sea
And cradles of mud that rocked
The wet and sloth of infancy.

A stripe of tiger, curled
And sleeping on the ribs of reason
Prints as clear
As Eve and Adam, pearled
With sweat, staring at an apple core;

And death, in black and white
Or politic in green and Easter film,
Lands on steely points, a dancer
Disciplined to the foolscap stage,
The property of poets
Who command his robes, expose
His moving likeness on the page.

1955

In June and Gentle Oven

ANNE
WILKINSON

In June and gentle oven
Summer kingdoms simmer
As they come
And flower and leaf and love
Release
Their sweetest juice.

No wind at all
On the wide green world
Where fields go stroll-
ing by
And in and out
An adder of a stream
Parts the daisies
On a small Ontario farm.

And where, in curve of meadow,
Lovers, touching, lie,
A church of grass stands up
And walls them, holy, in.

Fabulous the insects
Stud the air
Or walk on running water,
Klee-drawn saints
And bright as angels are.

Honeysuckle here
Is more than bees can bear
And time turns pale
And stops to catch its breath
And lovers slip their flesh
And light as pollen
Play on treble water
Till bodies reappear
And a shower of sun
To dry their languor.

Then two in one the lovers lie
And peel the skin of summer
With their teeth

And suck its marrow from a kiss
ANNE
WILKINSON
So charged with grace
The tongue, all knowing
Holds the sap of June
Aloof from seasons, flowing.

1955

Daily the Drum

'If we had a keen vision and feeling . . .
it would be like hearing the grass grow
or the squirrel's heart beat,
and we should die of that roar
which lies on the other side of silence.'
GEORGE ELIOT

I
Daily the drum is burst
It is not only or foremost
The din of squirrel hearts
Or the spangled noise of grass
These are simple sounds
Like bird love,
Not the sounds we die of.

II
On the other side of silence
I can hear the bones
Of bold and trembling girls
Clacking castanets
In dance of fire and fear

And who is deaf enough
When young men cry
And hailstones break the panes
That glaze the lovers' eye,
Or terror's tin scream rises,
Not from a throat
But from the key that locks
The sickness in the mouth?

The service at our graves
Comes clear, and bells,
But who can bear
The hidden grinding mirth
When etiquette conceals
The date and nature of our death?

And every hour a child's
Black coal of trouble
Picks at the poet's ear
Sharper than any other,
For child and poet wind
A one-day clock. 'NOW,'
It strikes, 'NOW is forever.'

These are the sounds that murder.

1955

Nature be Damned

I
Pray where would lamb and lion be
If they lay down in amity?
Could lamb then nibble living grass?
Lamb and lion both must starve;
Bird and flower, too, must die of love.

II
I go a new dry way, permit no weather
Here, on undertaker's false green sod
Where I sit down beneath my false tin tree.
There's too much danger in a cloud,
In wood or field, or close to moving water.
With my black blood—who can tell?
The dart of one mosquito might be fatal;

Or in the flitting dusk a bat
Might carry away my destiny,
Hang it upside down from a rafter
In a barn unknown to me.

I hide my skin within the barren city
Where artificial moons pull no man's tide,
And so escape my green love till the day
Vine breaks through brick and strangles me.

III
I was witch and I could be
Bird or leaf
Or branch and bark of tree.

In rain and two by two my powers left me;
Instead of curling down as root and worm
My feet walked on the surface of the earth,
And I remember a day of evil sun
When forty green leaves withered on my arm.

And so I damn the font where I was blessed,
Am unbeliever; was deluded lover; never
Bird or leaf or branch and bark of tree.
Each, separate as curds from whey,
Has signature to prove identity.

And yet we're kin in appetite;
Tree, bird in the tree and I.
We feed on dung, a fly, a lamb
And burst with seed
Of tree, of bird, of man,
Till tree is bare
And bird and I are bone
And feaster is reborn
The feast, and feasted on.

IV
Once a year in the smoking bush
A little west of where I sit
I burn my winter caul to a green ash.
This is an annual festival,
Nothing to stun or startle;
A coming together—water and sun
In summer's first communion.

Today again I burned my winter caul
Though senses nodded, dulled by ritual.

One hundred singing orioles
And five old angels wakened me;
Morning sky rained butterflies
And simple fish, bass and perch,
Leapt from the lake in salutation.
St. Francis, drunk among the daisies,
Opened his ecstatic eye.
Then roused from this reality I saw
Nothing, anywhere, but snow.

ANNE
WILKINSON

1968

WILFRED
WATSON

b. 1911

Lines: I Praise God's Mankind
in an Old Woman

I praise God's mankind in an old woman:
I hear him rattle the body of an old wife
Dry and brown, and bitter as bracken,
Her stalk womb-cancelled, sere with seedgone;
With shrivel fingers clutching upon her life,
Wrestling for the empty pod and the dry leaf.
But still in her mildewed eyes moist's last token—
But oh, ever in her eyes the flash and strife,
Husk edge, cruel and sharp as any knife
Which not God's death itself can unsharpen.
Not all the frosts marching to this last March
Frost, not all the suns flaming to August
The last, dry-dried her spirit to adust;
She her own frost and sun at last must
Fetch—to blaze within and her soul's spirit parch
Into a desert—her own contracted flame;
Her radical sin, this sin at last to tame.
May she like the fathers by the desert broken
In her own desert find at last salvation.

1955

147

Emily Carr

WILFRED
WATSON

Like Jonah in the green belly of the whale
Overwhelmed by Leviathan's lights and liver
Imprisoned and appalled by the belly's wall
Yet inscribing and scoring the uprush
Sink vault and arch of that monstrous cathedral,
Its living bone and its green pulsing flesh—
Old woman, of your three days' anatomy
Leviathan sickened and spewed you forth
In a great vomit on coasts of eternity.
Then, as for John of Patmos, the river of life
Burned for you an emerald and jasper smoke
And down the valley you looked and saw
All wilderness become transparent vapour,
A ghostly underneath a fleshly stroke,
And every bush an apocalypse of leaf.

1955

IRVING
LAYTON

b. 1912

The Cold Green Element

At the end of the garden walk
the wind and its satellite wait for me;
their meaning I will not know
              until I go there,
but the black-hatted undertaker

who, passing, saw my heart beating in the grass,
is also going there. Hi, I tell him,
a great squall in the Pacific blew a dead poet
              out of the water,
who now hangs from the city's gates.

Crowds depart daily to see it, and return
with grimaces and incomprehension;

if its limbs twitched in the air
      they would sit at its feet
peeling their oranges.

And turning over I embrace like a lover
the trunk of a tree, one of those
for whom the lightning was too much
      and grew a brilliant
hunchback with a crown of leaves.

The ailments escaped from the labels
of medicine bottles are all fled to the wind;
I've seen myself lately in the eyes
      of old women,
spent streams mourning my manhood,

in whose old pupils the sun became
a bloodsmear on broad catalpa leaves
and hanging from ancient twigs,
      my murdered selves
sparked the air like the muted collisions

of fruit. A black dog howls down my blood,
a black dog with yellow eyes;
he too by someone's inadvertence
      saw the bloodsmear
on the broad catalpa leaves.

But the furies clear a path for me to the worm
who sang for an hour in the throat of a robin,
and misled by the cries of young boys
      I am again
a breathless swimmer in that cold green element.

1955

The Improved Binoculars

IRVING
LAYTON

Below me the city was in flames:
the firemen were the first to save
themselves. I saw steeples fall on their knees.

I saw an agent kick the charred bodies
from an orphanage to one side, marking
the site carefully for a future speculation.

Lovers stopped short of the final spasm
and went off angrily in opposite directions,
their elbows held by giant escorts of fire.

Then the dignitaries rode across the bridges
under an auricle of light which delighted them,
noting for later punishment those that went before.

And the rest of the populace, their mouths
distorted by an unusual gladness, bawled thanks
to this comely and ravaging ally, asking

Only for more light with which to see
their neighbour's destruction.

All this I saw through my improved binoculars.

1956

The Fertile Muck

There are brightest apples on those trees
    but until I, fabulist, have spoken
they do not know their significance
or what other legends are hung like garlands
    on their black boughs twisting
like a rumour. The wind's noise is empty.

Nor are the winged insects better off
    though they wear my crafty eyes
wherever they alight. Stay here, my love;

you will see how delicately they deposit
    me on the leaves of elms
or fold me in the orient dust of summer.

And if in August joiners and bricklayers
    are thick as flies around us
building expensive bungalows for those
who do not need them, unless they release
    me roaring from their moth-proofed cupboards
their buyers will have no joy, no ease.

I could extend their rooms for them without cost
    and give them crazy sundials
to tell the time with, but I have noticed
how my irregular footprint horrifies them
    evenings and Sunday afternoons:
they spray for hours to erase its shadow.

How to dominate reality? Love is one way;
    imagination another. Sit here
beside me, sweet; take my hard hand in yours.
We'll mark the butterflies disappearing over the hedge
    with tiny wristwatches on their wings:
our fingers touching the earth, like two Buddhas.

1956

From Colony to Nation

A dull people,
but the rivers of this country
are wide and beautiful

A dull people
enamoured of childish games,
but food is easily come by
and plentiful

Some with a priest's voice
in their cage of ribs: but

on high mountain-tops and in thunderstorms
the chirping is not heard

Deferring to beadle and censor;
not ashamed for this,
but given over to horseplay,
the making of money

A dull people, without charm
or ideas,
settling into the clean empty look
of a Mountie or dairy farmer
as into a legacy

One can ignore them
(the silences, the vast distances help)
and suppose them at the bottom
of one of the meaner lakes,
their bones not even picked for souvenirs.

1956

For Mao Tse-Tung:
A Meditation on Flies and Kings

So, circling about my head, a fly.
Haloes of frantic monotone.
Then a smudge of blood smoking
On my fingers, let Jesus and Buddha cry.

Is theirs the way? Forgiveness of hurt?
Leprosariums? Perhaps. But I
Am burning flesh and bone,
An indifferent creature between
Cloud and a stone;
Smash insects with my boot,
Feast on torn flowers, deride
The nonillion bushes by the road
(Their patience is very great)
Jivatma, they endure,
Endure and proliferate.

And the meek-browed and poor
In their solid tenements
(Etiolated, they do not dance.)
Worry of priest and of commissar:
None may re-create them who are
Lowly and universal as the moss
Or like vegetation the winds toss
Sweeping to the open lake and sky.
I put down these words in blood
And would not be misunderstood:
They have their Christs and their legends
And out of their pocks and ailments
Weave dear enchantments
Poet and dictator, you are as alien as I.

On this remote and classic lake
Only the lapsing of the water can I hear
And the cold wind through the sumac.
The moneyed and their sunburnt children
Swarm other shores. Here is ecstasy,
The sun's outline made lucid
By each lacustral cloud
And man naked with mystery.
They dance best who dance with desire,
Who lifting feet of fire from fire
Weave before they lie down
A red carpet for the sun.

I pity the meek in their religious cages
And flee them; and flee
The universal sodality
Of joy-haters, joy-destroyers
(O Schiller, wine-drunk and silly!)
The sufferers and their thick rages;
Enter this tragic forest where the trees
Uprear as if for the graves of men,
All function and desire to offend
With themselves finally done;
And mark the dark pines farther on,
The sun's fires touching them at will,
Motionless like silent khans
Mourning serene and terrible
1958   Their Lord entombed in the blazing hill.

A Tall Man Executes a Jig

IRVING
LAYTON

I

So the man spread his blanket on the field
And watched the shafts of light between the tufts
And felt the sun push the grass towards him;
The noise he heard was that of whizzing flies,
The whistlings of some small imprudent birds,
And the ambiguous rumbles of cars
That made him look up at the sky, aware
Of the gnats that tilted against the wind
And in the sunlight turned to jigging motes.
Fruitflies he'd call them except there was no fruit
About, spoiling to hatch these glitterings,
These nervous dots for which the mind supplied
The closing sentences from Thucydides,
Or from Euclid having a savage nightmare.

II

Jig jig, jig jig. Like minuscule black links
Of a chain played with by some playful
Unapparent hand or the palpitant
Summer haze bored with the hour's stillness.
He felt the sting and tingle afterwards
Of those leaving their orthodox unrest,
Leaving their undulant excitation
To drop upon his sleeveless arm. The grass,
Even the wildflowers became black hairs
And himself a maddened speck among them.
Still the assaults of the small flies made him
Glad at last, until he saw purest joy
In their frantic jiggings under a hair,
So changed from those in the unrestraining air.

III

He stood up and felt himself enormous.
Felt as might Donatello over stone,
Or Plato, or as a man who has held
A loved and lovely woman in his arms
And feels his forehead touch the emptied sky
Where all antinomies flood into light.
Yet jig jig jig, the haloing black jots
Meshed with the wheeling fire of the sun:

Motion without meaning, disquietude
Without sense or purpose, ephemerides
That mottled the resting summer air till
Gusts swept them from his sight like wisps of smoke.
Yet they returned, bringing a bee who, seeing
But a tall man, left him for a marigold.

IV

He doffed his aureole of gnats and moved
Out of the field as the sun sank down,
A dying god upon the blood-red hills.
Ambition, pride, the ecstasy of sex,
And all circumstance of delight and grief,
That blood upon the mountain's side, that flood
Washed into a clear incredible pool
Below the ruddied peaks that pierced the sun.
He stood still and waited. If ever
The hour of revelation was come
It was now, here on the transfigured steep.
The sky darkened. Some birds chirped. Nothing else.
He thought the dying god had gone to sleep:
An Indian fakir on his mat of nails.

V

And on the summit of the asphalt road
Which stretched towards the fiery town, the man
Saw one hill raised like a hairy arm, dark
With pines and cedars against the stricken sun
—The arm of Moses or of Joshua.
He dropped his head and let fall the halo
Of mountains, purpling and silent as time,
To see temptation coiled before his feet:
A violated grass snake that lugged
Its intestine like a small red valise.
A cold-eyed skinflint it now was, and not
The manifest of that joyful wisdom,
The mirth and arrogant green flame of life;
Or earth's vivid tongue that flicked in praise of earth.

VI

And the man wept because pity was useless.
'Your jig's up; the flies come like kites,' he said
And watched the grass snake crawl towards the hedge,

Convulsing and dragging into the dark
The satchel filled with curses for the earth,
For the odours of warm sedge, and the sun,
A blood-red organ in the dying sky.
Backwards it fell into a grassy ditch
Exposing its underside, white as milk,
And mocked by wisps of hay between its jaws;
And then it stiffened to its final length.
But though it opened its thin mouth to scream
A last silent scream that shook the black sky,
Adamant and fierce, the tall man did not curse.

VII
Beside the rigid snake the man stretched out
In fellowship of death; he lay silent
And stiff in the heavy grass with eyes shut,
Inhaling the moist odours of the night
Through which his mind tunnelled with flicking tongue
Backwards to caves, mounds, and sunken ledges
And desolate cliffs where come only kites,
And where of perished badgers and racoons
The claws alone remain, gripping the earth.
Meanwhile the green snake crept upon the sky,
Huge, his mailed coat glittering with stars that made
The night bright, and blowing thin wreaths of cloud
Athwart the moon; and as the weary man
Stood up, coiled above his head, transforming all.

1963

Butterfly on Rock

The large yellow wings, black-fringed,
were motionless

They say the soul of a dead person
will settle like that on the still face

But I thought: the rock has borne this;
this butterfly is the rock's grace,
its most obstinate and secret desire

to be a thing alive made manifest

IRVING
LAYTON

Forgot were the two shattered porcupines
I had seen die in the bleak forest.
Pain is unreal; death, an illusion:
There is no death in all the land,
I heard my voice cry;
And brought my hand down on the butterfly
And felt the rock move beneath my hand.

1963

For Musia's Grandchildren

I write this poem
for your grandchildren
for they will know of your loveliness
only from hearsay,
from yellowing photographs
spread out on table and sofa
for a laugh.

When arrogant
with the lovely grace you gave their flesh
they regard your dear frail body pityingly,
your time-dishonoured cheeks
pallid and sunken
and those hands
that I have kissed a thousand times
mottled by age
and stroking a grey ringlet into place,
I want them suddenly
to see you as I saw you
—beautiful as the first bird at dawn.

Dearest love, tell them
that I, a crazed poet all his days
who made woman
his ceaseless study and delight,
begged but one boon
in this world of mournful beasts

that are almost human:
to live praising your marvellous eyes
mischief could make glisten
like winter pools at night
or appetite put a fine finish on.

1967

Grand Finale

I've seen the grey-haired lyrists come down from the hills;
they think because they howl with eloquence and conviction
the townspeople will forgive their disgraceful sores
and not care how scandalous and odd they look;
how vain their contrite blurtings over booze and women
or the senescent itch for the one true faith.

Not for me sorrowful and inglorious old age
not for me resignation and breastbeating
or reverbing of guilts till one's limbs begin to tremble
and a man's brought to his knees whimpering and ashamed;
not for me if there's a flicker of life still left
and I can laugh at the gods and curse and shake my fist.

Rather than howl and yowl like an ailing cat
on wet or freezing nights or mumble thin pieties
over a crucifix like some poor forsaken codger
in a rented room, I'll let the darkness come only when I
an angry and unforgiving old man yank the cloth of heaven
and the moon and all the stars come crashing down.

1978

GEORGE
WOODCOCK

b. 1912

Imagine the South

Imagine the South from which these migrants fled,
Dark-eyed, pursued by arrows, crowned with blood,
Imagine the stiff stone houses and the ships
Blessed with wine and salt, the quivering tips
Of spears and edges signalling in the sun
From swords unscabbarded and sunk in brine,
Imagine the cyclamen faces and yielding breasts
Hungered after in a dead desert of icy mists,
Imagine, for though oblivious, you too are cast
Exile upon a strange and angry coast.

Going into exile away from youth,
You too are losing a country in the South,
Losing, in the red daylight of a new shore
Where you are hemmed by solitude and fear,
The loving faces far over a sea of time,
The solid comfort and the humane dream
Of a peaceful sky, the consoling patronage
And the golden ladder to an easy age,
All these are lost, for you too have gone away
From your southern home upon a bitter journey.

There is no home for you marked on the compass.
I see no Penelope at the end of your Odysseys,
And all the magic islands will let you down.
Do not touch the peaches and do not drink the wine,
For the Dead Sea spell will follow all you do,
And do not talk of tomorrow, for to you
There will only be yesterday, only the fading land,
The boats on the shore and tamarisks in the sand
Where the beautiful faces wait, and the faithful friends.
They will people your mind. You will never touch their hands.

1949

Poem for Garcia Lorca

GEORGE
WOODCOCK

Count on dead fingers of time the years that pass
Since Lorca sang his last of Spain
And fell beneath the hard inhuman paw,
Gasping between white walls in Granada.

Lorca, the song of men whose emptying hearts
Sang out the seconds of their death in blood,
The song of women whose bloodless futures lay
Twisted under the roof of tyranny.

Remember Lorca as Spain's noblest bull,
Not in the sunlight of Mithraic rings
Spurting his life to matadors and crowds
But in numb secrecy to the knacker's laugh.

Remember Lorca as the earth of Spain,
Lined with valleys as an old man's hand,
In each valley the gun lurking and the dead waiting
For the dawn that will not break their empty sleep.

Remember Lorca as the poor of Spain,
Rising once from their alleys of quiet death
To wash with blood the roots of barren trees
That do not bloom this year and one year will fall for ever.

Remember Lorca, who died only for being Lorca.

1967

Paper Anarchist Addresses
the Shade of Nancy Ling Perry

Out of our daylight into death you burn,
    For words once lit you, sparks struck out of books,
And as you char to memory I learn
    How words life-tempered bend to cruel hooks.

Among those words perhaps some were my own,

Written within the fiery coil of youth,
When ambiguity was left unknown
    And consequences seemed no bar to truth:

Truth as then seen, sharp white and shadow black,
    And as you saw it, leading through flame's dawn,
        The only causes time and fear and place
Why you, not I, enter that violent dark
    And I look on, appalled, ashamed, and mourn
        Terrible children, comrades, enemies.

GEORGE
WOODCOCK

1975

Pacifists

The icy, empty dawn cracks in the fields
Under our labouring feet. We cross the fallow
With billhooks on our shoulders sloped like guns,
Drawing dark lines in rime white as we go.

Standing in filthy ditches in leaking boots,
We fell the towering hedges like Jericho walls
Under the blast of day. Around our feet
The water seeps and numbs through invisible holes.

Strange we have come, from library and office.
Hands that had never toiled, myopic eyes
And sloping backs revolt in an alien time.
Under a dead sky we expiate our oddness.

Having left friends and substitutes for love
In the leaning fragments of a distant city
We tread the furrows of infertile fields
And rediscover our pasts in a wet country.

Under our ineffectual misery, our boredom
And the empty sequence of unprivate days,
The lost squalors of the city become our end.
The cause that brought us dwindles. We hate blank skies,

Biting wind and the black bones of trees,

The promise of spring as a green omen of toil.
We rest our billhooks and talk of starlit town
As the weak sun breaks on the land without a hill.

GEORGE
WOODCOCK

1975

GEORGE
JOHNSTON

b. 1913

War on the Periphery

Around the battlements go by
Soldier men against the sky,
Violent lovers, husbands, sons,
Guarding my peaceful life with guns.

My pleasures, how discreet they are!
A little booze, a little car,
Two little children and a wife
Living a small suburban life.

My little children eat my heart;
At seven o'clock we kiss and part,
At seven o'clock we meet again;
They eat my heart and grow to men.

I watch their tenderness with fear
While on the battlements I hear
The violent, obedient ones
Guarding my family with guns.

1959

Cathleen Sweeping

GEORGE
JOHNSTON

The wind blows, and with a little broom
She sweeps against the cold clumsy sky.
She's three years old. What an enormous room
The world is that she sweeps, making fly
A little busy dust! And here am I
Watching her through the window in the gloom
Of this disconsolate spring morning, my
Thoughts as small and busy as her broom.

Do I believe in her? I cannot quite.
Beauty is more than my belief will bear.
I've had to borrow what I think is true:
Nothing stays put until I think it through.
Yet, watching her with her broom in the dark air
I give it up. Why should I doubt delight?

1959

Bliss

The less said about Edward's slut the better,
Nobody knows who she is or how he met her
With her waterfall of yellow-coloured hair
And feet like scissor points, a spiky pair.

Melancholy of love improves her lies,
Melancholy of gin makes deep her eyes,
Melancholy of streets refines her touch,
Sweet melancholy of tongue and teeth and such.

When summer evenings come across the tracks
We spread ourselves with beer and paperbacks:
Down comes Edward, powder on his face,
To take his slut out smooching every place.

Bliss is nice, but a little bit will do;
Edward has had too much, and his slut has too:
Only to see the hoof-marks in their eyes
And hear them wheeze would make a fellow wise.

1972

Veterans

GEORGE
JOHNSTON

There are seventy times seven kinds of loving
    None quite right:
One is of making, one of arguing,
    One of wheedling in the night
And all the others one can think of, none quite right.

Yet they are good,
    Paying attention, giving the low-down kiss;
Answering back in the heart is always good
    And coming out of a sulk is almost bliss.

There is a kind of loving in grass and weeds,
    One in brass beds, another in corridors;
An uncanny kind that turns away and bleeds
    And a gorgeous kind, practised by saints and bores.

They are all hard,
    All seventy times seven, hard as can be:
Veterans of loving are wary-eyed and scarred
    And they see into everything they see.

1972

ANNE
MARRIOTT

b. 1913

Prairie Graveyard

Wind mutters thinly on the sagging wire
binding the graveyard from the gouged dirt road,
bends thick-bristled Russian thistle,
sifts listless dust
into cracks in hard grey ground.
Empty prairie slides away
on all sides, rushes toward a wide
expressionless horizon, joined
to a vast blank sky.

Lots near the road are the most expensive ANNE
MARRIOTT
where heavy tombstones lurch a fraction
tipped by splitting soil.
Farther, a row of nameless heaps
names weatherworn from tumbled sticks
remember now the six thin children
of a thin, shiftless home.

Hawk, wind-scouring, cuts
a pointed shadow in the drab scant grass.

Two graves apart by the far fence
are suicides, one with a grand
defiant tombstone, bruising at the heart
'Death is swallowed up in victory'.
(And may be, God's kindness being more large
than man's, to this, who after seven years
of drought, burned down his barn,
himself hanged in it.)
The second, nameless, set around
with even care-sought stones
(no stones on this section)
topped with two plants, hard-dried,
in rust-thick jam-tins set in the caked pile.

A gopher jumps from a round cave,
sprints furtively, spurts under fence, is gone.
Wind raises dead curls of dust, and whines
under its harsh breath on the limp dragged wires,
then leaves the graveyard stiff with silence, lone
in the centre of the huge lone land and sky.

1945

Beaver Pond

Not furred nor wet, the pointing words yet make
a feel of plush slip moistly through the mind.
Tires grate to gravelled stops; tourists, lumpy in jeans,
question and cluster round the still, small pool.
Twigs, peanuts flip

on the wrought island on the farther side—
its basket crown, cunningly cut,
entangles all eyes, but none in return
looks through the sealed lattice. Water absorbs
nut, cry and pebble, offers in reply
no waking head, and no binocular
searching route to the shelter but reveals
on the shut surface only its blind, mirrored eye.

And yet I feel the water in my ears,
nose sucks the strong root-smell
and light refracts among the embroidered weeds
in rich deep greens and brown that grow
more coloured with acquaintance.
The velvet bodies of our infrequent kind
press here beside me. Deep beaver I
greet you under the masked water from my secret house,
neither will break the public surface against my wish
for sticks or stones or softest coaxing words.

1981

As You Come In

The building
illuminates itself
light breaks outside the windows
stripes you with a dozen
swelling colours.

I love you.
There—it burst out
a huge flower opening
inside my skin
bone and flesh and tissue turned
all to one giant bloom.

I button up my coat
afraid the people around will see
the petals curving
note the unique perfume.

ANNE
MARRIOTT

A year from now,
I may not love you, either—
but as you come in
I'm a rich stalk
a honeyed pole
a tree thick with leaves
long closed
opened by this new sun.

1981

DOUGLAS
LePAN

b. 1914

A Country Without a Mythology

No monuments or landmarks guide the stranger
Going among this savage people, masks
Taciturn or babbling out an alien jargon
And moody as barbaric skies are moody.

Berries must be his food. Hurriedly
He shakes the bushes, plucks pickerel from the river,
Forgetting every grace and ceremony,
Feeds like an Indian, and is on his way.

And yet, for all his haste, time is worth nothing.
The abbey clock, the dial in the garden,
Fade like saint's days and festivals.
Months, years, are here unbroken virgin forests.

There is no law—even no atmosphere
To smooth the anger of the flagrant sun.
November skies sting sting like icicles.
The land is open to all violent weathers.

Passion is not more quick. Lightnings in August
Stagger, rocks split, tongues in the forest hiss,
As fire drinks up the lovely sea-dream coolness.
This is the land the passionate man must travel.

Sometimes—perhaps at the tentative fall of twilight— DOUGLAS
LePAN
A belief will settle that waiting around the bend
Are sanctities of childhood, that melting birds
Will sing him into a limpid gracious Presence.

The hills will fall in folds, the wilderness
Will be a garment innocent and lustrous
To wear upon a birthday, under a light
That curls and smiles, a golden-haired Archangel.

And now the channel opens. But nothing alters.
Mile after mile of tangled struggling roots,
Wild-rice, stumps, weeds, that clutch at the canoe,
Wild birds hysterical in tangled trees.

And not a sign, no emblem in the sky
Or boughs to friend him as he goes; for who
Will stop where, clumsily constructed, daubed
With war-paint, teeters some lust-red manitou?

1948

Coureurs de bois

Thinking of you, I think of the *coureurs de bois*,
Swarthy men grown almost to savage size
Who put their brown wrists through the arras of the woods
And were lost—sometimes for months. Word would come back:
One had been seen at Crêve-coeur, deserted and starving,
One at Sault Sainte Marie shouldering the rapids.
Giant-like, their labours stalked in the streets of Quebec
Though they themselves had dwindled in distance: names only;
Rumours; quicksilvery spies into nature's secrets;
Rivers that seldom ran in the sun. Their resource
Would sparkle and then flow back under clouds of hemlock.

So you should have travelled with them. Or with La Salle.
He could feed his heart with the heart of a continent,
Insatiate, how noble a wounded animal,
Who sought for his wounds the balsam of adventure,
The sap from some deep, secret tree. But now

That the forests are cut down, the rivers charted,   DOUGLAS
LePAN
Where can you turn, where can you travel? Unless
Through the desperate wilderness behind your eyes,
So full of falls and glooms and desolations,
Disasters I have glimpsed but few would dream of,
You seek new Easts. The coats of difficult honour,
Bright with brocaded birds and curious flowers,
Stowed so long with vile packs of pemmican,
Futile, weighing you down on slippery portages,
Would flutter at last in the courts of a clement country,
Where the air is silken, the manners easy,
Under a guiltless and reconciling sun.
You hesitate. The trees are entangled with menace.
The voyage is perilous into the dark interior.
But then your hands go to the thwarts. You smile. And so
I watch you vanish in a wood of heroes,
Wild Hamlet with the features of Horatio.

1948

The Net and the Sword

Who could dispute his choice
That in the nets and toils of violence
Strangled his leafing voice
Enforced his own compassionate heart to silence,
Hunted no more to find the untangling word
And took a short, straight sword?

In this sandy arena, littered
And looped with telephone wires, tank-traps, mine-fields,
Twining about the embittered
Debris of history, the people whom he shields
Would quail before a stranger if they could see
His smooth as silk ferocity.

Where billowing skies suspend
Smoke-latticed rumours, enmeshed hypotheses
And mad transmitters send
Impossible orders on crossed frequencies,
His eyes thrust concentrated and austere.
Behind his lids, the skies are clear.

Not that he ever hopes
To strike the vitals of the knotted cloud.
But, to the condemned, those ropes
At least let in the sun. And he, grown proud,
Among the sun's bright retinue would die,
Whose care is how they fall, not why.

DOUGLAS
LePAN

1953

PATRICK
ANDERSON

1915-1979

From 'Poem on Canada'

Cold Colloquy

What are you . . ? they ask, in wonder.
And she replies in the worst silence of all her woods:
I am Candida with the cane wind.

What are you . . ? they ask again, their mouths full of gum,
their eyes full of the worst silence of the worst winter in a
    hundred years
and the frames of their faces chipped round the skaters' picture—
What are you . . ? they ask.
And she replies: I am the wind that wants a flag.
I am the mirror of your picture
until you make me the marvel of your life.
Yes, I am one and none, pin and pine, snow and slow,
America's attic, an empty room,
a something possible, a chance, a dance
that is not danced. A cold kingdom.

Are you a dominion of them? they ask, scurrying
home on streetcars, skiing the hill's shoulder
and hurrying where the snow is heaping colder and colder.
Are you a dominion of them? they ask.
Most loyal and empirical, she says, in ice ironic,
and subject of the king's most gratuitous modesty, she says.

What do you do then?   PATRICK
ANDERSON
Lumbering is what I do and whitening is what I wheat,
but I am full of hills and sadness;
snow is where I drift and wave my winds
and as silence my doom, distance is my dream.
Mine are the violet tones of the logs in rivers,
my tallness is the tallness of the pines and the grain elevators
tubular by the scarps of coal, at Quebec.
My caves are the caves of ice but also the holes of Cartier
where the poor squat, numb with winter,
and my poverty is their rags and the prairies' drought.

What is the matter then . . ? they ask, and some are indifferent,
What is the matter then . . ? they ask.

The matter is the sections and the railways, she replies,
and the shouting lost by the way and the train's whistle
like wild-life in the night.
The matter is the promise that was never taken, she replies,
above your heads the cool and giant air
and the future aching round you like an aura—
land of the last town and the distant point,
land of the lumber track losing itself
petering out in the birches, the half-wish
turning back in the wastes of winter or slums
and the skiers lovely and lonely upon the hills
rising in domes of silence. The matter is
the skiers, she replies, athletically lonely,
drowsed in their delight, who hunt and haunt
the centres of their silence and excitement:
finding the cirrus on the high sierras
sluice down the dangers of their dear content—
the matter is being lost in a dream of motion
as larks are in their lights, or bees and flies
glued on the humpbacked honey of summertime.

What should we do then, what should we do . . ? they ask,
out of the factories rattling a new war,
on all the Sundays time has rocked to motion.
What should we do then . . ? they ask, English and
French,
Ukrainians, Poles, Finns, at drugstore corners
of streets extended to the ultimate seas
of their defended but ambiguous city.

—Suffer no more the vowels of Canada
to speak of miraculous things with a cleft palate—
let the Canadian,
with glaciers in his hair, straddle the continent,
in full possession of his earth and north
dip down his foot and touch the New York lights
or stir the vegetable matter of the Bahamas
within the Carib gutter. Let
the skiers go with slogans of their eyes
to crowd a country whose near neighbourhood's
the iron kindness of the Russian coasts—
through deserts of snow or dreary wastes of city,
the empty or the emptily crowded North.

And see, she says, the salmon pointing home
from the vast sea, the petalled plethora
and unplumbed darkness of the sea, she says:
gliding along their silvery intuitions
like current on its cables, volt upon volt,
to flash at last, sparking the mountain falls
of Restigouche—spawning a silver million.

1946

Houses Burning: Quebec

A house on fire! We stumbled over the snow
crackling under our feet to the hills' applause
clapping our faces furious and rose—
our breath hung round our necks like steaming meals
in fodder bags, and we were clumsy as horses
from bedded straws that cough and jingle brass.
But, drawing near, amongst the crowding people
where crisis drew the ragged gesture, the raw
impotent laughing answer, we heard
the base of the praying clouds go brisk with fire
as shrivel and flit of flames swept board on board.

And how the house was soft with heat that, cold,

had tinkled ice and drawn its tingling edge—
it was all air and bars like the dirty cage
where a bird on a perch no longer sustains the world.
Not only timbers fell but space fell through
and was no longer space. Design decayed
that had made the little big, as the bird is bold.
We saw a flare of sparks float downward, drift
from top to sump, as though a burglar came
down stairs that would not hold, with nothing to lift,
no one to fear, and burgled his childhood home,
his ghostly prison, the slum sunk under the flame.

PATRICK
ANDERSON

Four times in that week of violent winter
houses burned. One in a great blow,
in the heart of a blizzard, one that I have named
and two at night, flooding the snow
with blood and yellow and black of that swarm
of watching people. There was no chance of water
and each took only twenty minutes of flame.
When summer comes the ruins will be green
with weed. Only a ragged chimney will
be left to say this isn't a curious pond
but was three months a house, one night a game—
for no one died, or cried to see them go,
and what flared up and joined the serious climb
inside our faces no one will ever know.

1953

R.A.D.
FORD

b. 1915

Twenty Below

The woman watches her husband rubbing his nose,
frozen while chopping a hole in the river's ice,
now thawing slowly between his hands and snow—
sitting by the stove with his peasant eyes nowhere
and his feet in their ribbed grey homespun stockings placed
in the oven, the fire roaring with the top grate raised,
the pipes and flues across the room near white
with heat. The mongrel restless at his side
creeps closer to the fire. The children doze,
half living only through the frozen days.

The woman goes to the window and presses her hand
against the glacial pane, and leans her head
against the frame. Her breath has made a hole
in the frost. She can see outside the northern cold
smothering the world; and an impossible sleep
and silence falling from a sky of slate,
even the pines grey and rigid and still,
the mighty hills mere shadows on the pale
immeasurable horizon.

       Without reason,
feeling only her heart oppressive within her
and her life stopped dead and motionless in the hoar
and drifted week, she weeps, and the tears become
cold rivulets that cut across her cheeks.

       The cold presses into the room
from every side through the logs and stones and chinks
between the logs, so the circle of people sinks
into sopor, and the woman takes her sadness
and thaws it before the flames.

1956

Sakhara

R.A.D.
FORD

Here the eye is inevitably cast
Down, fixed on the desert
Floor, staring myopic at the grains
Of sand, until each one
Looks as large and hard as a boulder,
As smooth as a hundred clichés,
All true enough in the sun.

They are like the dogs of the nomads,
Distracting us from the lofty
Contemplation of history. Who cares
Or even hears when the guide
Stumbles through the life story
Of Queen Ti'. We are not overwhelmed
By the palaces and tombs,
Nor burial mounds, nor a majesty
That is as distant as the eyes
Of the bedouin child.
It is a majesty that numbs.

Fascinated rather by the alabaster
Fragments in the rubble of sand
And all the other unimportant
Details that stick in the memory,
While the background of nonsense clings
To the sticky air like thunder
In our own summer country:
The coca-cola vendor in the shade,
The tourist camels, the pure
Geometry of Kings.

And one cliché not forgot—
Under the fragile nomad tent,
The half-starved children
In the desert slums.

1969

Earthquake
R.A.D.
FORD

The seasons burn. The wind is dry,
Like the tongue of a sickly dog.
The eyes of the fishermen's wives
Are buried in their dark faces
And the children are all armed with knives.

Nothing in the sensuous street gives
Us warning, even cruelty posted
Everywhere, slinking in the shade,
Or unashamed in the meadows
Of cactus that press upon the dead.

Nothing except love—a warning that
Runs before the earthquake to say
That the streets are opening, the fire
Prepared and the waters of the bay
Ready to resume their empire.

It was in the end a small one, the killed
Very few, the fires soon put out. But not
The memory of the woman running above
The blast with her too late warning
And testimony of love.

1969

ELDON
GRIER

b. 1917

Mountain Town—Mexico

Arms at my side like some inadequate sign,
I lie awake in a dark room in an alien country.
While plates of frost slide past my face, and needles
cluster in the crêpe-like air, my friend who has made
his adjustment, urinates into a bucket with a thunderous ring.

I must impress myself with certain things;
the honesty of mountain people, the lightheartedness
of a people never conquered by arms—and yet
the monster of the mines lies dead beneath their homes,
its scattered mouths decaying in a final spittle of stones.

Into this piled-up town beneath astringent stars
what did we bring with us that is simple and hopeful—
into this confusion of times? Breadcrumbs for the blister
of the floor, bottles crowding off the ebbing surfaces,
memories of love, perhaps the gentle trauma of our intrusion.

A jukebox rumbles out a tune, the singer
holds her sex against my abstract form. We are the angels
of ironic movement, she and I. Our pleasures
are more permanent than the mountains here whose marrows
fired in a day form quickly into sediments of tragic angularity.

I lie awake until the blackness burns to filaments
of tired red. A horse sparks up the cobblestones.
A voice speaks cleanly from the stage of cold beyond.
No spout of sunlight ever entered to my bed, but stealthily
an orange cat comes snaking through the door in search of food.

1971

Kissing Natalia

Invention begs from door to door in the indescribable darkness,
a chorus of animals like canned laughter. I had it planned,
drunk though I was, to drive you to the edge of the town
and when you said 'thank you' as you always did, I was going to
   kiss you.

This was the plan and in the calm of decision I got you in,
passed houses drawn up like fanatical serfs, my thin excuse
trailing lifelessly after us like a rodent tail. (The general's
coming, boys, and his aide-de-camp and faceless mariachis from
   the 'gatos'.)

The engine slowed as my heart rose, your profile, dumb in the
   light,
came to the edge of town, looked off to stepping stones
which glowed in the shallows, to total darkness, and Lord knows
   where.
You said, 'thank you,' and so I put my hand there and kissed you.

Were you scared? It must have come like a moon pie in the face,
and unprepared for an instant, the trembling ring of your lips
held me as a lover. The place reeked of the chemistry of rivers
I remember now, and your mouth left the slightest aftertaste of
   earth.

1971

My Winter Past

I owe nothing to winter
because it is not my way to be cold
or to be covered like furniture in a deserted house:
my father was flickering warmth;
feelings poached in the living white of my mother's passionate
   isolation;
my brother's hands said what he had to say (and died without
   saying).
I wore down the evenings with mirrors of flesh and wool.
I trampled a landscape of frozen hysteria,
cried out fear with my winter joy.

A child with needle in brain,
I armed myself with the physical sweat of kitchens and drugstores
and gravies and lightbulbs and dreams . . .

What was queer
was an all-deceptive peace:
midnights of burgeoning snow, charcoal cupboards of heat,
the actor's clap of the door—a knock on wood,
a single breaking wave in the family of stillnesses;
smoke behind the trees so pure so very far, tumescent, imperially
    weak.

> . . . Beneath a continental grey
> inside the brilliant tear of cold
> in the visceral voices of women
> in the fossil of the windows
> in the ragged nostalgia of sugar, of fever
> in the fruity dampness of wool
> in the licorice veins of my sensuality.

1971

P.K.
PAGE

b. 1916

Stories of Snow

Those in the vegetable rain retain
an area behind their sprouting eyes
held soft and rounded with the dream of snow
precious and reminiscent as those globes—
souvenir of some never-nether land—
which hold their snow-storms circular, complete,
high in a tall and teakwood cabinet.

In countries where the leaves are large as hands
where flowers protrude their fleshy chins
and call their colours,
an imaginary snow-storm sometimes falls
among the lilies.
And in the early morning one will waken

to think the glowing linen of his pillow
a northern drift, will find himself mistaken
and lie back weeping.
And there the story shifts from head to head,
of how in Holland, from their feather beds
hunters arise and part the flakes and go
forth to the frozen lakes in search of swans—
the snow-light falling white along their guns,
their breath in plumes.
While tethered in the wind like sleeping gulls
ice-boats wait the raising of their wings
to skim the electric ice at such a speed
they leap jet strips of naked water,
and how these flying, sailing hunters feel
air in their mouths as terrible as ether.
And on the story runs that even drinks
in that white landscape dare to be no colour;
how flasked and water clear, the liquor slips
silver against the hunters' moving hips.
And of the swan in death these dreamers tell
of its last flight and how it falls, a plummet,
pierced by the freezing bullet
and how three feathers, loosened by the shot,
descend like snow upon it.
While hunters plunge their fingers in its down
deep as a drift, and dive their hands
up to the neck of the wrist
in that warm metamorphosis of snow
as gentle as the sort that woodsmen know
who, lost in the white circle, fall at last
and dream their way to death.

And stories of this kind are often told
in countries where great flowers bar the roads
with reds and blues which seal the route to snow—
as if, in telling, raconteurs unlock
the colour with its complement and go
through to the area behind the eyes
where silent, unrefractive whiteness lies.

[1945] 1946

Photos of a Salt Mine

How innocent their lives look,
how like a child's
dream of caves and winter, both combined;
the steep descent to whiteness
and the stope
with its striated walls
their folds all leaning as if pointing to
the greater whiteness still,
that great white bank
with its decisive front,
that seam upon a slope,
salt's lovely ice.

And wonderful underfoot the snow of salt
the fine
particles a broom could sweep,
one thinks
muckers might make angels in its drifts
as children do in snow,
lovers in sheets,
lie down and leave imprinted where they lay
a feathered creature holier than they.

And in the outworked stopes
with lamps and ropes
up miniature matterhorns
the miners climb
probe with their lights
the ancient folds of rock—
syncline and anticline—
and scoop from darkness an Aladdin's cave:
rubies and opals glitter from its walls.

But hoses douse the brilliance of these jewels,
melt fire to brine.
Salt's bitter water trickles thin and forms,
slow fathoms down,
a lake within a cave,
lacquered with jet—
white's opposite.
There grey on black the boating miners float

to mend the stays and struts of that old stope
and deeply underground
their words resound,
are multiplied by echo, swell and grow
and make a climate of a miner's voice.

So all the photographs like children's wishes
are filled with caves or winter,
innocence
has acted as a filter,
selected only beauty from the mine.
Except in the last picture,
it is shot
from an acute high angle. In a pit
figures the size of pins are strangely lit
and might be dancing but you know they're not.
Like Dante's vision of the nether hell
men struggle with the bright cold fires of salt,
locked in the black inferno of the rock:
the filter here, not innocence but guilt.

[1951] 1954

The Snowman

Ancient nomadic snowman has rolled round.
His spoor: a wide swathe on the white ground
signs of a wintry struggle where he stands.

Stands? Yes, he stands. What snowman sat?
Legless, indeed, but more as if he had
legs than had not.

White double 0, white nothing nothing, this
the child's first man on a white paper, his
earliest and fistful image is

now three-dimensional. Abstract. Everyman.
Of almost manna, he is still no man
no person, this so personal snowman.

O transient un-inhabitant, I know
no child who, on seeing the leprous thaw
undo your whitened torso and face of snow

would not, had he the magic
call you back
from that invisible attack

even knowing he can, with the new miracle
of another and softer and whiter snowfall
make you again, this time more wonderful.

Innocent single snowman. Overnight
brings him—a bright
omen—a thunderbolt of white.

But once I saw a mute in every yard
come like a plague; a stock-still multitude
and all stone-buttoned, bun-faced and absurd.

And next day they were still there but each
had changed a little as if all had inched
forward or back, I barely knew which;

and greyed a little too, grown sinister
and disreputable in their sooty fur,
numb, unmoving and nothing moving near.

And as far as I could see the snow was scarred
only with angels' wing marks or the feet of birds
like twigs broken upon the snow or shards

discarded. And I could hear no sound
as far as I could hear except a round
kind of an echo without end

rung like a hoop below them and above
jarring the air they had no need of
in a landscape without love.

[1967] 1967

After Rain

The snails have made a garden of green lace:
broderie anglaise from the cabbages,
chantilly from the choux-fleurs, tiny veils—
I see already that I lift the blind
upon a woman's wardrobe of the mind.

Such female whimsy floats about me like
a kind of tulle, a flimsy mesh,
while feet in gum boots pace the rectangles—
garden abstracted, geometry awash—
an unknown theorem argued in green ink,
dropped in the bath.
Euclid in glorious chlorophyl, half drunk.

I none too sober slipping in the mud
where rigged with guys of rain
the clothes-reel gauche
as the rangey skeleton of some
gaunt delicate spidery mute
is pitched as if
listening;
while hung from one thin rib
a silver web—
its infant, skeletal, diminutive,
now sagged with sequins, pulled ellipsoid,
glistening.

I suffer shame in all these images.
The garden is primeval, Giovanni
in soggy denim squelches by my hub
over his ruin,
shakes a doleful head.
But he so beautiful and diademmed,
his long Italian hands so wrung with rain

I find his ache exists beyond my rim
and almost weep to see a broken man
made subject to my whim.

O choir him, birds, and let him come to rest
within this beauty as one rests in love,

till pears upon the bough
encrusted with
small snails as pale as pearls
hang golden in
a heart that knows tears are a part of love.

And choir me too to keep my heart a size
larger than seeing, unseduced by each
bright glimpse of beauty striking like a bell,
so that the whole may toll,
its meaning shine
clear of the myriad images that still—
do what I will—encumber its pure line.

[1956] 1967

T-bar

Relentless, black on white, the cable runs
through metal arches up the mountain side.
At intervals giant pickaxes are hung
on long hydraulic springs. The skiers ride
propped by the axehead, twin automatons
supported by its handle, one each side.

In twos they move slow motion up the steep
incision in the mountain. Climb. Climb.
Somnambulists, bolt upright in their sleep
their phantom poles swung lazily behind,
while to the right, the empty T-bars keep
in mute descent, slow monstrous jigging time.

Captive the skiers now and innocent,
wards of eternity, each pair alone.
They mount the easy vertical ascent,
pass through successive arches, bride and groom,
as through successive naves, are newly wed
participants in some recurring dream.

So do they move forever. Clocks are broken.
In zones of silence they grow tall and slow,

inanimate dreamers, mild and gentle-spoken
blood-brothers of the haemophilic snow
until the summit breaks and they awaken
imagos from the stricture of the tow.

Jerked from her chrysalis the sleeping bride
suffers too sudden freedom like a pain.
The dreaming bridegroom severed from her side
singles her out, the old wound aches again.
Uncertain, lost, upon a wintry height
these two, not separate, but no longer one.

Now clocks begin to peck and sing. The slow
extended minute like a rubber band
contracts to catapult them through the snow
in tandem trajectory while behind
etching the sky-line, obdurate and slow
the spastic T-bars pivot and descend.

[1953] 1974

The Permanent Tourists

Somnolent through landscapes and by trees
nondescript, almost anonymous,
they alter as they enter foreign cities—
the terrible tourists with their empty eyes
longing to be filled with monuments.

Verge upon statues in the public squares
remembering the promise of memorials
yet never enter the entire event
as dogs, abroad in any kind of weather,
move perfectly within their rainy climate.

Lock themselves into snapshots on the steps
of monolithic bronze as if suspecting
the subtle mourning of the photograph
might later conjure in the memory
all they are now incapable of feeling.

And search all heroes out: the boy who gave

his life to save a town; the stolid queen;
forgotten politicians minus names
and the plunging war dead, permanently brave,
forever and ever going down to death.

Look, you can see them nude in any café
reading their histories from the bill of fare,
creating futures from a foreign teacup.
Philosophies like ferns bloom from the fable
that travel is broadening at the café table.

Yet somehow beautiful, they stamp the plaza.
Classic in their anxiety they call
all sculptured immemorial stone
into their passive eyes, as rivers
draw ruined columns to their placid glass.

[1948] 1974

Evening Dance of the Grey Flies

For Chris

Grey flies, fragile, slender-winged and slender-legged
scribble a pencilled script across the sunlit lawn.

As grass and leaves grow black
the grey flies gleam—
their cursive flight a gold calligraphy.

It is the light that gilds their frail
bodies, makes them fat and bright as bees—
reflected or refracted light—
as once my fist
burnished by some beam I could not see
glowed like gold mail and conjured Charlemagne

as once your face

grey with illness and with age—
a silverpoint against the pillow's white—

shone suddenly like the sun
before you died.

[1978] 1981

.K.

PAGE

MIRIAM
WADDINGTON

b. 1917

Icons

Suddenly
in middle age
instead of withering
into blindness
and burying myself
underground
I grow delicate
and fragile
superstitious;
I carry icons
I have begun
to worship
images.

I take them out
and prop them up
on bureau tops
in hotel rooms
in Spain
I study them
in locked libraries
in Leningrad
I untie them
from tourist packages
in Italy

they warm me
in the heatless winters
of London in the
hurry-up buses
of Picadilly.

My icons are not
angels or holy
babies they have
nothing to do
with saints or
madonnas, they
are mostly of
seashores summer
and love which I no
longer believe in
but I still believe
in the images,
I still preserve
the icons:

a Spanish factory
worker talks to me
in a street behind
the cathedral he

188

offers me *un poco
amor,* the scars on
his hand, his wounded
country and the black-
jacketed police; he
touches me on the
arm and other places,
and the alcoholic
in the blazing square
drinks brandy, confides
that fortunes can still
be made in Birmingham
but he has a bad
lung is hard of
hearing and owns
an apartment in Palma.

In Montreal a man
in a white shirt
with his sleeves
rolled up is reading
a book and waiting
for me in a room
with the door ajar,
the light falls
through the open
door the book
falls from his
open hand and he
stands up and
looks at me with
open eyes.

Of course I know
these are only
icons; there is
no such thing
as love left in
the world but
there is still
the image of it
which doesn't let
me wither into
blindness which
doesn't let me
bury myself
underground which
doesn't let me
say yes to the
black-leather police
or the empty libraries
or the lonely rooms
or the foggy windows
of cold London buses.

The world is getting
dark but I carry
icons, I remember
the summer
I will never forget
the light.

1969

Old Women of Toronto

MIRIAM
WADDINGTON

All old women sometimes come to this:
they go to live away, they cross ravines,
mornings they ride the subway, later look below
to read the red of dogwood and the print of snow.
They tread upon the contours of each month
with delicate feet that hardly sense its shape,
explore the mouth of March and with a hiss,
they spit at myth and swallow counter-bliss.

Their brows beetle, their plush hats tremble
they specially deplore without preamble
the palomino carpets on the lawns
steamy with manure in frosty air;
against all evidence and witnesses they'll swear
they never argued once or schemed to take
the room in front with the old Morris chair,
and partial view, at least, of the bright lake.

1972

The Women's Jail

This garden is outlandish
with its white picket fence
and straggling orchard;
who would guess this painted house
with convent walks
is a women's jail?

Unless you had seen their faces,
old women grey as sponges
drooping in this habitat
young ones sullen
with a worm gnawing them.
I often wonder why the drug-takers
have such skyblue eyes.

And the cheque-forgers:
how velvet they are

how apples and cream,
secretly I envy them
their blossoming bodies
and their talents with men.

Being especially human
I am no judge of evil
but hear how it has
a singing life in them
how it speaks out
with an endowed voice.

Doubt my poor, my gentle one
my overtrained, my fine
my inner ear.

I have been insufficiently dowered
my limbs are pale as winter
sun-starved
my blood is free from alcohol
I am law-abiding, I am completely
resistible—is there anything
praiseworthy in that?

1972

Advice to the Young

1
Keep bees and
grow asparagus,
watch the tides
and listen to the
wind instead of
the politicians
make up your own
stories and believe
them if you want to
live the good life.

2
All rituals
are instincts
never fully
trust them but
study to im-
prove biology
with reason.

3
Digging trenches
for asparagus
is good for the
muscles and
waiting for the
plants to settle
teaches patience
to those who are
usually in too
much of a hurry.

4
There is morality
in bee-keeping
it teaches how
not to be afraid
of the bee swarm
it teaches how
not to be afraid of
finding new places
and building in them
all over again.

1972

Ten Years and More

MIRIAM
WADDINGTON

When my husband
lay dying a mountain
a lake three
cities ten years
and more
lay between us:

There were our
sons my wounds
and theirs,
despair loneliness,
handfuls of un–
hammered nails
pictures never
hung all

The uneaten
meals and unslept
sleep; there was
retirement, and
worst of all
a green umbrella
he can never
take back.

I wrote him a
letter but all
I could think of
to say was: do you
remember Severn
River, the red canoe
with the sail
and lee-boards?

I was really saying
for the sake of our
youth and our love
I forgave him for
everything
and I was asking him
to forgive me too.

1976

BERTRAM
WARR

1917–1943

Working Class

We have heard no nightingales singing
in cool, dim lanes, where evening
comes like a procession through the aisles at passion-tide,
filling the church with quiet prayer dressed in white.
We have known no hills where sea-winds sweep up thyme
    perfume,
and crush it against our nostrils, as we stand by hump-backed
    trees.

We have felt no willow leaves pluck us timidly
as we pass on slack rivers;
a kiss, and a stealing away, like a lover who dares no more.
For we are the walkers on pavement,
who go grey-faced and given-up through the rain;
with our twice turned collars crinkled,
and the patches bunched coarsely in our crotches.
They have gashed the lands with cities,
and gone away afraid when the wounds turned blue.
Beauty has crept into the shelves of squat buildings,
to stare out strangely at us from the pages of Keats,
and the wan and wishful Georgian leaves.
These are our birthright, smoke and angry steel,
and long stern rows of stone, and wheels.
We are left with the churches, the red-necked men who eat
    oysters,
and stand up to talk at us in the approved manner.
We are left with the politicians who think poorly of us,
and who stand back with chaos in their pale old eyes
whimpering, 'That is not what we wanted. No,
it was not to have gone that way.'
They are very old, but we have been very ill,
and cannot yet send them away.

But there are things that still matter, something yet within us:
nights of love, bread and the kids,
and the cheek of the woman next door,
thoughts that glitter sometimes like a ruby on a mud-flat,

dreams that stir, and remind us of our blood.
Though the cities straddle the land like giants, holding us away,
we know they will topple some day,
and will lie over the land, dissolving and giving off gases.
But a wind will spring up to carry the smells away
and the earth will suck off the liquids and the crumbling flesh,
and on the bleached bones, when the sun shines,
we shall begin to build.

1970

MARGARET
AVISON

b. 1918

The Swimmer's Moment

For everyone
The swimmer's moment at the whirlpool comes,
But many at that moment will not say
'This is the whirlpool, then.'
By their refusal they are saved
From the black pit, and also from contesting
The deadly rapids, and emerging in
The mysterious, and more ample, further waters.
And so their bland-blank faces turn and turn
Pale and forever on the rim of suction
They will not recognize.
Of those who dare the knowledge
Many are whirled into the ominous centre
That, gaping vertical, seals up
For them an eternal boon of privacy,
So that we turn away from their defeat
With a despair, not for their deaths, but for
Ourselves, who cannot penetrate their secret
Nor even guess at the anonymous breadth
Where one or two have won:
(The silver reaches of the estuary).

1960

Snow

MARGARET
AVISON

Nobody stuffs the world in at your eyes.
The optic heart must venture: a jail-break
And re-creation. Sedges and wild rice
Chase rivery pewter. The astonished cinders quake
With rhizomes. All ways through the electric air
Trundle candy-bright disks; they are desolate
Toys if the soul's gates seal, and cannot bear,
Must shudder under, creation's unseen freight.
But soft, there is snow's legend: colour of mourning
Along the yellow Yangtze where the wheel
Spins an indifferent stasis that's death's warning.
Asters of tumbled quietness reveal
Their petals. Suffering this starry blur
The rest may ring your change, sad listener.

1960

Thaw

Sticky inside their winter suits
The Sunday children stare at pools
In pavement and black ice where roots
Of sky in moodier sky dissolve.

An empty coach train runs along
The thin and sooty river flats
And stick and straw and random stones
Steam faintly when its steam departs.

Lime-water and licorice light
Wander the tumbled streets. A few
Sparrows gather. A dog barks out
Under the dogless pale pale blue.

Move your tongue along a slat
Of a raspberry box from last year's crate.
Smell a saucepantilt of water
On the coal-ash in your grate.

Think how the Black Death made men dance,   MARGARET
AVISON
And from the silt of centuries
The proof is now scraped bare that once
Troy fell and Pompey scorched and froze.

    A boy alone out in the court
    Whacks with his hockey-stick, and whacks
    In the wet, and the pigeons flutter, and rise,
    And settle back.

1960

New Year's Poem

The Christmas twigs crispen and needles rattle
Along the windowledge.
        A solitary pearl
Shed from the necklace spilled at last week's party
Lies in the suety, snow-luminous plainness
Of morning, on the windowledge beside them.
And all the furniture that circled stately
And hospitable when these rooms were brimmed
With perfumes, furs, and black-and-silver
Crisscross of seasonal conversation, lapses
Into its previous largeness.
        I remember
Anne's rose-sweet gravity, and the stiff grave
Where cold so little can contain;
I mark the queer delightful skull and crossbones
Starlings and sparrows left, taking the crust,
And the long loop of winter wind
Smoothing its arc from dark Arcturus down
To the bricked corner of the drifted courtyard,
And the still windowledge.
        Gentle and just pleasure
It is, being human, to have won from space
This unchill, habitable interior
Which mirrors quietly the light
Of the snow, and the new year.

1960

Meeting Together of Poles
and Latitudes (In Prospect)

Those who fling off, toss head,
   Taste the bitter morning, and have at it—
   Thresh, knead, dam, weld,
   Wave baton, force
   Marches through squirming bogs,
   Not from contempt, but
   From thrust, unslakeably thirsty,
   Amorous of every tower and twig, and
   Yet like railroad engines with
   Longings for their landscapes (pistons pounding)
   Rock fulminating through
   Wrecked love, unslakeably loving—

   Seldom encounter at the Judgment Seat
Those who are flung off, sit
   Dazed awhile, gather concentration,
   Follow vapour-trails with shrivelling wonder,
   Pilfer, mow, play jongleur
   With mathematic signs, or
   Tracing the forced marches make
   Peculiar cats-cradles of telephone wire,
   Lap absently at sundown, love
   As the stray dog on foreign hills
   A bone-myth, atavistically,
   Needing more faith, and fewer miles, but
   Slumber-troubled by it,
   Wanting for death that
   Myth-clay, though
   Scratch-happy in these (foreign) brambly wilds;

But when they approach each other
   The place is an astonishment:
   Runways shudder with little planes
   Practising folk-dance steps or
   Playing hornet,
   Sky makes its ample ruling
   Clear as a primary child's exercise-book
   In somebody else's language,
   And the rivers under the earth
   Foam without whiteness, domed down,

As they foam indifferently every
Day and night (if you'd call that day and night)
Not knowing how they wait, at the node, the
Curious encounter.

MARGARET
AVISON

1960

Civility a Bogey
OR, TWO CENTURIES OF CANADIAN CITIES

Chinashop at seaborde,
a speckled chinashop
in the hard-wheat flat-land,
a red-sand chinashop
in pine-scrub:
and inbetween the granite cup dangled by the pump.

Came big bull buildings,
sharded and shoaled
even the moustache-cup,
held a board-meeting,
stood, or sat smoking,
cratered the moonlight.
Mouseholes rustled with paper
and by then Hallowe'en was a prance of reeking horses.

Chinashops tame bulls
in time,
glass and enamel
annealed have the glitter
of schist, or a gunmetal
sheen. The ceilings
tilt, and the filled ground flounders.

Earth, air, firewater
crack their joints, daring
a dust-up;
no man can shape his own rump
though the seats of the mighty swing   sunlight.
                                        claw   in the
                                        and crane

Where was bullshop, boardroom
sky laps leisurely
round wrack and jetty.
Pigeons chuckle at
plunging and all the fuss and feathers,
and the docks of seaborde, flatland, pinescrub
shine through the windy night in their dark moorings.

To walk the earth
Is to be immersed,
Slung by the feet
In the universe:

The blessed heads learn smiling upside down
shored on a crumb
whether in hinterland or town.
It's all one.

1960

In a Season of Unemployment

These green painted park benches are
all new. The Park Commissioner had them
planted.
Sparrows go on
having dust baths at the edge of
the park maple's shadow, just where
the bench is cemented down, planted
and then cemented.

Not a breath moves
this newspaper.
I'd rather read it by the Lapland sun at midnight. Here we're
bricked in early by a
stifling dark.

On that bench a man in a
pencil-striped white shirt
keeps his head up and steady.

The newspaper-astronaut says
    'I feel excellent under the condition of weightlessness.'
And from his bench a
scatter of black bands in the hollow-air
ray out—too quick for the eye—
and cease.

    'Ground observers watching him on a TV circuit said
    At the time of this report he
    was smiling,' Moscow ra-
    dio reported.
I glance across at him, and mark that
he is feeling
excellent too, I guess, and
weightless and
'smiling'.

1966

The Dumbfounding

When you walked here,
took skin, muscle, hair,
eyes, larynx, we
withheld all honor: 'His house is clay,
how can he tell us of his far country?'

Your not familiar pace
in flesh, across the waves,
woke only our distrust.
Twice-torn we cried 'A ghost'
and only on our planks counted you fast.

Dust wet with your spittle
cleared mortal trouble.
We called you a blasphemer,
a devil-tamer.

The evening you spoke of going away
we could not stay.

All legions massed. You had to wash, and rise,
alone, and face
out of the light, for us.

MARGARET
AVISON

You died.
We said,
'The worst is true, our bliss
has come to this.'

When you were seen by men
in holy flesh again
we hoped so despairingly for such report
we closed their windpipes for it.

Now you have sought
and seek, in all our ways, all thoughts,
streets, musics—and we make of these a din
trying to lock you out, or in,
to be intent. And dying.

Yet you are
constant and sure,
the all-lovely, all-men's-way
to that far country.

Winning one, you again
all ways would begin
life: to make new
flesh, to empower
the weak in nature
to restore
or stay the sufferer;

lead through the garden to
trash, rubble, hill,
where, the outcast's outcast, you
sound dark's uttermost, strangely light-brimming, until
time be full.

1966

A Nameless One

MARGARET
AVISON

Hot in June a narrow winged
long-elbowed-thread-legged
living insect lived
and died within
the lodgers' second-floor bathroom here.

At six a.m.
wafting ceilingward,
no breeze but what it living made there;

at noon standing
still as a constellation of spruce needles
before the moment of
making it, whirling;

at four a
wilted flotsam, cornsilk, on the linoleum:

now that it is
over, I
look with new eyes
upon this room
adequate for one to
be, in.

Its insect-day
has threaded a needle
for me for my eyes dimming
over rips and tears and
thin places.

1966

Unspeakable

MARGARET
AVISON

> The beauty of the unused
> > (the wheatear among birds, or
> > > stonechat)
> the unused in houses (as a
> > portion of low roof swept by the
> > > buttery leaves of a pear tree
> > > where a manx cat is
> > > discovered—just now—blinking his
> > > > sunned Arctic sea-eyes in the
> > > > sun-play)
> the beauty of the
> > unused in one I know, of
> > excellent indolence
> > > from season into
> > > > skywide wintering
> should be
> confidently, as it is
> copious and new into the morning,
> celebrated.

1966

LOUIS
DUDEK

b. 1918

Garcia Lorca

It was as if the devil of evil had got
the God of all that is good by the throat
and shot
Adam the boy and Eve his girl,
scorched like a but through space.

The end of a world.

And yet, just as the fascists, firing, were only
an ignorant audience, breaking
to bits his stage,
that was such a friendly comedy
of loving creatures, of flowers and happy people,

and the poet
with notes in his fingers
was something on a stem,

a fire
in cups of flowers,

so, of us, many wise as candle wicks
in our halos while round us the insect wheels
in violence, kill what we can
alone, with subtle and selfish claws;
set up ourselves a single majority,
usurp the soul with a dollar,
the dictator for the ruling class of greeds;
and intent on the growth of percentage
and drawing a little blood from friends,
prepare the squeaking gallows
where soon, like innocent lilies, our children
will weep, bewildered and wondering why.

Each man's struggle against the pack
is the futile and dispersed class war. Could we but
concentrate violence, press out this pus
in one shock! But we make
a nest for germs, saving our inch of skin,
a home for killers paid by generous bankers,
ready to belt on their holsters and say, 'I am the law.'

So it grows to insanity, the furious stars
in our ears ringing, the poet's roses
ripped and scattered apart, as Federico
Garcia Lorca was shot that morning,
an agile songster dropped in the damp grass.

What if from bloody Granada
the black bullets sped
like lights from a mirror, knocking

at doors and at window ledges
with knuckles bleeding and red?

LOUIS
DUDEK

The news is a prophecy
no one heard:
a child had been taken from bed
and broken in our hands.

1946

Coming Suddenly to the Sea

Coming suddenly to the sea in my twenty-eighth year,
to the mother of all things that breathe, of mussels and whales,
I could not see anything but sand at first
and burning bits of mother-of-pearl.
But this was the sea, terrible as a torch
which the winter sun had lit,
flaming in the blue and salt sea-air
under my twenty-eight-year infant eyes.
And then I saw the spray smashing the rocks
and the angry gulls cutting the air,
the heads of fish and the hands of crabs on stones:
the carnivorous sea, sower of life,
battering a granite rock to make it a pebble—
love and pity needless as the ferny froth on its long smooth
    waves.
The sea, with its border of crinkly weed,
the inverted Atlantic of our unstable planet,
froze me into a circle of marble, sending the icy air out in
        lukewarm waves.
And so I brought home, as an emblem of that day
ending my long blind years, a fistful of blood-red weed in my
        hand.

1971

The Dead

After we knew that we were dead we sat down and cried a little,
only we found that our eyes were now empty and we were
without any feeling of sadness.
'We had it coming, it was bound to happen,' said one.
'I am thinking of the future,' said a lady beside him.
'There is no future,' an old man affirmed.
'I'm glad,' said one, looking back toward the earth. 'I'm free of it,
I'm no longer one of them. I am glad.'
'So am I' someone echoed.
'So am I.'
'So am I . . . So am I,' the echo travelled along the plain and
beyond. I did not know whether it was an echo, or whether
others were there repeating the sound.
'So am I, so am I' . . . it went on, the whole valley and plain
resounded.
I turned my eyes around to see, but there was only a grey
transparency without end, and empty, that was like a wall
before me. I could see as far as I wanted but I wanted to see
nothing, and there was nothing.
One of the dead beside me stirred, and as if a memory had
awakened him he said, 'They are always on edge down there.
We were always on edge.'
'And there was also the fear of death,' said a man of middle age.
'Someone there dies every day, every hour.
Think of the bird in the teeth of the hunter, beating its wings,
crying out—
That was the way we were.' He fell into a deep silence. We all sat
for a long time in silence.
Below us stretched the endless plain, and in the foreground, still
near, the earth hung, like a sad town in a grey mist.
'There they sit, the beautiful women and the young men in their
prime; time passes over them, and they shrivel in ugliness,
looking at one another in amazement. O, I am glad to be out of
it. Glad to be rid of it.'
'But the worst is that even the innocent suffer,' said a lady.
'They are all innocent,' the old man muttered.
Then, raising his head, one poor skinflint beside me made a face
like a devil who had done a good deed, and said, 'All this is
important. I never worried about important things. The worst
of it was, as I see it now' . . . (he looked out across the plain
into the grey distance without obstacle) 'was to be caught in a
net that did not even exist.'

'When you are caught in a net,' said the man of middle age,
     'whether it exists or doesn't exist, it is still a net, and you are
     caught in it.'
'I don't even want to think of it,' said the wizened man, as if
     losing interest;
'I remember,' and here he bit his lip out of ancient habit, 'that
     even love was painful.'
And just as he said this, a dark cloud passed over us, and the earth
     was blotted out.
It brightened. But the figures beside me, and the earth that had
     formed a dark figure, receded, in no determinate direction, until
     I could see no longer. And then we were bathed in a morning
     light of sudden gladness. And there was nothing.

1971

AL
PURDY

b. 1918

Remains of an Indian Village

Underfoot rotten boards, forest rubble, bones. . .
Animals were here after the plague,
after smallpox to make another ending:
for the tutelary gods of decay
acknowledge aid from any quarter. . .

Here the charging cotyledons of spring
press green forefingers
on femurs, vertebrae, and delicate
belled skulls of children;
the moon's waylaid light does not shrink
from bone relics and other beauties of nature. . .

Death is certainly absent now,
at least in the overwhelming sense
that it once walked at night in the village
and howled thru the mouths of dogs—
But everything fades
and wavers into something else,

the seasonal cycle and the planet's rhythm
vary imperceptibly into the other;
spirits of the dead are vanished,
only great trees remain,
and the birth certificate of cedars
specifies no memory of a village. . .

(And I have seen myself fade
from a woman's eyes
while I was standing there,
and the earth was aware of
me no longer—)
But I come here as part of the process
in the pale morning light,
thinking what has been thought by no one
for years of their absence,
in some way continuing them—
And I observe the children's shadows
running in this green light from
                        a distant star
into the near forest—
wood violets and trilliums of
a hundred years ago
blooming and vanishing—
the villages of the brown people
toppling and returning—
What moves and lives
        occupying the same space,
what touches what touched them
                        owes them. . .

Standing knee-deep in the joined earth
of their weightless bones,
in the archaeological sunlight,
the trembling voltage of summer,
in the sunken reservoirs of rain,
standing waist-deep in the criss-cross
rivers of shadows,
in the village of nightfall,
the hunters silent and women
bending over dark fires,
I hear their broken consonants. . .

1962

Night Song for a Woman

AL
PURDY

A few times only, then away,
leaving absence akin to presence
in the changed look of
buildings
      an inch off centre—

All things enter
into me so softly I am
aware of them
        not myself
the mind is sensuous
        as the body
        I am a sound
out of hearing past
Arcturus
      still moving outward

—if anyone were to listen
they'd know
      about humans

1962

The Cariboo Horses

At 100 Mile House the cowboys ride in rolling
stagey cigarettes with one hand reining
half-tame bronco rebels on a morning grey as stone
—so much like riding dangerous women
      with whiskey coloured eyes—
such women as once fell dead with their lovers
with fire in their heads and slippery froth on thighs
—Beaver or Carrier women maybe or
      Blackfoot squaws far past the edge of this valley
on the other side of those two toy mountain ranges
      from the sunfierce plains beyond

But only horses
      waiting in stables

hitched at taverns
standing at dawn
pastured outside the town with
jeeps and fords and chevvys and
busy muttering stake trucks rushing
importantly over roads of man's devising
over the safe known roads of the ranchers
families and merchants of the town
On the high prairie
are only horse and rider
wind in dry grass
clopping in silence under the toy mountains
dropping sometimes and
lost in the dry grass
golden oranges of dung

Only horses
no stopwatch memories or palace ancestors
not Kiangs hauling undressed stone in the Nile Valley
and having stubborn Egyptian tantrums or
Onagers racing thru Hither Asia and
the last Quagga screaming in African highlands
lost relatives of these
whose hooves were thunder
the ghosts of horses battering thru the wind
whose names were the wind's common usage
whose life was the sun's
arriving here at chilly noon
in the gasoline smell of the
dust and waiting 15 minutes
at the grocer's

1965

The Country North of Belleville

Bush land scrub land—
>Cashel Township and Wollaston
Elzevir McClure and Dungannon
green lands of Weslemkoon Lake
where a man might have some
>opinion of what beauty
is and none deny him
>>for miles—

Yet this is the country of defeat
where Sisyphus rolls a big stone
year after year up the ancient hills
picnicking glaciers have left strewn
with centuries' rubble
>>backbreaking days
>>in the sun and rain
when realization seeps slow in the mind
without grandeur or self deception in
>>noble struggle
of being a fool—

A country of quiescence and still distance
a lean land
>not like the fat south
with inches of black soil on
>earth's round belly—
And where the farms are
>it's as if a man stuck
both thumbs in the stony earth and pulled

>>it apart
>>to make room
enough between the trees
for a wife
>and maybe some cows and
>room for some
of the more easily kept illusions—
And where the farms have gone back
to forest
>are only soft outlines
>shadowy differences—

AL
PURDY

Old fences drift vaguely among the trees
        a pile of moss-covered stones
gathered for some ghost purpose
has lost meaning under the meaningless sky
        —they are like cities under water
and the undulating green waves of time
        are laid on them—

This is the country of our defeat
        and yet
during the fall plowing a man
might stop and stand in a brown valley of the furrows
        and shade his eyes to watch for the same
        red patch mixed with gold
        that appears on the same
        spot in the hills
        year after year
        and grow old
plowing and plowing a ten-acre field until
the convolutions run parallel with his own brain—

And this is a country where the young
        leave quickly
unwilling to know what their fathers know
or think the words their mothers do not say—

Herschel Monteagle and Faraday
lakeland rockland and hill country
a little adjacent to where the world is
a little north of where the cities are and
sometime
we may go back there
        to the country of our defeat
Wollaston Elzevir and Dungannon
and Weslemkoon lake land
where the high townships of Cashel
        McClure and Marmora once were—
But it's been a long time since
and we must enquire the way
        of strangers—

1965

Wilderness Gothic

Across Roblin Lake, two shores away,
they are sheathing the church spire
with new metal. Someone hangs in the sky
over there from a piece of rope,
hammering and fitting God's belly-scratcher,
working his way up along the spire
until there's nothing left to nail on—
Perhaps the workman's faith reaches beyond:
touches intangibles, wrestles with Jacob,
replacing rotten timber with pine thews,
pounds hard in the blue cave of the sky,
contends heroically with difficult problems
of gravity, sky navigation and mythopeia,
his volunteer time and labour donated to God,
minus sick benefits of course on a non-union job—

Fields around are yellowing into harvest,
nestling and fingerling are sky and water borne,
death is yodelling quiet in green woodlots,
and bodies of three young birds have disappeared
in the sub-surface of the new county highway—

That picture is incomplete, part left out
that might alter the whole Durer landscape:
gothic ancestors peer from medieval sky,
dour faces trapped in photograph albums escaping
to clop down iron roads with matched greys:
work-sodden wives groping inside their flesh
for what keeps moving and changing and flashing
beyond and past the long frozen Victorian day.
A sign of fire and brimstone? A two-headed calf
born in the barn last night? A sharp female agony?
An age and a faith moving into transition,
the dinner cold and new-baked bread a failure,
deep woods shiver and water drops hang pendant,
double yolked eggs and the house creaks a little—
Something is about to happen. Leaves are still.
Two shores away, a man hammering in the sky.
Perhaps he will fall.

1968

Poem

You are ill and so I lead you away
and put you to bed in the dark room
—you lie breathing softly and I hold your hand
feeling the fingertips relax as sleep comes

You will not sleep more than a few hours
and the illness is less serious than my anger or cruelty
and the dark bedroom is like a foretaste of other darknesses
to come later which all of us must endure alone
but here I am permitted to be with you

After a while in sleep your fingers clutch tightly
and I know that whatever may be happening
the fear coiled in dreams or the bright trespass of pain
there is nothing at all I can do except hold your hand
and not go away

1971

Alive or Not

It's like a story
because it takes so long to happen:

a block away on an Ottawa street
I see this woman about to fall
and she collapses slowly
in sections the way you read about
and there just might be time
for me to reach her
running as fast as I can
before her head hits the sidewalk
Of course it's my wife
I am running toward her now
and there is a certain amount of horror
a time lag in which other things happen
I can almost see flowers break into blossom
while I am running toward the woman
my wife it seems

orchids in the Brazilian jungle
exist like unprovable ideas
until a man in a pith helmet
steps on one and yells Eureka or something
—and while I am thinking about this
her body splashes on the street
her glasses fall broken beside her
with a musical sound under the traffic
and she is probably dead too
Of course I cradle her in my arms
a doll perhaps without life
while someone I do not know
signals a taxi
as the bystanders stare
What this means years later
as I grow older and older
is that I am still running toward her:
the woman falls very slowly
she is giving me more and more time
to reach her and make the grab
and each time each fall she may die
or not die and this will go on forever
this will go on forever and ever
As I grow older and older
my speed afoot increases
each time I am running and reach
the place before she falls every time
I am running too fast to stop
I run past her farther and farther
it's almost like a story
as an orchid dies in the Brazilian jungle
and there is a certain amount of horror

1976

The Dead Poet

I was altered in the placenta
by the dead brother before me
who built a place in the womb
knowing I was coming:
he wrote words on the walls of flesh
painting a woman inside a woman
whispering a faint lullaby
that sings in my blind heart still

The others were lumberjacks
backwoods wrestlers and farmers
their women were meek and mild
nothing of them survives
but an image inside an image
of a cookstove and the kettle boiling
—how else explain myself to myself
where does the song come from?

Now on my wanderings:
at the Alhambra's lyric dazzle
where the Moors built stone poems
a wan white face peering out
—and the shadow in Plato's cave
remembers the small dead one
—at Samarcand in pale blue light
the words came slowly from him
—I recall the music of blood
on the Street of the Silversmiths

Sleep softly spirit of earth
as the days and nights join hands
when everything becomes one thing
wait softly brother
but do not expect it to happen
that great whoop announcing resurrection
expect only a small whisper
of birds nesting and green things growing
and a brief saying of them
and know where the words came from

1981

Spinning

For Colleen Thibaudeau

'Can't see out of my left eye
nothing much happens on the left anyway'
—you have to spin around right quickly
then just catch a glimpse
of coat tails leaving the room
(lace doilies on the settee)
light foot rising and disappearing
the last shot fired at Batoche
or maybe it was Duck Lake
—thought I saw someone I knew
and turned faster and faster
said wait for me
it was my grandmother I never knew
before I was born she died
—sometimes I turned fast enough
and nearly caught up with the sun
it bounded like a big red ball
forward and then went backwards
over the mountains somewhere
—thought I saw someone I knew
she was young in an old summer
I tried to remember very carefully
balanced on one foot
and concentrated and concentrated
lightfoot white feet in the long grass
running to meet her lover
I couldn't stop turning then
wait for me wait for me

1981

RAYMOND
SOUSTER

b. 1921

The Man Who Finds That
His Son Has Become a Thief

Coming into the store at first angry
At the accusation, believing in
The word of his boy who has told him:
I didn't steal anything, honest.

Then becoming calmer, seeing that anger
Will not help in the business, listening painfully
As the other's evidence unfolds, so painfully slow.

Then seeing gradually that evidence
Almost as if tighten slowly around the neck
Of his son, at first vaguely circumstantial, then gathering damage,
Until there is present the unmistakable odour of guilt
Which seeps now into the mind and lays its poison.

Suddenly feeling sick and alone and afraid,
As if an unseen hand had slapped him in the face
For no reason whatsoever: wanting to get out
Into the street, the night, the darkness, anywhere to hide
The pain that must show in the face to these strangers, the fear.

It must be like this.
It could hardly be otherwise.

1952

Lagoons, Hanlan's Point

RAYMOND
SOUSTER

Mornings
before the sun's liquid
spilled gradually, flooding
the island's cool cellar,
there was the boat
and the still lagoons,
with the sound of my oars
the only intrusion
over cries of birds
in the marshy shallows,
or the loud thrashing
of the startled crane
rushing the air.

And in one strange
dark, tree-hung entrance,
I followed the sound
of my heart all the way
to the reed-blocked ending,
with the pads of the lily
thick as green-shining film
covering the water.

And in another
where the sun came
to probe the depths
through a shaft of branches,
I saw the skeletons
of brown ships rotting
far below in their burial-ground,
and wondered what strange fish
with what strange colours
swam through these palaces
under the water. . . .

A small boy
with a flat-bottomed punt
and an old pair of oars
moving with wonder
through the antechamber
of a waking world.

1952

Flight of the Roller Coaster

Once more around should do it, the man confided. . .

And sure enough, when the roller-coaster reached the peak
Of the giant curve above me—screech of its wheels
Almost drowned by the shriller cries of the riders—

Instead of the dip and plunge with its landslide of screams
It rose in the air like a movieland magic carpet, some wonderful
   bird,

And without fuss or fanfare swooped slowly across the
   amusement park,
Over Spook's Castle, ice-cream booths, shooting-gallery; and
   losing no height

Made the last yards above the beach, where the cucumber-cool
Brakeman in the last seat saluted
A lady about to change from her bathing-suit.

Then, as many witnesses duly reported, headed leisurely over the
   water,
Disappearing mysteriously all too soon behind a low-lying flight
   of clouds.

1955

The Hunter

I carry the ground-hog along by the tail
all the way back to the farm, with the blood
dripping from his mouth a couple of drops at a time,
leaving a perfect trail for anyone to follow.

The half-wit hired man is blasting imaginary rabbits
somewhere on our left. We walk through fields steaming after
   rain,
jumping the mud: and watching the swing of your girl's hips
ahead of me, the proud way your hand holds the gun,

and remembering how you held it
up to the hog caught in the trap and blew his head in

wonder what fate you have in store for me.

1964

On the Rouge

I can almost see
my father's canoe
pointing in from the lake,
him paddling,
mother hidden
in a hat of fifty years ago.

Turning now up a stream
clear-flowing through marsh
(not mud-brown like today):

gliding under the same
railway bridge we cross under,
slipping by the same giant
stepping-stones of rock
standing up so like ramparts:

moving on to those quieter
summer-singing reaches,
the calling of birds
making speech difficult.

Lost finally, perhaps forever,
behind ferns swallowing banks,
bent trees overarching sky,

drifting the summer
labyrinths of love.

1967

b. 1922

Great-Aunt Rebecca

I remember my mother's Aunt Rebecca
Who remembered very well Confederation
And what a time of mourning it was.
She remembered the days before the railway,
And how when the first train came through
Everybody got on and visited it,
Scraping off their shoes first
So as not to dirty the carriage.
She remembered the remoteness, the long walks between
    neighbours.
Her own mother had died young, in childbirth,
But she had lived till her eighties,
Had borne eleven children,
Managed to raise nine of them,
In spite of scarlet fever.
She had clothed them with the work of her own fingers,
Wool from her own sheep, spun at home,
Woven at home, sewed at home
Without benefit of machine.
She had fed them with pancakes and salt pork
And cakes sweetened with maple sugar.
She had taught them one by one to memorize
'The chief end of man is to know God,'
And she had also taught them to make porridge
And the right way of lighting a wood fire,
Had told the boys to be kind and courageous
And the girls never to raise their voices
Or argue with their husbands.

I remember her as an old woman,
Rheumatic, with folded hands,
In a rocking chair in a corner of the living room,
Bullied (for her own good) by one of her daughters.
She marveled a little, gently and politely,
At radios, cars, telephones;
But really they were not as present to her
As the world of her prime, the farmhouse

223

In the midst of woods, the hayfields
Where her husband and the boys swung their scythes
Through the burning afternoon, until she called for supper.

For me also, the visiting child, she made that world more real
Than the present could be. I too
Wished to be a pioneer,
To walk on snowshoes through remote pastures,
To live away from settlements an independent life
With a few loved people only; to be like Aunt Rebecca,
Soft as silk and tough as that thin wire
They use for snaring rabbits.

1969

If I Could Walk Out into the Cold Country

If I could walk out into the cold country
And see the white and innocent dawn arise:
The mist stealing away, leaving the low hills
Bathed in pale light; the pink, unreal sun;
The jagged trees stabbing the cold, bright sky;
If I could walk over stubble fields white with frost
And see each separate small beaded blade
Loaded and edged with white; or climb the fence
Of grey and twisted wood, to find and eat
The crab-apples in the pasture, sharp with frost;
If I could shelter, shivering in a clump of woods
To watch the chill and beautiful day go past;
Perhaps I might find again my lost childhood,
A ghost blowing with the November wind,
Or buried in the wood, like those dead pioneers
Whose tumbled tombstones I found overgrown with brambles,
Their names erased, in an unfrequented way.

1969

Death by Drowning

ELIZABETH
BREWSTER

Plunging downward through the slimy water
He discovered, as the fear grew worse,
That life, not death, was what he had been after:
Ironic to die in life's symbol and source.

Drowning was not so easy as it looked from shore.
He had thought of sinking down through layers of peace
To depths where mermaids sang. He would be lapped over
By murmuring waves that lulled him into rest.

But all death is a kind of strangulation,
He had been told once and remembered now,
Choking on water like a rope, and coughing
Its bloody taste from his mouth. He had not known
Before how the body struggled to survive
And must be forced, and forced again, to die.

1969

Anti-Love Poems

I
No, I don't love you
in spite of what I say
in the ecstasy of the act.

Don't preen,
don't worry.
It isn't
the way you think it is.
(How do I know
what you think?)

Why do I feel guilty
that I am sometimes bored?
That I compare your
hands with other hands?
That I remember other faces
better than I remember yours?

It's not your fault.
Love is never deserved,
is mostly imagination anyway.

It's only fretfulness that I complain
you are not warmer, gayer, tenderer,
don't have brown eyes,
have the same faults I have.

Now that I have opened
all my doors to you,
could I close them again?
Would I really love you, maybe,
only if you went away?

Is unrequited love
what I have always wanted
because it takes less time
than the other kind?

2
Yet I do sympathize,
try to understand
the scared small boy in a bleak boarding school
with all those dotty and perverse masters

boy who killed a bird once
not knowing why

(the story frightened me,
   bird-woman that I am,
   perched
   assailable
   always scared
   of having my wings maimed)

but you wanted then to be punished,
maybe still do.

I understand better
the time you stole
the model sailing ship
(because once I stole

a beaded purse from my cousin's box of popcorn
and Grandmother said
I would end up in prison
eating bread and water)

and the way you idolized
your reckless charmer
disreputable father
who went from job to job
and wife to wife

and that sailor
who dared you to swim
in the shark-infested sea
(you felt he would scorn you forever
    because you could not do it)

always punishing yourself
by failing,
not daring,
not wanting to hope too much.

I wonder, do you see me
as bird, or ship, or shark?

1977

b. 1922

From the North Saskatchewan

when on the high bluff discovering
the river cuts below
                          send messages
we have spoken to those on the boats

I am obsessed by the berries they eat
all night odour of Saskatoon
and an unidentifiable odour
something baking
                          the sun
never reaches the lower bank

I cannot read the tree markings
today the sky is torn by wind:
a field after a long battle
strewn with corpses of cloud

give blessings to my children
speak for us to those who sent us here
say we did all that could be done
we have not learned
what lies north of the river
or past those hills that look like beasts

1967

Houdini

ELI
MANDEL

I suspect he knew that trunks are metaphors,
could distinguish between the finest rhythms
unrolled on rope or singing in a chain
and knew the metrics of the deepest pools

I think of him listening to the words
spoken by manacles, cells, handcuffs,
chests, hampers, roll-top desks, vaults,
especially the deep words spoken by coffins

escape, escape: quaint Harry in his suit
his chains, his desk, attached to all attachments
how he'd sweat in that precise struggle
with those binding words, wrapped around him
like that mannered style, his formal suit

and spoken when? by whom? What thing first said
'there's no way out?'; so that he'd free himself,
leap, squirm, no matter how, to chain himself again,
once more jump out of the deep alive
with all his chains singing around his feet
like the bound crowds who sigh, who sigh.

1967

Envoi

my country is not a country
                              but winter
rivers of ice
from St. Hubert terrible knives
run through the whiteness of my veins

politics pierce my heart
on a floor littered with history
I shiver while wardens shovel in
lunatic sentences, rag upon rag

it must be cold in prison, in québec

and your heart hurt singer
what do you see through its pane

icy slaves circle the river
montréal tense against the steel of its manacles
your words drifting   frozen wounds
                                    blessing

a sick bride
a murderous bridegroom
                    that wedding
whose children will be colder killers
than the words of this or any other song

1973

On the 25th Anniversary of the Liberation of Auschwitz: Memorial Services, Toronto, January 25, 1970 YMHA Bloor & Spadina

the name is hard
a German sound made out of
the gut guttural throat
y scream yell   ing open
voice mouth growl
                and sweat
'the only way out of Auschwitz
is through the chimneys'
                        of course
that's second hand   that's told
again Sigmund Sherwood (Sobolewski)
twisting himself into that sentence
before us on the platform
                        the poem
shaping itself late in the after
noon later than it would be:

Pendericki's 'Wrath of God'
moaning electronic Polish theatric
the screen silent
                framed by the name
looking away from/pretending not there

no   name   no   not name no

         Auschwitz
    in GOTHIC lettering
                   the hall
a parody a reminiscence a nasty memory
the Orpheum in Estevan before Buck Jones
the Capitol in Regina before Tom Mix
waiting for the guns
waiting for the cowboy killers
one two three
                  Legionnaires
Polish ex-prisoners Association
Legions
         their medals their flags
so the procession, the poem gradual
ly insistent beginning to shape itself
with the others
              walked with them
into the YMHA Bloor & Spadina
thinking apocalypse shame degradation
thinking bones and bodies melting
thickening thinning melting bones and bodies
thinking not mine/must speak clearly
the poet's words/Yevtyshenko at Baba-Yar

there   this January   snow
heavy wet   the wind   heavy wet
the street grey white slush melted concrete
bones and bodies melting slush
                             saw
with the others
              the prisoner
in the YMHA hall Bloor & Spadina
arms wax stiff body stiff unnatural
coloured face blank eyes
                      walked
with the others toward the screen
toward the picture
                 SLIDES
       this is mother
       this is father
       this is

the one who is

waving her arms like that
is the one who
                    like
I mean running with her breasts bound
ing
          running
                    with her hand here and there
with her here and
                              there
hands
          that   that is
the poem becoming the body
becoming the faint hunger
ing body
              prowling
                          through
words the words words the words
opening   mouths ovens
the generals smiling saluting
in their mythic uniforms god-like
generals uniforms with the black leather
with the straps and the intricate leather
the phylacteries and the prayer shawl
corsets and the boots and the leather straps

and the shining faces of the generals in their boots
and their stiff wax bodies their unnatural faces
and their blank eyes and their hands their stiff hands
and the generals in their straps and wax and stiff
staying standing
                          melting bodies and thickening
                          quick flesh on flesh handling
                          hands
          the poem flickers, fades
the four Yarzeit candles guttering one
          each four million lights dim
my words drift
                    smoke from chimneys and ovens
          a bad picture, the power failing
     pianist clattering on and over and through
the long Saturday afternoon in the Orpheum
          while the whitehatted star spangled cowboys
               shot the dark men and shot the dark men

and we threw popcorn balls and grabbed
        each other and cheered:
the lowheach other and cheered:
me jewboy yelling
for the shot town and the falling men
        and the lights come on
                                and
        with the others
standing in silence

the gothic word hangs
over us on a shroud-white screen

and we drift away
                to ourselves
                        to the late Sunday Times
                                the wet snow
                                the city

                        a body melting

1973

ELI
MANDEL

The Madwomen of the Plaza de Mayo

They wear white scarves and shawls.
They carry pictures on strings about their necks.
I have seen their faces elsewhere:
in Ereceira, fishermen's wives
walking in dark processions
to the sea, its roaring,
women of Ireland
wearing their dark scarves
hearing the echo of guns, bombs

Identities
the *desaparecidos*
lost ones
the disappeared

in the Plaza the Presidential Palace
reveals soldiers like fences with steel spikes
the rhythm of lost bodies
the rhythm of loss

A soldier is a man who is not a man.
A fence, a spike
A nail in somebody's eye.
Lost man.

Why are the women weeping?
For whom do they cry
under the orange moon
under the lemon moon of Buenos Aires?

'If only for humanitarian reasons
tell the families of the living
where are they
tell the families of the dead
what they need
what they deserve to know.'

No one speaks.
The junta says nothing.
The *desaparecidos* remain silent.
The moon has no language.

1981

MILTON
ACORN

b. 1923

The Fights

What an elusive target
the brain is! Set up
like a coconut on a flexible stem
it has 101 evasions.
A twisted nod slews a punch
a thin gillette's width

past a brain, or
a rude brush-cut to the chin
tucks one brain safe under another.
Two of these targets are
set up to be knocked down
for 25 dollars or a million.

In that TV picture in the parlor
the men, tho linked move to move
in a chancy dance,
are abstractions only.
Come to ringside, with two
experts in there! See
each step or blow pivoted,
balanced and sudden as gunfire.
See muscles wriggle, shine
in sweat like windshield rain.

In stinking dancehalls, in
the forums of small towns,
punches are cheaper but
still pieces of death.
For the brain's the target
with its hungers
and code of honor. See
in those stinking little towns,
with long counts, swindling judges,
how fury ends with the last gong.
No matter who's the cheated one
they hug like a girl and man.

It's craft and
the body rhythmic and terrible,
the game of struggle.
We need something of its nature
but not this;
for the brain's the target
and round by round it's whittled
til nothing's left of a man
but a jerky bum, humming
with a gentleness less than human.

1967

I've Tasted My Blood

MILTON
ACORN

If this brain's over-tempered
consider that the fire was want
and the hammers were fists.
I've tasted my blood too much
to love what I was born to.

But my mother's look
was a field of brown oats, soft-bearded;
her voice rain and air rich with lilacs:
and I loved her too much to like
how she dragged her days like a sled over gravel.

Playmates? I remember where their skulls roll!
One died hungry, gnawing grey perch-planks;
one fell, and landed so hard he splashed;
and many and many
come up atom by atom
in the worm-casts of Europe.

My deep prayer a curse.
My deep prayer the promise that this won't be.
My deep prayer my cunning,
my love, my anger,
and often even my forgiveness
that this won't be and be.
I've tasted my blood too much
to abide what I was born to.

1969

On Saint-Urbain Street

My room's bigger than a coffin
but not so well made.
The couple on my left drink, and
at two a.m. the old man shouts
of going back to Russia.
About five he or his wrung-out wife
puke up their passage money.

The janitor (pay, five a week

MILTON
ACORN

plus a one-bed apartment
with furnace in kitchen) has
one laughing babe at home
and two girls, for lack of room,
in the orphanage.
On holidays they appear
with their soul-smashed faces.

Upstairs the Negro girl
answers the phone, sings my name
in a voice like a bad angel's.
Her boyfriends change
every weekend, like the movies.
But my room's cheap, tho'
when the wind shifts north
I wear my overcoat
to type this bitter little poem.

1969

Knowing I Live in a Dark Age

Knowing I live in a dark age before history,
I watch my wallet and
am less struck by gunfights in the avenues
than by the newsie with his dirty pink chapped face
calling a shabby poet back for his change.

The crows mobbing the blinking, sun-stupid owl;
wolves eating a hamstrung calf hindend first,
keeping their meat alive and fresh . . . these
are marks of foresight, beginnings of wit:
but Jesus wearing thorns and sunstroke
beating his life and death into words
to break the rods and blunt the axes of Rome:
this and like things followed.

Knowing that in this advertising rainbow   MILTON
ACORN
I live like a trapeze artist with a headache,
my poems are no aspirins . . . they show
pale bayonets of grass waving thin on dunes;
the paralytic and his lyric secrets;
my friend Al, union builder and cynic,
hesitating to believe his own delicate poems
lest he believe in something better than himself:
and history, which is yet to begin,
will exceed this, exalt this
as a poem erases and rewrites its poet.

1969

You Growing

You growing and your thought threading
The delicate strength of your focus
Out of a clamour of voices
Demanding faces and noises
Apart from me but vivid
As when I kissed you and chuckled

Wherever you are be fearless
And wherever I am I hope to know
You're moving vivid beyond me
So I grow by the strength
Of you fighting for your self,
Many selves, your life, many lives, your people.

1975

b. 1924

The Lizard

Do you remember the lizard?

I remember the dark man
squatting turbaned in the garden,
the hard hot earth,
the green parrots that came suddenly
in thousands out of nowhere
into the green peepul tree.

Do you remember the lizard?

I remember the three-fingered man;
he stood under a banyan tree
circled with cement to keep away snakes.
He was strange, they said;
he did not always know what he did.
One day when the dog lay still in the heat
and bananas hung on the banana tree
he was jailed out of the garden.
To me he was not strange.

Do you remember the lizard?

I remember the baby.
It had been left on the floor
of a white and empty house
on a hill across the bed of the dried river.
When they brought it to
my young and dancing mother
its skin was pitted by lime.
It was a girl.
They fed her milk with an eye-dropper.

Do you remember the lizard?

I remember the porcupine quills
the rabbit fur

the snake my father killed
the scarlet poinsettia growing high
into a pitiless sky.

Do you remember the lizard?

Under the jacaranda tree
the dark man in his white turban
cut the lizard into two pieces
across the middle;
two clawed feet and a tail
scrabbled under some leaves,
two clawed feet and a bright, unblinking head
went in another direction.
The parrots were making a great noise
and the man said,
staring intently at a smear of colourless blood,
—You see, it does not hurt him;
he is not dead.

1974

ROBIN
SKELTON
───────────
b. 1925

Lakeside Incident

For Herbert Siebner

Slowly the vision grows.
A hand and then a hand
reach up through the ice,
a face, a blinded face,
mouthing, that cannot speak,
a helpless tongue that turns
around forgotten words,

a sleeve of crystal blue
lying upon the scarred
grey mirror of the cold
that can reflect no hint,
a body inching up,
a figure from a page
of quattrocento dream
suddenly obscured
by nothing but my stare.
I watch the cloak extend
slowly from nape to heel.
Upright, the man begins
to speak again. The mouth
repeats an ancient tune
I cannot understand.
The face is half my own
and half a lucid beast's,
as words, untroubled, lost
only to meaning, spin
a pattern that repeats
the patterns of the frost
upon the bracken's crisp
I brush with helpless boot.
The lake reflects the sky
and dazzles in the sun
which burns the page; a hole,
the size, first, of a coin,
grows angry at its edge;
the vellum twists and browns
into a wall of rock.
I stand before the rock.
There is no cave or door.
The sky is grey as lead.

And far below me, where
I stand upon a shelf
of breaking rock, the waters
race in brackish foam.
I beat upon the rock.
There is no answering voice.
Only a tattered rag
of blue hangs on a thorn.

1974

Eagle

ROBIN
SKELTON

Vertigo is my territory. Man
only another movement, another shift
in the arrangement of shadows beneath my shadow,
angular, thick-boned, cumbersome, and bad meat.

I do not trouble him or the larger kind,
having no love of eating on the ground;
I kill what I can bring into my height,
what I can raise up until, terror-stunned,

they watch the dwindling of their day, perceive
the small earth small, self-cancelling, and share
the shock that is the last discovery; here
they learn abandonment of every word

and are self-rent before I rend and eat
what they already have forgotten, locked
on fear and splendour. Image me as God.
I am the final judgement and the rock.

1974

Wart Hog

Moon-tusked, wrenching at roots,
I dream of women.

Once there were sacred boars
in the sacred wood,

eaters of corpses,
guardians of the groves

under the wand of the goddess.
Now I grub,

trample, and squeal,
bulk-shouldered, warted, haired

rank as the sweat of terror,
sour as shame,

ROBIN
SKELTON

guardian of no ritual
but the thrust

through darkness
of the bald horn of the moon.

1974

COLLEEN
HIBAUDEAU

b. 1925

The Green Family

I will begin to delineate the green family.
Under the shade of the mother sat the father
small weedy and seedy
wearing his light hair daubed on his forehead;
he was a salvation army man, weekdays
he moved ashcans for the city.

His children were all mouths diligent with love of honey.
They could have spelled down anybody's child.
Sitting in the front row at the library hour
they let their darned black legs hang down,
all of them thin as water spiders, and the gold
dream of his trumpet kept them whole.

Summer sand could have held them
like five smooth stones. Off to one side
was the mother being a flowering-bush in her housedress.
They consulted about the special ride; at twilight
he took the three biggest ones aboard
that marvel of a varnished speedboat and went off in a wave.

He could not walk on water. When the shock came COLLEEN
THIBAUDEAU
he was a gallant giving his arm
in perfect faith to his three small daughters,
told them the longest story they had ever heard;
going along that hollow wooden walk by the lake
they came to the all-gold sugar bush of the tale.

The airforce dragged
him up pale as a weed-draped Shiva;
one of the other mothers told that she was knitting
a wee red jacket for her Rita that would have been
more mere red flesh though and no sort of preserver.
Henry had been an angel.

I cannot bring my heart to mourn
his unreturn,
nor can the remnant that remember him
remembering he looked last into the sun
that was a golden gabriel and sang him home.

1977

The Brown Family

All round the Browns stretched forty acres of potatoes.
They lived like squatters in my father's little chicken-house
That grew to lean-tos and then to a whole shack-town where
    married Browns
Slept God-knows-how hilled in the darkness all night long,
Mornings how rolled out to breakfast on the lawn
Sitting in crumbs and clover, their eyes still glozed over
With dufferish sleep, and all stuffing away like Eskimos.

Brown boys had greasy jeans and oilcloth school-bags made at
    home
And sneakers for quick escapes through orchard gates,
Tom had two left thumbs while Ted was tough and dumb, but
    there was much
Of army sadness to the way all their heads got furry as muskrats
    by March.

Well after meagre spells Fall was their full season when they
dropped
Partridge, pheasant and squirrel—shooting as if they would never
stop
As later they crazily shot up even the apple-trees at Caen.

Their sisters inevitably called Nellie or Lily were deliberately pale,
Silly incestuous little flirts whose frilly skirts were dirty
From every ditch in the county. On lonely country roads under
the moon
Their sadness lit like incense their sweet ten-cent perfume.
But at hint of insult their cheeks took on fiery tints those summers
When they hired-out to cook. And their eyes often had that
strange blue look
Of the blue willow plates round a rich farmer's plate-rail.

'What I can touch and take up in these two hands,' said Mrs
Brown,
'Is what I trust!' Accordingly on the bashed piano and on the
floor, dust
And rich potato-coloured light everywhere mingled: scraps,
fronds, gourds,
Teazle, fossils, hazel wands, turkey feathers and furs . . . goods
All lovingly hers tangled. And all could be taken up, stroked,
cajoled
In the same manner as her Old Man: for Mr Brown's heart was
pure glossy gold
By tender handling, of all that's drossy, slowly, suvendibly,
rendered down.

But as alike as Anna Pauker's brood so that it tears the heart to see
Was that last lot and will all Browns ever be,
Picking and pecking at life, scratching where something is cached.
What are they looking for? Not lots to eat or wear. Not lots in
town.
Strangely, the same thing *we* want would satisfy a Brown—
Something of the sort God gives us every day
Something we can take up in our hands and bear away.

1977

Poem

COLLEEN
THIBAUDEAU

I do not want only
The shy child with the shock of slippery wheatlike hair
Standing alone after her first communion
By the white picket fence,
She is light and airy
She is for once still and stilled her shrill voice,
She is like a beefy window curtain
Or a lacy Breughel
And must be trained in the right way
Lest she twist and turn like a very poem.
I want the others too.
I want the baby in—
He who sits under the hollyhocks
His behind the exact same shade as the Purple King hollyhock at
   the very top.

I want too the neighbour looking over with a leer
At the big sister got up to look like Rita Hayworth
White as white as in a restaurant.
I want the young Socialist on the corner with his cough
I want the mother
Though they tell me she lies in the churchyard
That is halfway up Montreal Mountain.
I want the man who sits on the steps of the Mayfair Washing
   Machine Co.
This morning and every morning
Wearing a dirty hockey sweater and holding his head in his hands.

And I too
After adjusting the focus
I shall go just as natural among them all;
Why must the lover and the sufferer be out?
I do not want the shy child only
Aloof for the one minute of her life;
I want it to be like a lacy Breughel.

1977

PHYLLIS
GOTLIEB

b. 1926

Late Gothic

From the window of my grandfather's
front room above the store I could see
over the asylum wall through the barred window
a madwoman raving, waving
pink arm sleeves. From the kitchen at the back
faceted skylights lay, grown quartz among the sooty
stalagmite chimneys. Two faces of despair.

My grandmother and grandfather cultivated
in the scoured yard of their love
a garden of forget-me.

My grandmother was a golden
turbulence, my goldwin, giver of all
lovehated vortex. Like all children I looked
twenty-five years later at her picture and found
the woman, monstrously coarse and obese
a drowned reaching beauty.

My grandfather, crumpled old Jew, read Hebrew
through a magnifying glass, crawled
to the park for sun, swore, told old tales
babbled of green fields and died.

My father sold that legendary
furniture for twelve dollars
                    and we smelled the stench
of the furs the old man had made his shapeless coats of
and went down the narrow walled stair for the last time
into the bright street between the wall upflung
against the howling chimney of the madwoman's throat
on the one side
and the redbrick rampart of shoddy stores against the
reaching blackened arms of the chimneys on the other.

1964

247

Three-handed Fugue

PHYLLIS
GOTLIEB

Into Suburbia between eight and nine
the army of cleaning-women marches,
knot-haired browbeaten
arbiters of mop and bucket, eaten
by acid lines about the mouth. Armpit-sweating
handmaidens of Godliness, they let down
great fuming freshets of hot water, pour
libations of Olddutch to the Allhigh
and praise Jehovah in terms of bleaches and starches.

Polisher and vacuum-cleaner roar
like the bellmouth of Moses at idolsfall
and MENE, MENE in noseprints on the windows
vanish, and TEKEL UPHARSIN the writing on the wall.

Burnished doorknobs sing
Hosannah! In white enamel
they build slender arches of worship, Bacchian eyries
of handworn wood, boneclean, glittering.

Exalted, stayed with cups of tea they make decorous
retreat by four.

                     As the golden light
burns through crystal panes, insidiously the mote
falls in the beam, turning like a feather.

And you and I, climbing the stairs by midnight
leave stubfilled ashtrays, islands in a sea of shards
and celebrating in criscrisp sheets together
pull down the house of cards.

1964

A Cocker of Snooks

PHYLLIS
GOTLIEB

We kept him an hour in the
bottom of a bushel basket, a
flourish fit for a john hancock, not particularly
brainy, his trowelhead
narrower than the lithe surprising
bulk, like a stretchsock holds
any size frog or toad *blip*
the red tongue, in hand skinshabby
the snake ideal of boneplate
hidden, he needed a new
coat or maybe a dose of
Plantshine, but released
he turned into grassblade leaf stone twig
blip the red tongue said, *that*
for you! he
owed us nothing but the grace of God.

1964

This One's on Me

1. The lives and times of Oedipus and Elektra
   began with bloodgrim lust and dark carnality
   but I was born next to the Neilson's factory
   where every piece is different, and that's how I got
   my individuality.

2. I lived on Gladstone Avenue,
   2 locations on Kingston Rd.
   2 crescents, Tennis and Chaplin
   Xanadu, Timbuktu,
   Samarkand & Ampersand
   and many another exotic locality.

3. My grandparents came from the ghettos
   of Russia and Poland with no mementos
   one grandfather was a furrier, one a tailor,
   grey men in dark rooms tick tack to
   gether dry snuffy seams of fur and fibre
   my father managed a theatre

4. which one day (childhood reminiscence indicated) passing
   on a Sunday ride, we found
   the burglar alarm was ring
   alingaling
   out jumped my father and ran for the front door
   Uncle Louie ran for the back
   siren scream down the cartrack Danforth
   and churchbells ding dong ding
   (ting a ling)
   and brakescreech whooee
   six fat squadcars filled with the finest
   of the force of our fair city
   brass button boot refulgent
   and in their plainclothes too
   greysuit felthat and flat black footed
   and arrested Uncle Louie
   Oh what a brannigan
   what a brouhaha
   while Mother and Aunt Gittel and me
   sat in the car and shivered
   delicious
   ly

   because a mouse bit through a wire.

5. For some the dance of the sugar-plum fairies
   means that.
   but the Gryphons and Gorgons of my dreams
   dance in the salon of Miss Peregrine Peers
   stony eyed, stone footed on Church Street
   up grey stairs
   where two doors down at Dr Weams I
   gnawed his smoky fingers and followed
   the convolutions of his twisted septum
   as he stretched and knotted little twines of silver
   on the rack of my oral cavity
   and all the while Miss Peregrine Peers
   tum tiddy tum tiddy TUM TUM TUM
   O Peregrine O Miss Peers
   I find you no longer in life's directories
   may you rest in peace
   and I do mean

6. Where, oh where are the lovely ladies who taught me PHYLLIS GOTLIEB
    to break the
    Hearts And trample the *Flowers* of the muses?
                                                    Mrs Reeves
    gracile, a willow on a Chinese plate, who
    winced with an indrawn gasp when I struck a wrong
    note, or blew my nose in her handkerchief
    absentmindedly?
    Miss Marll, under whose tutelage icecubes
    popped from the pores of my arm
    pits and slid down to drop from my
    ELBOWS HELD HIGH FINGERS CURVED ON THE KEYS
    may you rot in hell
    subtly, Miss Marll.

7. O child of the thirties
    of stonewarm porches and spiraea snowfalls
    in print cotton dress with matching panties hanging well down
    (the faded snapshot says)
    hand on the fender of the Baby Austin
    (feel the heat and glare)
    gaptooth grin to be converted by braces
    myopic eyes fit for glasses
    and tin ears waiting to be bent
    by the patient inexorable piano teacher
    the postered car advertises in innocence:
    LADIES OF LEISURE
    See it at the Eastwood Theatre, friends,
    next time 1930 rolls around.

1964

Death's Head

PHYLLIS
GOTLIEB

at 3 a.m. I run my tongue
around my teeth (take in a breath)
(give out a breath) take one more step
approaching death. my teeth are firm
and hard and white (take in a breath)
incisors bite and molars grind
(give out a breath) the body lying
next to mine is sweet and warm
I've heard that worms (take in a breath)
don't really eat (give out a breath)
the coffin meat of human kind
and if they did I wouldn't mind
that's what I heard (take in a breath)
(and just in time) I think it's all
a pack of lies. I know my flesh
will end in slime. the streets are mean
and full of thieves. the children in
the sleeping rooms (give out a breath)
walk narrowly upon my heart
the animal beneath the cloth
submerged rises to any bait
of lust or fury, love or hate
(take in a breath) my orbic skull
is eminently frangible
so delicate a shell to keep
my brains from spillage. still my breath
goes in and out and nearer death

and yet I seem to get to sleep

1969

JAMES
REANEY

b. 1926

The School Globe

Sometimes when I hold
Our faded old globe
That we used at school
To see where oceans were
And the five continents,
The lines of latitude and longitude,
The North Pole, the Equator and the South Pole—
Sometimes when I hold this
Wrecked blue cardboard pumpkin
I think: here in my hands
Rest the fair fields and lands
Of my childhood
Where still lie or still wander
Old games, tops and pets;
A house where I was little
And afraid to swear
Because God might hear and
Send a bear
To eat me up;
Rooms where I was as old
As I was high;
Where I loved the pink clenches,
The white, red and pink fists
Of roses; where I watched the rain
That Heaven's clouds threw down
In puddles and rutfuls
And irregular mirrors
Of soft brown glass upon the ground.
This school globe is a parcel of my past,
A basket of pluperfect things.

And here I stand with it
Sometime in the summertime
All alone in an empty schoolroom
Where about me hang
Old maps, an abacus, pictures,
Blackboards, empty desks.

If I raise my hand
No tall teacher will demand
What I want.
But if someone in authority
Were here, I'd say
Give me this old world back
Whose husk I clasp
And I'll give you in exchange
The great sad real one
That's filled
Not with a child's remembered and pleasant skies
But with blood, pus, horror, death, stepmothers, and lies.

1949

The Upper Canadian

I wish I had been born beside a river
Instead of this round pond
Where the geese white as pillows float
In continual circles
And never get out.

Sometimes I wish that I
Hadn't been born in this dull township
Where fashion, thought and wit
Never penetrate,
Unless the odd quotation from *Handy Andy*
Is really what I demand,
What I want.

The river, the railroad,
And His Majesty's Highways
Number Seven and Eight
Go through town
And never are the same again.
But this pond and I
Go through and become
Nothing different.
Now if I went away
And left this little lake,

If I struck out for the railroad and the river, JAMES
REANEY
I might lose my way.
I would have to win a scholarship
Or build a Punch and Judy Show.
I'd better not,
I'd better stay.

And watch the darning-needle flies
Fly and glitter in the shining wind
Of summer by this pond.
At night I'll read
The Collected Works of William Shakespeare
By an empty stove
And think at least there's this
Although I'll never see it acted.
I'll hear the rain outside
And, if it's August,
A cricket's sharp chirp in the pantry.
I won't go away
Unless it rains and rains
Making the pond so large
That it joins the river,
But it never will.
I shall always sit here in this hovel
Weeping perhaps over an old Victorian novel
And hear the dingy interwinding tunes
Of country rain and wind
And lame fires of damp wood.
Especially shall I hear that starved cricket
My mind, that thinks a railway ticket
Could save it from its enclosed, cramped quality.
That mind where thoughts float round
As geese do round a pond
And never get out.

1949

Granny Crack

JAMES
REANEY

I was a leather skinned harridan
I wandered the county's roads
Trading and begging and fighting
With the sun for hat and the road for shoes.

You played a pigsty Venus
When you were young, old dame,
In the graveyard or behind the tavern.
The burdock girl was your name.

She talked vilely it is remembered,
Was a moving and walking dictionary
Of slang and unconventional language
The detail of her insults was extraordinary.

We dozen scoundrels laid you
For a quarter each in the ditch
To each you gave the sensation
That we were the exploited bitch.

You saw me freckled and spotted
My face like a killdeer's egg
When, berry-picking kids, you ran from me
Frightened down the lane by the wood.

They saw her as an incredible crone
The spirit of neglected fence corners,
Of the curious wisdom of brambles
And weeds, of ruts, of stumps and of things despised.

I was the mother of your sun
I was the sister of your moon
My veins are your paths and roads
On my head I bear steeples and turrets
I am the darling of your god.

1959

The Lost Child

JAMES
REANEY

Long have I looked for my lost child.
I hear him shake his rattle
Slyly in the winter wind
In the ditch that's filled with snow.

He pinched and shrieked and ran away
At the edge of the November forest.
The hungry old burdock stood
By the dead dry ferns.

Hear him thud that ball!
The acorns fall by the fence.
See him loll in the St. Lucy sun,
The abandoned sheaf in the wire.

Oh Life in Death! my bonny nursling
Merry drummer in the nut brown coffin,
With vast wings outspread I float
Looking and looking over the empty sea

And there! in the—on the rolling death
Rattling a dried out gourd
Floated the mysterious cradle
Filled with a source.

I push the shore and kingdom to you,
Oh winter walk with seedpod ditch:
I touch them to the floating child
And lo! Cities and gardens, shepherds and smiths.

1959

FRANCIS
SPARSHOTT

b. 1926

The Naming of the Beasts

In that lost Caucasian garden
where history began
the nameless beasts paraded
in front of the first man.

Who am I? they asked him
and what shall I be
when you have left the garden?
Name me. Name me.

Poverty cruelty lechery
rage hate shame
each stalked past the podium
seeking his name.

Adam stood to attention
unable to speak
his life too short to utter
what was made that week.

The glum parade stumbles
from risen to set sun
past their dumfounded patron.
But he knows each one

and at last a strange dampness
salts either cheek.
That was the language of Eden.
Not Hebrew, not Greek:

in groans, grunts, howls
as the first tears fall
the inarticulate brute
finds names for them all.

1979

Reply to the Committed Intellectual

FRANCIS
SPARSHOTT

(On a theme by Otto René Castillo)

Stalin stood committed to peasant hunger.
Hitler numbered among his commitments death
for Jews and Gypsies.
This commitment you ask of me now:
is it to put bread
on a man's table, pride in his mind,
or lead in his back?
And if any should ask me
among fallen barricades
citizen where did you stand
in the time of our hunger
I shall have to tell them
I stood to one side
holding neither your face nor another's
in the sight of my gun.
I shall endure the reproaches
of devoted murderous men
that with tasks to perform I performed them
with work to be done I did my share
and will ask no more of you then than to stand aside
as I have done, forgoing the stern beauty
of a white face framed in your avid gunsight.

1979

Three Seasons

AUGUST
A loon's long night call
over the waves' low continued roar
floats and I wake
finding the fog cleared and the night starry.
Naked I turn to embrace
my warm sleeping lover.

NOVEMBER
You come to me where I sit reading
quietly this winter evening.

You kiss my mouth, your arms hold me.
When you leave me I return to my book
where I read of the halycon loves
of young people beautiful in imagined sunshine.

FEBRUARY
Toward the end of his twentieth married year
he sits after supper at the kitchen table
and thinks of her eyes. Her eyes are eye colour.
What colour would they be? He looks in her eyes
but the light is behind them and he cannot see.
She rests her cigarette carefully in the tin ashtray
and walks to him round the table,
holding to her thin breast his bald weeping head.

1979

ANNE
SZUMIGALSKI

b. 1926

Visitors' Parking

O Mary Mary lying on the wheel
looking up through rafters
yes you can see through the ceiling
the beams of your eyes dissolve
the joists and the tiles
and though you may writhe and scream
yet calmly you watch the clouds
circling our planet
tears drip from your open eyes
but you are a wax woman
a supple and yellow image
somehow they have managed
to embalm you yelling

kind Doctor Lawson puts his arm round my shoulders
(he is the fatherly type with springing gray hair)
'it's just that she's a broken loony girl'
he says *'the whole damn place is full of them
those are shock treatments we're giving her'*

So then I remembered the day in the woods
when the wheels crunched and crackled
the twigs and the leaves
I remembered the scratch of the branches
along the cartop as we slowly drove away
it was a roofless camp   the trees
grew straight upwards towards the shining sky
as we lay side by side on pine needles

there are two old women with my Mary now
one cackles and the other titters
as they walk her up and down on the mown grass
each holding a hand *'we know her better
than you do dearie'* the fat one says

        I peer at Mary through green porthole glass
        she is smiling the smile of a clever fish
        'in summer' she says *'when all the doors are open
        this place is a madhouse'* and then she sits
        down on the steps of the white bandstand
        hoping the huge brass noise
        will drown out the voices
        shouting inside her head

'forget it son' says the old doc benignly
*'get your self another bit   once the pants
are off them what's the difference?'*

1974

A Midwife's Story: Two

ANNE
SZUMIGALSKI

an experienced wife
(this wasn't her first pregnancy)
was lying on a trolley
shaved and draped for delivery
        as she panted correctly
in the intervals between pangs
she tried to convince herself
and those around her
that this whole thing
was some kind of joyous picnic

what was her surprise
when the head showed red fur
and after a minute
a fox struggled out
jumped to the floor
and ran out the door
that one of the nurses
was holding open for him

he ran out into the city
crying for food and care
and he found a woman in a doorway
who took pity on him
she fed him every day
from a grey pot dogdish
she would not let him
in the house of course

the mother had no more trouble
except once on the bus
someone sat down beside her
and said *I know you*
you are the lady who gave birth
to a fox on TV   don't feel
badly   it could happen
to anyone

1980

Angels

ANNE
SZUMIGALSKI

have you noticed
how they roost in trees?
not like birds
their wings fold the other way

my mother, whose eyes are clouding
gets up early to shoo them
out of her pippin tree
afraid they will let go their droppings
over the lovely olive
of the runnelled bark

she keeps a broom by the door
brushes them from the branches
not too gently
go and lay eggs she admonishes

they clamber down
jump clumsily to the wet ground
while she makes clucking noises
to encourage them to the nest

does not notice how they
bow down low before her anger
each lifting a cold and rosy hand
from beneath the white feathers
raising it in greeting
blessing her and the air
as they back away into the mist

1980

ROBERT
KROETSCH

b. 1927

Stone Hammer Poem

1
This stone
become a hammer
of stone, this maul

is the colour
of bone (no,
bone is the colour
of this stone maul).

The rawhide loops
are gone, the
hand is gone, the
buffalo's skull
is gone;

the stone is
shaped like the skull
of a child.

2
This paperweight on my desk

where I begin
this poem   was

found in a wheatfield
lost (this hammer,
this poem).

Cut to a function,
this stone was
(the hand is   gone—

3
Grey, two-headed,
the pemmican maul

fell from the travois or
a boy playing   lost it in
the prairie wool or
a squaw   left it in
the brain of a buffalo or

It is a million
years older than
the hand that
chipped stone or
raised slough
water (or blood) or

4
This stone maul
was found.

In the field
my grandfather
thought
was his

my father
thought was his

5
It is a stone
old as the last
Ice Age, the
retreating/the
recreating ice,
the retreating
buffalo, the
retreating Indians

(the saskatoons bloom
white (infrequently
the chokecherries the
highbush cranberries the
pincherries bloom
white along the barbed
wire fence (the
pemmican   winter

6
This stone maul
stopped a plow
long enough for one
Gott im Himmel.

The Blackfoot (the
Cree?) not

finding the maul
cursed.

?did he curse
?did he try to
go back
?what happened
I have to/I want
to know (not know)
?WHAT HAPPENED

7
The poem
is the stone
chipped and hammered
until it is shaped
like the stone
hammer, the maul.

8

Now the field is
mine because
I gave it
(for a price)

to a young man
(with a growing son)
who did not

notice that the land
did not belong

to the Indian who
gave it to the Queen
(for a price) who
gave it to the CPR
(for a price) which
gave it to my grandfather
(for a price) who
gave it to my father
(50 bucks an acre
Gott im Himmel I cut
down all the trees I
picked up all the stones) who

gave it to his son
(who sold it)

9
This won't
surprise you.

My grandfather
lost the stone maul.

10
My father (retired)
grew raspberries
He dug in his potato patch.
He drank one glass of wine
each morning.
He was lonesome
for death.

He was lonesome for the
hot wind on his face, the smell
of horses, the distant
hum of a threshing machine,
the oilcan he carried, the weight
of a crescent wrench in his hind pocket.

He was lonesome for his absent
son and his daughters,
for his wife, for his own
brothers and sisters and
his own mother and father.

He found the stone maul
on a rockpile in the
north-west corner of what
he thought of
as his wheatfield.

He kept it (the
stone maul) on the railing
of the back porch in
a raspberry basket.

11
I keep it
on my desk
(the stone).

Sometimes I use it
in the (hot) wind
(to hold down paper)

smelling a little of cut
grass or maybe even of
ripening wheat or of
buffalo blood hot
in the dying sun.

Sometimes I write
my poems for that

stone hammer.

1975

b. 1927

Poetics Against the Angel of Death

I am sorry to speak of death again
(some say I'll have a long life)
but last night Wordsworth's 'Prelude'
suddenly made sense—I mean the measure,
the elevated tone, the attitude
of private Man speaking to public men.
Last night I thought I would not wake again
but now with this June morning I run ragged to elude
the Great Iambic Pentameter
who is the Hound of Heaven in our stress
because I want to die
writing Haiku
or, better,
long lines, clean and syllabic as knotted bamboo. Yes!

1962

To Friends
Who Have Also Considered Suicide

PHYLLIS
WEBB

It's still a good idea.
Its exercise is discipline:
to remember to cross the street without looking,
to remember not to jump when the cars side-swipe,
to remember not to bother to have clothes cleaned,
to remember not to eat or want to eat,
to consider the numerous methods of killing oneself,
that is surely the finest exercise of the imagination:
death by drowning, sleeping pills, slashed wrists,
kitchen fumes, bullets through the brain or through
the stomach, hanging by the neck in attic or basement,
a clean frozen death—the ways are endless.
And consider the drama! It's better than a whole season
at Stratford when you think of the emotion of your
family on hearing the news and when you imagine
how embarrassed some will be when the body is found.
One could furnish a whole chorus in a Greek play
with expletives and feel sneaky and omniscient
at the same time. But there's no shame
in this concept of suicide.
It has concerned our best philosophers
and inspired some of the most popular
of our politicians and financiers.
Some people swim lakes, others climb flagpoles,
some join monasteries, but we, my friends,
who have considered suicide take our daily walk
with death and are not lonely.
In the end it brings more honesty and care
than all the democratic parliaments of tricks.
It is the 'sickness unto death'; it is death;
it is not death; it is the sand from the beaches
of a hundred civilizations, the sand in the teeth
of death and barnacles our singing tongue:
and this is 'life' and we owe at least this much
contemplation to our western fact: to Rise,
Decline, Fall, to futility and larks,
to the bright crustaceans of the oversky.

1962

The Days of the Unicorns

PHYLLIS
WEBB

I remember when the unicorns
roved in herds through the meadow
behind the cabin, and how they would
lately pause, tilting their jewelled
horns to the falling sun as we shared
the tensions of private property
and the need to be alone.

Or as we walked along the beach
a solitary delicate beast
might follow on his soft paws
until we turned and spoke the words
to console him.

It seemed they were always near
ready to show their eyes and stare
us down, standing in their creamy
skins, pink tongues out
for our benevolence.

As if they knew that always beyond
and beyond the ladies were weaving them
into their spider looms.

I knew where they slept
and how the grass was bent
by their own wilderness
and I pitied them.

It was only yesterday, or seems
like only yesterday when we could
touch and turn and they came
perfectly real into our fictions.
But they moved on with the courtly sun
grazing peacefully beyond the story
horns lowering and lifting and
lowering.

I know this is scarcely credible now
as we cabin ourselves in cold
and the motions of panic

and our cells destroy each other
performing music and extinction
and the great dreams pass on
to the common good.

1980

From 'The Kropotkin Poems'

Syllables disintegrate ingrate alphabets
          lines decline into futures and limbos
            intentions and visions fall

and fall like bad ladders.

I shaft my needle again and again
        into hell's veins and heaven's
          listening for messages pulsing

on whose bloody hopes?

Whose love, tell me, o love's divine airs
          elaborates the oratorio?

His dream. His exile. His imprisonments. Shadows

of his brother fixed in handiwork, letters, lexicons,

          lessons, bereavements.

          Alexander.

And him growing old. Peter. Who loved him before his marriage
at age thirty-six? Who did he lust for or sleep with
and who shifted his decorous sweetness into plain-song
          pain-song, body to body?

        Peter.

The state of affairs so bad, the sufferings
        power in things awry
          crooked

and perilous orders, forcing his language.

He cut his own vein
                              stateless in grace
                                        o love words flow

on love whose airs are his own oratorio.

                                        In Adam's garden

he plants all his blood.

1980

Spots of Blood

I am wearing absent-minded red
slippers and a red vest—
spots of blood
to match the broken English
of Count Dracula being interviewed
on the radio in the morning sun.
I touch the holes in my throat
where the poppies bud—spots of blood
spots of womantime. '14,000 rats,'
Dracula is saying, and the interviewer
echoes, '14,000 rats! So beautiful,'
he sighs, 'The Carpathian Mountains—
the photography, so seductive!' The Count
also loves the film; he has already seen it
several times. He tells in his dreamy voice
how he didn't need direction, didn't want
makeup, how he could have done it with his own
teeth. He glided in and out of this role
believing in reincarnation, in metamorphosis.
Yet 14,000 rats and the beleaguered
citizens of the Dutch town where those scenes
were shot (without him) are of no interest.
'And Hollywood?' the interviewer asks, himself
an actor, 'Hollywood next?' Who knows?
Who knows?

The blood pounds at my temples.
The women of the world parade before me
in red slippers and red vests, back and
forth, back and forth, fists clenched.
My heart emerges from my breast for
14,000 rats and the citizens of Delft,
for the women of the world in their menses.

Yet I too imitate a crime of passion:
Look at these hands. Look at the hectic
red painting my cheekbones as I metamorphose
in and out of the Buddha's eye, the *animus
mundi*.

In the morning sun Count Dracula leans
against my throat with his own teeth.
Breathing poppies. Thinking.

1980

Imperfect Sestina

I
So what if Lowry got spooked by sea-birds and volcanoes
    crossing,
his alter-ego stood beside him in the double mirror,
showed him Eden and flapped off darkest Raven,
who, cawing, took her mask and showed his twin.
Who can survive that mad illumination
shining in eyes, pouring over the stone.

II
We who have dreamt our demons into stone,
caught at our groins, screamed and fell at the crossing,
find mercy and loving-beholding illumination.
Hide the mirrors. Break them. There are more mirrors.
See how the crucial stork rides off with its twin.
Over the world the Paraclete, the holy Raven.

III
Mind you, there may be more to a bird than its name Raven.
I have often wondered about a rhyme with stone.
There is a nest and there is nesting and something about the
    birthday of a twin.
I have seen both open and closed eyes at the double crossing,
and even as I lay there dying I saw the mirror.
Shall you or I smash out that multiple illumination?

IV
Oh yes, Death came, and, oh yes, there was illumination.
Death sang a song, one grand delusion of Raven
got up in feathers and a mask of stone.
Now give me back that mirror, give me the mirror,
and I will show the path and why it is a crossing.
And you and I shall lie there buying illumination.

V
Did I say buying illumination? Illumination,
twin beat of flinty wings, one-eyed illumination?
Can I really say I found even two cents at the crossing?
There I was stabbed and pecked by spirit Raven.
There in that marriage I turned into stone,
and did not understand he carved me at his mirror.

VI
Six times six I multiplied the vision by the mirror.
Now any mask can show me all those twins.
Loving beholding and mercy pecked upon a stone
until the moon came down and said, 'Il'umination.'
The pool stood still, but I think earth hovered under Raven,
and on the path the signs of love and crossing.

VII
Laughing and crying, twin meets at the crossing twin.
They do not ask the mirror. Gold licks of illumination.
Eden smells of cedar. Raven holds his wings and sucks his stone.

1980

b. 1928

Photograph in a Stockholm Newspaper
for March 13, 1910

Here is a family so little famous
their names were not recorded. They stand,
indistinct as though they know
it's right, in the slum courtyard
in weak sunlight. The darksuited father's hand
rests on his small son's shoulder,
mother & daughter are on either side
of the open door. It is a Sunday
or we may suppose they would not be
together like this, motionless
for the photographer's early art.

To be moved by these people must seem
sentimental. We come years too late
to hope their blurred faces will unpack
into features we can side with
or against, or expect these bodies
will continue into those next shapes
on which we'll base a plot.

But that's it: not here they are, but
there they were. Safe now from even
their own complexities—what luck
not to be asked their names!—& proof
against our most intricate pursuit,
they stand in a blur that seems
no error of focus but an inspired rendering
of how they chose to last,
admitting nothing except that once
they were there. That hand rested
on that shoulder. The four of them stood there.
There was a little sunlight.

We shall never learn more. They seem
miraculous. They persuade me
all will be well.

1975

Natalya Nikolayevna Goncharov

DON
COLES

(she will marry, on February 18, 1831,
Alexander Sergeyevich Pushkin)

Another of the placid beauties!
Whose mother flaunts her before
The poet—clamberer among words,
His monkey-trellis of language,
Toxic dexterity. It is all he has.
Le pauvre, c'est déjà trop.
Her white skin, if he would stop
Here where others have but, ah,
Imperial softnesses in her blouse,
The swelling, shaded baskers. Who
Could ask for more? *Than two?* Hear
How last year's irreverence now
Falls short. His words against
That same restraining silk
Her soft body butts—of course
It's no contest. Inside her head,
Not a sound. Instead, a shape,
Shapes within shapes, her stately
Shoulders, a mirrored torso half-
Turns, ripples whitely. These forms
Both mimic and predict his dreams,
Which have no other guides. Try
Arguing with that. Her thighs,
Proffered, see, see, on the low divan
Where they stream. They are endless
As Homer. The light slides on them,
Firmpacked emblems, serene martyrs.
To pour images is fine, drowning however
Is no joke. Onegin, of course, had
The same problem. Or think of,
Inside *his* huge story,
Pierre Bézuhov: Hélène, brainless,
As he knew, but mitigatingly
Décolletaged, bending towards him
Over the dinner-table, *déesse!* World-
Altering. And now Natalya Nikolayevna
Offers her word-monkey 'Her whole body
Only veiled by her grey gown'. At which
All roads out of this place—

277

Gone! Until death! Because
What a place it is, for a poet.
'Her whole body'—and all of it
Dumb. Amazing. No rhymes
But are his own. *Odalisque,*
Risque. All directions to this
Lavish property, his. Such
White abundance. Her thighs. She
'Doesn't like poetry'. When they.
When she opens them. Ah. The Church.
Bless it. Soon. Can she talk?

D. G.
JONES

b. 1929

These Trees Are No Forest of Mourners

They had dragged for hours.
The weather was like his body,
Cold, though May. It rained.

It had rained for three days—
In the grass, in the new leaves,
In the black boughs against the sky.

The earth oozed,
Like the bottom of the lake—
Like a swamp. They stared

At the drowned grass, at the leaves
That dripped in the water—aware
Of their own death, heavy

As the black boughs of the spruce
Moving in a current under the grey
Surface of the sky—aware

Of a supreme ugliness, which seemed
In its very indifference,
Somehow, to defy them:

The sodden body of the world
And of their only son.

Let them be. Oh hear me,

Though it cannot help you. They exist
Beyond your grief; they have their own
Quiet reality.

1961

The River: North of Guelph

I

The river is so much mica
            running in its shallow course
            through dusty patchwork of the earth;
      It is not deep enough
            to mirror clouds, or drown
            the pebbles in its bed.
      Downstream
            a concrete bridge
            yawns to find a minnow in its mouth.

Lost beyond these banks, the distant farms
            spin out the networks of the fields;
            there, day long, pasturing herds
      browse in the sunlight until thirst
            brings them in a paling sky
      down the cowpath to the river's edge,
            their horny feet
            splashing in the mud between the stones.

Through the flat land
            under the old, redundant sun
            the river flows

quietly, as if the mirror of those hours
  unfolding on the whitened stones
  in country churchyards—as if death,
birth, marriage with its fleshly joys, the bright
  waterfalls within the blood,
  here
amid the endless repetitions of the earth
  grew thin and trite—merely
  these shadows, shifting lights
moved by the wind, or broken
  by the hot
  calm, in which the stone, once more,
asserts itself.

Sex, alcohol, the infrequent murder
  cry out
    make a sudden flood
    rattling the pebbles in their bed;
  then the land again beneath an empty sky
  skrinks the river to its own dry crust.

II
Quiet river, brief
    image of my boredom,
    you reflect
  the flatness of my soul, my comfort,
    my own lack
    of sensual joy—
  yet you are strangely bright.

So let my mind
    be, like this river,
    thin as glass
  that thunder, dark clouds, rain,
    the violent winds, may pass
  and leave no lasting darkness in their wake:

let it be
    sheer, like crystal,
    clear, that each
  tree or stone, each

        whistling bird or shrill
        face, in field or street,
may be itself, seen,
        undistorted, may be itself,
        revealed, as in the wild
brilliance of the sun. O thin stream
        if you must be the image of my mind
        let me be that glass through which the light
shines—O mind,
        be nothing, be
        that translucent glass:

A crow, grown tired of cawing,
        lights
        on a dead branch;
he folds his wings; the sun
        gleams black.
        A fallen leaf
drifts and catches on a twig.
        A tin
        funnel,
pitched into the middle of the stream,
        catches the light
        and sends it back.

1961

On a Picture of Your House

The first pale shoots
the plants make flower
into the picture of your house:

full summer reigns
there in the silence where the sun
showers cataracts of light,

shuts out all other sound.

Only in extremes like that
can I protect you, touch—
as lately, in your presence,

I could not. Only
after you'd gone, fallen,
the street so steep and dark,

could I look after you.

As spring is here
never so intense
as at the end of winter with the ice

still breathing off the lake,

so I attend you in that house
consumed by light,
that garden to which flowers

point, and which is not,

no place. And I confess
what I protect is your
capacity for loss,

your freedom to be no one, look
so naked from that window
you are lost in light.

1967

For Spring

Earth holds the sunlit
locks of the snow
tenderly

like a dying love,
her death
leaving raw earth, stones.

The long-stemmed grass
quivers
in the chill breeze;

evening
cannot conceal the stark
nudity of trees.

1967

D.G.
JONES

'From sex, this sea . . .'

From sex, this sea, we have emerged
into a quiet room
our bodies bare

We have been washed by tides
the glacial waters welling up
to shudder and subside, the broad streams

wandering to the pole

The climate of the flesh
is temperate here
though we look out on a winter world

We are the islanders
between two seasons, and a garden where
we are the botanists

of our own flowers. And yet

I am led into the winter air
by certain nameless twigs, as bare
as we are. I would find

them also in our mouths

1977

The Ark

Ark to Noah

I wait, with those that rest
In darkness till you come,
Though they are murmuring flesh
And I a block and dumb.

Yet when you come, be pleased
To shine here, be shown
Inward as all the creatures
Drawn through my bone.

Ark Articulate

Shaped new to your measure
From a mourning grove,
I am your sensing creature
And may speak for love.

If you repent again
And turn and unmade, me,
How shall I rock my pain
In the arms of a tree?

Ark Anatomical

JAY
MACPHERSON

Set me to sound for you
The world unmade
As he who rears the head
In light arrayed,

That its vision may quicken
Every wanting part
Hangs deep in the dark body
A divining heart.

Ark Artefact

Between me and the wood
I grew in, you stand
Firm as when first I woke
Alive in your hand.

How could you know your love,
If not defined in me,
From the grief of the always wounded,
Always closing sea?

Ark Apprehensive

I am a sleeping body
Hulling down the night,
And you the dream I ferry
To shores of light.

I sleep that you may wake,
That the black sea
May not gape sheer under you
As he does for me.

Ark Astonished

JAY
MACPHERSON

Why did your spirit
Strive so long with me?
Will you wring love from deserts,
Comfort from the sea?

Your dove and raven speed,
The carrion and the kind.
Man, I know your need,
But not your mind.

Ark Overwhelmed

When the four quarters shall
Turn in and make one whole,
Then I who wall your body,
Which is to me a soul,

Shall swim circled by you
And cradled on your tide,
Who was not even, not ever,
Taken from your side.

Ark Parting

You dreamed it. From my ground
You raised that flood, these fears.
The creatures all but drowned
Fled your well of tears.

Outward the fresh shores gleam
Clear in new-washed eyes.
Fare well. From your dream
I only shall not rise.

1957

The Fisherman

JAY
MACPHERSON

The world was first a private park
Until the angel, after dark,
Scattered afar to wests and easts
The lovers and the friendly beasts.

And later still a home-made boat
Contained Creation set afloat,
No rift nor leak that might betray
The creatures to a hostile day.

But now beside the midnight lake
One single fisher sits awake
And casts and fights and hauls to land
A myriad forms upon the sand.

Old Adam on the naming-day
Blessed each and let it slip away:
The fisher of the fallen mind
Sees no occasion to be kind,

But on his catch proceeds to sup;
Then bends, and at one slurp sucks up
The lake and all that therein is
To slake that hungry gut of his,

Then whistling makes for home and bed
As the last morning breaks in red;
But God the Lord with patient grin
Lets down his hook and hoicks him in.

1957

The Beauty of Job's Daughters

JAY
MACPHERSON

The old, the mad, the blind have fairest daughters.
Take Job: the beasts the accuser sends at evening
Shoulder his house and shake it; he's not there,
Attained in age to inwardness of daughters,
In all the land no women found so fair.

Angels and sons of God are nearest neighbours,
And even the accuser may repair
To walk with Job in pleasures of his daughters:
Wide shining rooms more warmly lit at evening,
Gardens beyond whose secrets scent the air.

Not wiles of men nor envy of the neighbours,
Riches of earth, nor what heaven holds more rare,
Can take from Job the beauty of his daughters,
The gardens in the rock, music at evening,
And cup so full that all who come must share.

Perhaps we passed them? it was late, or evening,
And surely those were desert stumps, not daughters,
In fact we doubt that they were ever there.
The old, the mad, the blind have fairest daughters.
In all the land no women found so fair.

1968

A Lost Soul

JAY
MACPHERSON

Some are plain lucky—we ourselves among them:
Houses with books, with gardens, all we wanted,
Work we enjoy, with colleagues we feel close to—
    Love we have, even:

True love and candid, faithful, strong as gospel,
Patient, untiring, fond when we are fretful.
Having so much, how is it that we ache for
    Those darker others?

Some days for them we could let slip the whole damn
Soft bed we've made ourselves, our friends in Heaven
Let slip away, buy back with blood our ancient
    Vampires and demons.

First loves and oldest, what names shall I call you?
Older to me than language, old as breathing,
Born with me, in this flesh: by now I know you're
    Greed, pride and envy.

Too long I've shut you out, denied acquaintance,
Favoured less barefaced vices, hoped to pass for
Reasonable, rate with those who more inclined to
    Self-hurt than murder.

You were my soul: in arrogance I banned you.
Now I recant—return, possess me, take my
Hands, bind my eyes, infallibly restore my
    Share in perdition.

1974

They Return

JAY
MACPHERSON

Long desired, the dead return.
—Saw our candle and were safe,
Bought from darkness by our care?
Light from ours has touched their eyes,
Blood of ours has filled their veins.
Absence, winter, shed like scales.

They return, but they are changed.
Armoured each in private shade,
Sullen, helmed against the light,
Their resentment fills our arms,
Sifting from their ribs like night.
Absence, winter, is their name.

Change comes slowly, where they were.
Pain, exclusion, long endured,
Ate their human places out,
Sold to darkness by our fear.
They, returning, bring us back.
Absence, winter, what we gave.

1974

b. 1939

If

Like that dying woman in Mexico
who fed her family by fucking a burro
on a wooden stage in Tiajuana
you are alone and I am drunk again
on tequila, refusing to die,
hearing the madness of the burro
as the woman wept with pain . . . you are
naked and I no longer want you.
If I could choose a last vision
it would be the dream of the knife,
the dream of the death of pain.
Put on your clothes.
I am obscene.
I am one of those who laughed
when the burro dropped her on the floor.

1978

Passing into Storm

Know him for a white man.
He walks sideways into wind
allowing the left of him

to forget what the right
knows as cold. His ears
turn into death what

his eyes can't see. All day
he walks away from the sun
passing into storm. Do not

mistake him for the howl you hear
or the track you think you
follow. Finding a white man

in snow is to look for the dead.
He has been burned by the wind.
He has left too much

flesh on winter's white metal
to leave his colour as a sign.
Cold white. Cold flesh. He leans

into wind sideways; kills without
mercy anything to the left of him
coming like madness in the snow.

1978

Stigmata

For Irving Layton

What if there wasn't a metaphor
and the bodies were only bodies
bones pushed out in awkward fingers?
Waves come to the seawall, fall away,
children bounce mouths against the stones
that man has carved to keep the sea at bay
and women walk with empty wombs
proclaiming freedom to the night.
Through barroom windows rotten with light
eyes of men open and close like fists.

I bend beside a tidal pool and take a crab from the sea.
His small green life twists helpless in my hand
the living bars of bone and flesh
a cage made by the animal I am.
This thing, the beat, the beat of life
now captured in the darkness of my flesh
struggling with claws as if it could tear its way
through my body back to the sea.
What do I know of the inexorable beauty,
the unrelenting turning of the wheel I am inside me?
Stigmata. I hold a web of blood.

I dream of the scrimshawed teeth of endless whales, PATRICK LANE
the oceans it took to carve them. Drifting ships
echo in fog the wounds of Leviathin
great grey voices giving cadence to their loss.
The men are gone
who scratched upon white bones their destiny.
Who will speak of the albatross in the shroud of the man,
the sailor who sinks forever in the Mindanao Deep?
I open my hand. The life leaps out.

1978

At the Edge of the Jungle

At the edge of the jungle
I watch a dog bury his head
in the mud of the Amazon
to drive away the hovering
mass of flies around his eyes.
The swarm expands like a lung
and settles again on the wound.

I turn to where orchids gape
like the vulvas of hanged women.
Everything is madness:
a broken melon bleeds a pestilence
of bees; a woman squats and pees
balancing perfectly her basket
of meat; a gelding falls to its knees
under the goad of its driver.

Images catch at my skull like thorns.
I no longer believe
the sight I have been given
and live inside the eyes of a rooster
who walks around a pile of broken bones.
Children have cut away his beak
and with a string have staked him
where he sees but cannot eat.

Diseased clouds bloom in the sky.
They throw down roots of fire.
The bird drags sound from its skin.
I am grown older than I imagined:
the garden I dreamed does not exist
and compassion is only the beginning
of suffering. Everything deceives.

A man could walk into this jungle
and lying down be lost
among the green sucking of trees.
What reality there is resides
in the child who holds the string
and does not see
the bird as it beats its blunt head
again and again into the earth.

1978

PATRICK
LANE

The Measure

For P.K. Page

What is the measure then, the magpie in the field
watching over death, the dog's eyes hard as marbles
breath still frozen to his lips? This quiet repose,

the land having given up the battle against sleep,
the voices crying out beneath the snow.
It is the cold spear of the wind piercing me

that makes me sing of this, the hunger in your eyes.
It is the room of your retreat,
the strain in the hand when it reaches out to touch

the dried and frozen flowers brittle in their vase,
the strain when the mind desires praise . . .
the music as of soldiers wandering among their dead

or the poor dreaming of wandering as they break
their mouths open to sing as prisoners sing.
Or soldiers marching toward their devotions

294

or the poor marching or the rich in their dark
rooms of commerce saying this is finally the answer,
this will allow us the right to be and be. To be

anything. In the field the rare
stalks of grass stick stiffly into air.
The poor, the broken people, the endless suffering

we are heir to, given to desire and gaining little.
To fold the arms across the breast and fly
into ourselves. That painless darkness or stand

in the field with nothing everywhere and watch
the first flakes falling and pray for the deliverance
of the grass, a dog's death in the snow? Look

there. Stark as charred bone
a magpie stuns his tongue against the wind
and the wind steals the rattle of his cry.

1980

ALDEN
NOWLAN

1933–1983 *Beginning*

From that they found most lovely, most abhorred,
my parents made me: I was born like sound
stroked from the fiddle to become the ward
of tunes played on the bear-trap and the hound.

Not one, but seven entrances they gave
each to the other, and he laid her down
the way the sun comes out. Oh, they were brave,
and then like looters in a burning town.

Their mouths left bruises, starting with the kiss
and ending with the proverb, where they stayed;
never in making was there brighter bliss,
followed by darker shame. Thus I was made.

1961

In the Operating Room

ALDEN
NOWLAN

The anesthetist is singing
'Michael, row the boat ashore,
Hallelujah!'
And I am astonished
that his arms
are so hairy—
thick, red, curly hair
like little coppery ferns
growing out of
his flesh
from wrist
to shoulder.
I would like
to reach up
and touch
the hairy arm
of the anesthetist
because it may be
the last living thing
I will ever see
and I am glad
it is not
white and hairless
—but if I reached up
and wound
a few wisps
of his hair
around my forefinger
as I would like to do
they would think
their drugs
had made me silly
and might remember
and laugh
if I live,
so I concentrate
very hard
on the song
the anesthetist
is singing—
'The River Jordan

is muddy and cold,
Hallelujah!'
And soon
everything
is dark
and nothing
matters
and when I try
to reach up
and touch
the hair
which I think of
now as
little jets
of fire,
I discover
they've strapped
my arms
to the table.

1967

Suppose This Moment Some Stupendous Question

Suppose this moment some stupendous question
such as they asked of Lazarus. The dead
are secretive; they act like strangers
we ought to recognize but don't; and all
the secular accounts of resurrections
are horror stories. Grandmother recalled
how her grandmother prayed for seven nights,
cut off by grief, that she might see her dead
daughter who went blue-tongued and choking walk
into her bedroom, and maintained it happened
—though twice-great-grandmother was never certain:
she jerked the quilts over her head and screamed,
with every light gone out, the door blown open.

1967

ALDEN
NOWLAN

For Jean Vincent d'Abbadie,
Baron St.-Castin

Take heart, monsieur, four-fifths of this province
is still much as you left it: forest, swamp and barren.
Even now, after three hundred years, your enemies
    fear ambush, huddle by coasts and rivers,
the dark woods at their backs.

    Oh, you'd laugh to see
how old Increase Mather and his ghastly Calvinists
patrol the palisades, how they bury their money
under the floors of their hideous churches
lest you come again in the night
with the red ochre mark of the sun god
on your forehead, you exile from the Pyrenees,
    you baron of France and Navarre,
you squaw man, you Latin poet,
    you war chief of Penobscot
and of Kennebec and of Maliseet!

    At the winter solstice
your enemies cry out in their sleep
and the great trees throw back their heads and shout
    nabujcol!
Take heart, monsieur,
even the premier, even the archbishop,
even the poor gnome-like slaves
at the all-night diner and the service station
will hear you chant
    The Song of Roland
as you cross yourself
and reach for your scalping knife.

1967

The Bull Moose

ALDEN
NOWLAN

Down from the purple mist of trees on the mountain,
lurching through forests of white spruce and cedar,
stumbling through tamarack swamps,
came the bull moose
to be stopped at last by a pole-fenced pasture.

Too tired to turn or, perhaps, aware
there was no place left to go, he stood with the cattle.
They, scenting the musk of death, seeing his great head
like the ritual mask of a blood god, moved to the other end
of the field and waited.

The neighbours heard of it, and by afternoon
cars lined the road. The children teased him
with alder switches and he gazed at them
like an old tolerant collie. The women asked
if he could have escaped from a Fair.

The oldest man in the parish remembered seeing
a gelded moose yoked with an ox for plowing.
The young men snickered and tried to pour beer
down his throat, while their girl friends
took their pictures.

And the bull moose let them stroke his tick-ravaged flanks,
let them pry open his jaws with bottles, let a giggling girl
plant a little purple cap
of thistles on his head.

When the wardens came, everyone agreed it was a shame
to shoot anything so shaggy and cuddlesome.
He looked like the kind of pet
women put to bed with their sons.

So they held their fire. But just as the sun dropped in the river
the bull moose gathered his strength
like a scaffolded king, straightened and lifted his horns
so that even the wardens backed away as they raised their rifles.
When he roared, people ran to their cars. All the young men
leaned on their automobile horns as he toppled.

1970

JOE
ROSENBLATT

b. 1933

It's in the Egg
IN THE LITTLE ROUND EGG

We are continually bored with the air,
the round doors, the flat tables, the straight spoons,
the whole damned breakfast ritual, the toast floating in the air
and suspended above our heads and the egg, the little round egg,
the paranoid egg, laid by the round hen in isolation;
the egg, the hen, fertilized by unnatural forces,
the light, the ultra blue light working
first on the bird and
then the egg, the little round egg balanced
on its little bottom
on our square plates.
and now the impression of tiny fingers working
at the top or the bottom
of the egg, always the round egg—
and our fingers, our precise fingers
digging, probing the round egg
like a conspiracy
like the egg contained the secret of the Sunday bomb.
it's in the egg
in the yolk of the egg;
the little plans
the final solution for the human race
it's in the
yolk.

And now I can see it
the blue light working on us,
urging us to tell everything,
all our intimate living,
the colour of our bank accounts;
details, details, details,
it's in
the
yolk.

And now all our fingers work furiously,
all six tiny fingers probing, digging
deeper, deeper,
into the guts of the egg.
it's in the egg in the yolk of the egg in the yolk
of the egg in the yolk of the egg in the yolk —
                          of the little round egg.

JOE
ROSENBLATT

We are continually bored with the air, the round doors, the
flat tables, the straight spoons, the whole damned breakfast
ritual, the toast floating in the air and suspended above our
heads, the golden brown toast, the delirious sunny toast, the
toast begging to be anointed with margarine, the toast
dipped in the yolk of the egg, in the yolk that tells all.

1966

Ichthycide

My uncle was Sabbath crazed
wouldn't flick a switch on Saturday
but on the caudal fin of Friday evening
he'd be cutting up Neptune's nudist colony
into mean kingdom cutlets.
On Friday, Uncle Nathan lowered a butterfly net
to catch an Alcatraz shadow
dreaming myriads of muscled minnows:
spice cuisines of Esther Williams–fish pornography.

Lips ellipsing; a spiny Baptist lay on newspaper
blue leviathan with chopped up vertebrae
fanned fins in vendor's prayer
while scaly fingers mummified the prophet
-a fish head conjured Salome in a basket-

I too have knifed the sacred fish
have carnivored to please my palate:
a bass from a Chinese steam bath

lay in a puddle of Soya sauce.
This stranded swimmer on his oval casket
balanced death on optic centres;
animal penumbra expired for post mortem
I ghouled my way to the neck bone
then turned away from the Last Supper
for the eyes of Moby illuminated
or were they the fish eyes of Uncle Nathan?

Sleep Uncle Nathan, sexton in Narwhale's synagogue!

1968

JOE
ROSENBLATT

Of Dandelions & Tourists

Dandelions purr in their sleep.
The hillside is dotted with yellow cubs:
compromises of cat & gladiola.
They sway adagio; juices in the tubes
catch tigers & spiders; ghosts go into analysis
& meow of surplus love
to the earth alive with blissful fur.

1972

The Ant Trap

Brown semicolons move doggedly
through a round metal supermarket.
The summer's population carries home
tidbits of contaminated caviar
for an absolute picnic.
Home, sweet home,
I see a mound of dead animals.
God is death.

1972

Cat

JOE
ROSENBLATT

The grey psychopath in her season
scatters the birds into the shadows
where they flutter into yesterday.
They're question marks. The bootleggers
of worm are laid down like fractions of cemeteries.

Padding through her heaven
she measures us all: bird, or soul.
The asterisk, printed panic, vanishes.

1972

Fish

I touched the flesh with my eyes.
It was that of a woman with scales.
The lips were thick and closed.
It had swallowed all my symbols.

The phantom appeared and winked.
I kept hauling it up.
The eyes were bluer than mine.
She floundered on the sand
and the sea gleamed.

I pitched my wishes back into the black water.

1972

LEONARD
COHEN

b. 1934

A Kite Is a Victim

A kite is a victim you are sure of.
You love it because it pulls
gentle enough to call you master,
strong enough to call you fool;
because it lives
like a desperate trained falcon
in the high sweet air,
and you can always haul it down
to tame it in your drawer.

A kite is a fish you have already caught
in a pool where no fish come,
so you play him carefully and long,
and hope he won't give up,
or the wind die down.

A kite is the last poem you've written,
so you give it to the wind,
but you don't let it go
until someone finds you
something else to do.

A kite is a contract of glory
that must be made with the sun,
so you make friends with the field
the river and the wind,
then you pray the whole cold night before,
under the travelling cordless moon,
to make you worthy and lyric and pure.

1961

You Have the Lovers

LEONARD
COHEN

You have the lovers,
they are nameless, their histories only for each other,
and you have the room, the bed and the windows.
Pretend it is a ritual.
Unfurl the bed, bury the lovers, blacken the windows,
let them live in that house for a generation or two.
No one dares disturb them.
Visitors in the corridor tip-toe past the long closed door,
they listen for sounds, for a moan, for a song:
nothing is heard, not even breathing.
You know they are not dead,
you can feel the presence of their intense love.
Your children grow up, they leave you,
they have become soldiers and riders.
Your mate dies after a life of service.
Who knows you? Who remembers you?
But in your house a ritual is in progress:
it is not finished: it needs more people.
One day the door is opened to the lover's chamber.
The room has become a dense garden,
full of colours, smells, sounds you have never known.
The bed is smooth as a wafer of sunlight,
in the midst of the garden it stands alone.
In the bed the lovers, slowly and deliberately and silently
perform the act of love.
Their eyes are closed,
as tightly as if heavy coins of flesh lay on them.
Their lips are bruised with new and old bruises.
Her hair and his beard are hopelessly tangled.
When he puts his mouth against her shoulder
she is uncertain whether her shoulder
has given or received the kiss.

All her flesh is like a mouth.
He carries his fingers along her waist
and feels his own waist caressed.
She holds him closer and his own arms tighten around her.
She kisses the hand beside her mouth.
It is his hand or her hand, it hardly matters,
there are so many more kisses.
You stand beside the bed, weeping with happiness,

you carefully peel away the sheets
from the slow-moving bodies.
Your eyes are filled with tears, you barely make out the lovers.
As you undress you sing out, and your voice is magnificent
because now you believe it is the first human voice
heard in that room.
The garments you let fall grow into vines.
You climb into bed and recover the flesh.
You close your eyes and allow them to be sewn shut.
You create an embrace and fall into it.
There is only one moment of pain or doubt
as you wonder how many multitudes are lying beside your body,
but a mouth kisses and a hand soothes the moment away.

1961

Heirloom

The torture scene developed under a glass bell
such as might protect an expensive clock.
I almost expected a chime to sound
as the tongs were applied
and the body jerked and fainted calm.
All the people were tiny and rosy-cheeked
and if I could have heard a cry of triumph or pain
it would have been tiny as the mouth that made it
or one single note of a music box.
The drama bell was mounted
like a gigantic baroque pearl
on a wedding ring or brooch or locket.
    I know you feel naked, little darling.
I know you hate living in the country
and can't wait until the shiny magazines
come every week and every month.
Look through your grandmother's house again.
There is an heirloom somewhere.

1964

I Have Not Lingered in European Monasteries

LEONARD
COHEN

I have not lingered in European monasteries
and discovered among the tall grasses tombs of knights
who fell as beautifully as their ballads tell;
I have not parted the grasses
or purposefully left them thatched.

I have not released my mind to wander and wait
in those great distances
between the snowy mountains and the fishermen,
like a moon,
or a shell beneath the moving water.

I have not held my breath
·so that I might hear the breathing of God,
or tamed my heartbeat with an exercise,
or starved for visions.
Although I have watched him often
I have not become the heron,
leaving my body on the shore,
and I have not become the luminous trout,
leaving my body in the air.

I have not worshipped wounds and relics,
or combs of iron,
or bodies wrapped and burnt in scrolls.

I have not been unhappy for ten thousand years.
During the day I laugh and during the night I sleep.
My favourite cooks prepare my meals,
my body cleans and repairs itself,
and all my work goes well.

1965

'The killers that run . . .'

LEONARD
COHEN

The killers that run
            the other countries
are trying to get us
to overthrow the killers
            that run our own
I for one
prefer the rule
            of our native killers
I am convinced
            the foreign killer
will kill more of us
than the old familiar killer does
            Frankly I don't believe
anyone out there
really wants us to solve
our social problems
            I base this all on how I feel
about the man next door
I just hope he doesn't
            get any uglier
Therefore I am a patriot
I don't like to see
            a burning flag
because it excites
the killers on either side
to unfortunate excess
which goes on gaily
            quite unchecked
until everyone is dead

1972

E.D.
BLODGETT

b. 1935

Snails

theirs is a gesture of sorrow, infinite and taut:
some conceive the war that never begins—
they point, and beyond their hands nothing is wrought;
queens touch their hair and pose for kings,

and kings do not arrive, o egypt, airless,
who dreamt you, who made you, a horizontal gone
against a wall, your eyes as vacant circles
where nothing through a small abyss seems to yawn?

there stand your kings, their palms up.
they gaze nowhere: no heaven on high
hangs upon the wall, their hands cup
nothing. they die to live, they live to die.

time by fiat stops. they enter what has been,
a room as perfect as it ought to be,
and there from the side they stand in death akin
to life, and all time upon a frieze they see.

they open their mouths and hieroglyphic speak:
a room signals, still palinodes
unwinding, and everywhere they seek
themselves formal forever, they reflect in codes.

1980

Fossil

no branch nor the last grass
but the sky before me
opened on the ground,

and where the sky—all seasons
forgetting—began
as rivers in the early thaws
to split, a bird

before me fell, calling across
the rents of time, a bird
whose colour i could not tell,
no bird at all

but torn
from books of birds, and calling
to birds that he alone
recalls until the thaw had ceased.

a bird against the sun i saw
eclipsed, a disc of black
and pressed upon a page: it calls,

it prints silence

1980

GEORGE
JONAS

b. 1935

Portrait: The Freedom Fighter

In the streetcar conductor's uniform
The man tried to roll himself a cigarette
Without letting go of his machine gun.
'It's a dog's life,' he said, scratching himself with satisfaction,
'Rotten war,' he said, viewing with deliberate pleasure
The hulk of a burned-out streetcar among the torn cobblestones,
'Want a fag, kid?' he asked me, being an elder
For the first time in his life among his passengers.
Later the night came but he did not go to sleep
In the cool mist and total darkness the city belonged to him
'It will be a long time before we mop up the bastards,'
And he waited for approval and reassurance.
The barricades ran half way across the square,
When he turned his eyes toward me I hesitated to answer,
He looked at my face but he was looking at my skull.

1967

Temporal

GEORGE
JONAS

This is one of those Tuesdays
I want to be old.
Then you will be old too
For I wish you a long, long life.

Sometimes I will see you in the street
As I see other old women now
Who used to be desperately desired
By all sorts of old, dead men.
It is a comfort for me to see them
And oh, it will be a comfort for me to see you.
Grey strands of crinkly hair half-hiding
Long, flat ears
Thin legs ending in knotted ankles
Shuffling in black walking shoes
A quick glance at you
From top to bottom
That's all.

If doctors still permit me the odd cigar
I will light one after each such meeting
And sit by a window overlooking a street
A crowded street, full of young, nervous girls
Hurrying to meet their lovers
As you claimed to have hurried to meet me
Climbing the stairs on what might be called the same legs
Darting quick glances of promise
Through biologically the same eyes
But refusing my hand when I reached for the hips
You must have lost in a careless moment since.

Naturally I will have no pity
And no more reason for anger.
I will marvel, though
At the handiwork of God, at the fact
That I could have spent sleepless nights on account of this body
Which we both thought was yours
A comparatively short time ago.

1967

A Stone Diary

At the beginning I noticed
the huge stones on my path
I knew instinctively
why they were there
breathing as naturally
as animals
I moved them to ritual patterns
I abraded my hands
and made blood prints

Last week I became
aware of details
cubes of fool's gold
green and blue copper
crystal formations
fossils   shell casts
iron roses   candied gems

I thought of
the Empress Josephine,
the Burning of Troy
between her breasts,
of Ivan the Terrible lecturing
on the virtues of rubies.
They were dilettantes.

By the turn of the week
I was madly in love
with stone. Do you know
how beautiful it is
to embrace stone
to curve all your body
against its surfaces?

Yesterday I began
seeing you as
desirable as a stone

I imagined you coming
onto the path with me
even your mouth
a carved stone

Today for the first time
I noticed how coarse
my skin has grown
but the stones shine
with their own light,
they grow smoother
and smoother

1977

Last Letter to Pablo

Under the hills and veins water
comes out like stars;
your spirit
fleshy palpable
mines in the earth
dung and debris of generations;
curled shells
rags of leaves
impress your palms

I imagine you
a plateau city
spangled with frost,
a blue electric wind
before nightfall
that touches and takes
the breath away

How many making love
in the narrow darkness
between labours
how many bodies laid
stone upon stone

generations of fire and dirt
before you broke from us
a whole branch flowering

Cancer the newscast said,
and coma,   but
what of the sea
also full of bones
and miracles
they said was your
last prison?
What of your starward-riding
cities creaking again
with steel? How long
is death?

We are weary of atrocities;
the manure of blood
you said grows
something so frightful
only you could look:
you smoothing wounds
we shudder from—
bloody leather
face forming in mud

Always earth was
your substance:
grain, ores and bones
elements folded in power
humans patient as time
and weather;
now you too lie with skeletons
heaped about you;
our small crooked hands
touch you for comfort

From the deep hollows
water comes out like stars;
you are changing, Pablo,
becoming an element
a closed throat of quartz
a calyx
imperishable in earth

As our species bears
the minute electric
sting, possibility,
our planet carries Neruda
bloodstone
dark jewel of history
the planet carries you
a seed patient as time.

PAT
LOWTHER

1977

DARYL
HINE

b. 1936

A Bewilderment at the Entrance
of the Fat Boy into Eden

'L'art ne me connaît pas; je ne connais pas l'art.'
CORBIÈRE

i

Not knowing where he was or how he got there,
Led by the gentle sessions of his demons,
Now in the right and now in the left ear,
The fat boy trod ungarlanded in Eden.
Perhaps he knew of nowhere else to go.
Affairs of the heart, concerns of money, too,
Deprived him of all choosing of his route.
Dreaming of disaster, he set foot
At midnight in the earthly paradise.
The ice around him shattered like a shot,
The gates swung open, and an angel stood,
(His bright sword averted and put up),
To watch the fat boy lollop from the wood
He couldn't see because he was asleep.

ii

Within his head a rank and silent fortune
Gestured slowly. On the silver screen
Papier-mâché herds of buffalo
Pursued a cowboy over endless prairie,
While down his cheeks the glittering orbs of sorrow
Rolled their separate tracks to final ruin.
What password did his virtues and his powers
Whisper, that he awoke within the gates,
Preserved against his enemies the hours,
While we who, like the vultures near the towers,
Live at the expense of those who die of boredom,
Enchained by the strait enchantment of their longing,
Must pitch our camp beneath the walls of Sodom,
Detained within the sweet preserves of time?

iii

Always through the badlands of the heart
The invisible posse kept a secret watch.
Across the desert of the intellect,
Murmured his persuaders, Forward march!
Lest mirage of thought too intricate distract
The sight, or sound amuse the hearing
Whose ignorance alone they might instruct,
They guarded their somnambulist, and laid
His ears in stillness and his eyes in shade,
And on his tongue the sesame of love:
A little word so common in the world.
All doors were opened to him. What he meant:
The sentiment, the purpose, or the act,
He couldn't say and never understood.

iv

A little word. Unconsciousness is all.
But all our wisdom is unwillingness.
We cannot blink the lightning of the wit,
Or sink the ego's fragile paper boat.
We think too much. Our selves are ponderous.
Only the fat boy bounces like a ball
The law set rolling into the lawless park:
Contemptible, unintroduced to art.
His demon is our muse, when, after dark,
Each must choose a mask and play a part:

I'll be Hamlet or Polonius,
Or the deuce, whichever face will fit.
And I, Ophelia, who, in her distress,
Interbound the bitter with the sweet.

DARYL
HINE

1957

Fabulary Satire IV

The fox and crow, their dirty business finished,
Each in the aqueous landscape played his part,
Moved by the sun that shone on honour tarnished
And motivated by a love of art.
And through the leaves of trees their argument
Seemed to extend the empire of the heart;
Each claimed to be the other's monument,
And like the jack each called the queen a tart.

FOX
Was it you or some indifferent stranger
Put by my bed the bottle labelled Danger?

CROW
It was I. There never was a stranger
Could understand your hunger.
But who was it hid the bomb inside the bower
And wrote Fuck You across the bathroom mirror?

FOX
It was I, to crystallize your fever
With love's check and love's thermometer.

The crow considered talk ephemeral
And thought outmoded once the reed was broken.
The fox thought of the progress of the soul
And if indigestion meant the crow had spoken.
The cause of satire dying in his mind,
He turned the dialogue to those forsaken,
Whether they, like vox and trumpet in the wind,
Might someday talk of continence unshaken.

CROW
It is impossible to live in a world with animals
Who need a sunlit and immoral place,
To whom our problems are chimerical,
And who make right and wrong wait on table.

FOX
To animals the world is animal—
The only one that suffered was the cheese,
Who was after all the subject of the fall,
But who is seldom mentioned in the fable.

1957

Point Grey

Brought up as I was to ask of the weather
Whether it was fair or overcast,
Here, at least, it is a pretty morning,
The first fine day as I am told in months.
I took a path that led down to the beach,
Reflecting as I went on landscape, sex and weather.

I met a welcome wonderful enough
To exorcise the educated ghost
Within me. No, this country is not haunted,
Only the rain makes spectres of the mountains.

There they are, and there somehow is the problem
Not exactly of freedom or of generation
But just of living and the pain it causes.
Sometimes I think the air we breathe is mortal
And dies, trapped, in our unfeeling lungs.

Not too distant the mountains and the morning
Dropped their dim approval on the gesture
With which enthralled I greeted all this grandeur.
Beside the path, half buried in the bracken,
Stood a long-abandoned concrete bunker,
A little temple of lust, its rough walls covered
With religious frieze and votary inscription.

Personally I know no one who doesn't suffer

DARYL
HINE

Some sore of guilt, and mostly bedsores, too,
Those that come from scratching where it itches
And that dangerous sympathy called prurience.
But all about release and absolution
Lie, in the waves that lap the dirty shingle
And the mountains that rise at hand above the rain.
Though I had forgotten that it could be so simple,
A beauty of sorts is nearly always within reach.

1968

LIONEL
KEARNS

b. 1937

Foreign Aid

Relaxing all day in this tropical atmosphere
glass in hand, a mosquito net and fans at night
sweating a bit but never exerting yourself
you think how easy it would be to make it permanent

becoming a modern version of the old white planter
You've met a few of them, no pith helmets now but
they still observe the decencies, dressing for dinner
playing bridge at the Yacht Club, having cocktails

with our High Commissioner. Perhaps you could be
an oil-field specialist or missile tracking technician
British or American, even a Canadian might fit in
as bank manager or some kind of Foreign Aid expert

living on a small portion of your Canadian salary
with 4 servants and 3 cars and a house on the hill
with a sea breeze and white neighbours. So what if
your wife insists on flying to New York each month

and the cost of educating the children is ridiculous
at least you still enjoy fine liquor and imported food
and a view of the young maid servant on her knees
scrubbing the floor. She's a wonderful creature

strong, pretty and always cheerful. Yes she's asked you
to be god-father to her second child, and you are
so delighted you raise her wages to $40 a month. Oh
it's good to be good and still live the good life

And though your face grows redder each year
and your body gets flabbier and you lose your hair
and your paunch sticks out above your khaki shorts
at least the skin under your clothes seems to be

turning even whiter, and you joke about this
when you have guests visiting from home and you are
discussing interesting features of the local scene
the quaint behavior of the native population, their

innate laziness and lack of initiative, but they're
a happy lot generally. And finally, after years
of this pleasant life (and you're still an amiable
chap yourself) one night you are disturbed

by the air conditioner cutting out, and some
unrecognizable commotion, and you open your eyes
in time to meet death in the blackness
on the swift warm blade of a cutlass

1969

Environment

LIONEL
KEARNS

Bent old men and women and dirty children scavenging for
  scraps of paper to pack in immense bundles on their backs for
  a few centavos
They keep the streets clean
They are also shining your shoes and polishing your sports car
  and scrubbing out your toilet bowl
They are puking in their piles of rags
They are pawing through your garbage can for something to eat
They are so hungry they will do anything for a drink
They are selling their sick sisters to tourists
They are even pretending to smile
And you are so used to seeing all this that you hardly consider it
  anymore
Or maybe it's because their skins are darker than yours that you
  dismiss it as part of the natural order
But listen to me Fatty
They are living and dying and waiting the slow wait of the
  desperate
Degradation would finish them off if it wasn't for their hatred
And there is a rumour that something is going to happen
The police have begun searching for guns stored in the barrios
(It has happened before in other places, you know)
And don't go putting me down as just another one of those
  social-protest boys
Because I'm not protesting in the least
I'm just telling you what's going on
So you won't be too surprised when it happens

1969

b. 1935

Grandfather

Grandfather
   Jabez Harry Bowering
strode across the Canadian prairie
hacking down trees
     and building churches
delivering personal baptist sermons in them
leading Holy holy holy lord god almighty songs in them
red haired man squared off in the pulpit
reading Saul on the road to Damascus at them

Left home
   big walled Bristol town
at age eight
    to make a living
buried his stubby fingers in root snarled earth
for a suit of clothes and seven hundred gruelly meals a year
taking an anabaptist cane across the back every day
for four years till he was whipped out of England

Twelve years old
    and across the ocean alone
to apocalyptic Canada
      Ontario of bone bending child labor
six years on the road to Damascus till his eyes were blinded
with the blast of Christ and he wandered west
to Brandon among wheat kings and heathen Saturday nights
young red haired Bristol boy shoveling coal
in the basement of Brandon college five in the morning

Then built his first wooden church and married
a sick girl who bore two live children and died
leaving several pitiful letters and the Manitoba night

He moved west with another wife and built children and churches
Saskatchewan Alberta British Columbia Holy holy holy
lord god almighty
    struck his labored bones with pain

and left him a postmaster prodding grandchildren with crutches
another dead wife and a glass bowl of photographs
and holy books unopened save the bible by the bed

Till he died the day before his eighty fifth birthday
in a Catholic hospital of sheets white as his hair

1964

Dobbin

For Mike Ondaatje

We found dead animals in our sagebrush hills,
every day it seems now, deer, heads of
unimaginable elk. Or rattlesnake killed
by some kids we likely knew, upside down,
wrong coloured in the burnt couchgrass.

But my first dead horse. It was something
like mother, something gone wrong at home—
his opened & scattered body was tethered,
the old shit surrounded his tufted hair
& his skin, the oil gone, just twisted
leather without eyeballs. A horse, as if
someone had lost him, obeying the rope
thru his open-air starving.

I was then, then, no longer another one
of the animals come to look, this
was no humus like the others, this
was death, not merely dead: that rope
may now hang from some rotted fence.

1969

The House

GEORGE
BOWERING

I
If I describe my house
I may at last describe my self

but I will surely lie
about the house.

For there is the first lie.
It is not a house at all

but a fragment, a share
of a house, instinct drives me

to one door. As certain as
one hair lies beside another.

As certain as these rows of books
carry me from house to house,

arrange me to their will. I
squat for an hour, eye level

to those books, saying I will
read this, or I will read this,

& this way never succeed
in reading my self, no time

left in the hour between
the news & the pants on the floor.

II
In the morning the window
is bamboo & behind that

snow. (But here I am trying
to go outside the house, remember

what I said.) My bare feet
find no wood, the water

324

runs warm from the tap,
the coffee in the white cup

on which is painted a green
tree. There is a newspaper

on the floor inside the door,
& a woman in the chiffon

of the bed. A salt shaker
of glass & an aluminum

pepper shaker, & in the
farthest room, papers, orderly.

Those are the reason for the house
& its enemy. I am the fisher

who lays his fish side by side
in the pan. The noise of the pen

on paper is the drift of
cigarette smoke in the window's light.

III
The house has a refrigerator
& a stove, a painting & a

husband, & the husband
has fingers from which words

fall as the wine glass falls
unbroken on the rug.

The key fits into the door
as my feet step in snow, cutting

precise patterns & the silence
of wind, & from outside

the windows are glass, &
behind that the house is not empty.

1969

The Envies

GEORGE
BOWERING

I watcht as the flung screen door
slammed across our kitten's throat
& my father took it to the garage
to do what I didnt see
where I was still
in the porch.

I watcht as one brother fell
breaking his head on a rock
in the newly dug foundation & my father
took him to the hospital
& he later shared my bedroom,
a cast around his skull.

I sat & watcht as the other
opened the back door of the moving car
to step out over the pavement
& my father reacht back from the wheel
to pull him in.

& now I'm under that history
stored behind the eyes
where all household pets are forgotten
& I have contrived to
get my brothers out of a prairie jail.

They are both taller than I,
& we come together across our decade,
across the envies looking at one another,
men in a place
where smaller things die early.

1969

GEORGE
BOWERING

From 'Summer Solstice'

I am slowly dying, water evaporating
from a saucer. I saw my daughter this
morning, trying to walk, & it fell like a vial
of melted lead into my heart, my heart so
deep in my chest. She will have to do it now,
we have presented her with a world,
whose spectres take shapes before her eyes
have fully focust, poor voyager! For joy
she brings us every morning we exchange
an accelerating series of shocks. We are together
cannibals of her spirit, we feast to nurture
our tired bodies, turning music to shit, a shock
felt numbly here & radiating to collisions
at the rim of space. You dont believe me?
See her eyes when first she wakes. A visible
tyrant of light yanks their traces, demanding
they stride apace.

1976

In the Forest

They are in the forest
singing, they are in the
forest fucking, the colour in
your body is green
little daughter, dont look
for red of lion eating beast,

the colour in you is blue
that thinks to fall from the sky.
The marigold at your feet
is to eat, it will
colour your skin
yellow as a rainbow as it
gathers to a greatness.

GEORGE
BOWERING

The song they are singing
is for you for your
future which I fear but
prepare for I love you.

They are in the forest
naked & waiting for you
& here you are walking
on your new legs around
my house looking up at me
& out at the trees
with your eyes blue
like the bulge of little
souls, waiting to find out.

I cant quite tell you.
But there are the trees,
darling, over there.

1979

DAVID
HELWIG

b. 1938

For Edward Hicks

At least a hundred times,
there's the marvel,
a hundred times
as you travelled the green country,
you had to put away your sign painting
or turn from preaching the inner light
to the one picture,
the stiff animals gentle,
children among them,
men good.

You must have had violent hands
to have needed so often,
a hundred times at least,
the magic, the talisman,
the peaceable kingdom
made by your hands.

DAVID
HELWIG

1967

A Dead Weasel

Old snake, old hole in the corner man,
miniature killer, lithe and stinking,
now you are stiff as a broken stick
and I knock your body aside from the road.

How many sparrows, how many young rabbits
have you killed, have died in your sudden kiss,
have given you delight in their soft going,
held in your small cunning terrible teeth?

Now you are still, your sharp little teeth
harmless, your delicate cunning head
askew, the blood of your last passion,
your death under the wheels, in your mouth.

In you I see my terrible twin,
quick as lies, yet when I look down
at your stiff mean body, I must pity
even the destruction of such small life.

1967

Drunken Poem

DAVID
HELWIG

Afternoon is invading my eyes.
Between here and the barn
the fallen leaves lie untouched.
I never rake the lawn, I never
clean the car. The children
squabble all round me
as the day darkens and beer
darkens my brain and the thought
of you and a thousand confusions
darken my heart, and I find
a photograph on the table
of a newborn child. My child, I think,
my Kate who now stands near me,
grown, difficult, beloved, and I find
the threat of tears invading my eyes.

Oh sentimental absurd man, who
can you think you are, writing
this something, nothing, drunken words
that solve nothing and say
nothing, only that I know
nothing and that the earth
is the body of a god and you
and I are the body of a god.

The children laugh. I remember
the night that Kate was born.

All afternoon I have said to myself
that love is too simple, is only
an easy death. I think of the men
and women who are puzzled at me
and what they have heard me say.

I am the eyes of god, I am
the tongue of god and so are you
and you and you, even dying,
even hating the world to death.

Rhetoric, beer rhetoric, I have nothing
to claim but a willingness to lose.

I wear a child's Indian headdress.
I write with a ball-point pen.
My brain is addled by beer,
by the coming of dark, by the love
of death, by you, by all the times
that I didn't know what I was doing.

The trees are black against the blue air
as the paper boy does his rounds
and the day becomes gone. Time,
death, loving; we can only live
by being in love with loss, with disaster.

There is no conclusion to this poem. Ever.

1972

Considerations

Any country is only a way of failing,
and nationality is an accident of time,
like love.
            That I was born
in Toronto in an April snowstorm
makes nothing certain.
                        That I remember
ducks flying in the winter twilight
of Lake Ontario means only this,
that I was there, and I remember it.

Still, to have a country is to have
a way to encounter history in the streets
of a burning city whose fire is our own.
That we have less killing, more absurdities,
some luck, a bit of time,
and memories like those winter ducks
is about as much as a man can ask for,
a place to start.

1972

Words from Hell

DAVID
HELWIG

(For Brian Ensor, killed in Kingston Penitentiary 18 April 1971)

I was eighteen when I came in these gates
on a sentence of indeterminate duration.
I was eighteen and twisted, and your courts
sent me away from sexual temptation.

I could not keep my fingers off your children.
Your little girls set all my flesh on fire.
I did some things I knew you had forbidden.
You put me in a cell and closed the door.

My need was hideous to the violent men
around me, and they changed my face to mud,
my prisoned life to freedom in the land
of death. Coloured their weapons with my blood.

They beat the life from me with iron bars.
They beat me in a dance of joyous hate.
I cannot count the wounds my body bears.
I was eighteen when I came in these gates.

1972

TOM
MARSHALL

b. 1938

Summer

Sun blooms in our bodies
like a soft death,
a warmth that is far
more permanent than love.

We imagine that sun
becomes part of us.
Fools not to know
we must fall into it.

For now the park
opens within, living trees
unlock their secrets
to the whole silence or fire.

And do not ask to love me
but love through me
as now through the ripe tree
the bruise of life burns outward.

1969

Interior Monologue #666

'Hydrocephalics are holy, too,
they have
a certain
bloated beatitude . . .'

I think I am becoming
a tree. At any rate
something slow, lethargic,
vegetable. I am said
to resemble a rutabaga.

Do rutabagas have leaves
I wonder? I should like
to have leaves at least.
Slow ones. Leaves of pain
perhaps. Leaves of sleep.

It is said the gods
descend at last. In UFOs
perhaps. In BVDs for all
I care. Who cares if gods
descend? They are leaves

of sky, my leaves. Mine,
perhaps yours, I would be generous.
Every day the sky has leaves.
The sky-tree has grey leaves.
The sky-tree is ours.

1969

From 'Politics'

TOM
MARSHALL

1
They will win, I thought once,
because they have a myth.
The myth shapes their hunger.
And shapes also the faceless
beast made of many longings
who now coalesces in all of us
and surfaces crying 'Liberty!'

He is not good or evil.He is there, simply,
under the snow, under the white eye
of the dream continent
into which we sink further and further
an ancient pain grown ever more urgent
because we thought we left it behind
in Africa, Asia and Europe.

2
An almost monochrome snowscape
is the beginning of our myth.
Against it I have set
the brown and gold richness
of a room, a large room
with three large windows. Snow
flickers like cinema in all of them.

Hypnotic snow. Eradicating time
and banishing history from consciousness
you deceive us and begin us.
How shall we live with such blankness?
Shall we invoke the unjust past
or the equally false Utopian future?
Blood flows: a film on our eyes.

1971

JOHN
NEWLOVE

b. 1938

What Do You Want?

I want a good lover
who will not mistreat me
and suffers indignities willingly;
who is so good in bed
she covers my faults and will claim
the skill's mine, and love me,
and gossip too
to enhance my sexual fame—

what do you want,
what do you want?

I want a good lover
who will cook good meals
and listen respectfully;
shine my shoes, back my lies
with invented statistics at parties;
suffer indignities willingly
and be at my heels—

what do you want,
what do you want?

I want a good lover
who will keep her mouth shut
except for my praise to my face
or loudly behind my back;
who hates my enemies
and willingly suffers indignities—

what do you want,
what do you want?

I want a lover
who suffers indignities.

1968

Samuel Hearne in Wintertime

JOHN
NEWLOVE

1
In this cold room
I remember the smell of manure
on men's heavy clothes as good,
the smell of horses.

It is a romantic world
to readers of journeys
to the Northern Ocean

especially if their houses are heated
to some degree, Samuel.

Hearne, your camp must have smelled
like hell whenever you settled down
for a few days of rest and journal-work:

hell smeared with human manure,
hell half-full of raw hides,
hell of sweat, Indians, stale fat,
meat-hell, fear-hell, hell of cold.

2
One child is back from the doctor's while
the other one wanders about in dirty pants
and I think of Samuel Hearne and the land—

puffy children coughing as I think,
crying, sick-faced,
vomit stirring in grey blankets
from room to room.

It is Christmastime—
the cold flesh shines.
No praise in merely enduring.

3
Samuel Hearne did more
in the land (like all the rest

full of rocks and hilly country,
many very extensive tracts of land,
tittimeg, pike and barble,

and the islands:
the islands, many
of them abound

as well as the main
land does
with dwarf woods,

chiefly pine
in some parts intermixed
with larch and birch) than endure.

The Indians killed twelve deer.
It was impossible to describe
the intenseness of the cold.

4
And, Samuel Hearne,
I have almost begun to talk

as if you wanted to be
gallant, as if you went
through that land for a book—

as if you were not SAM, wanting
to know, to do a job.

5
There was that Eskimo girl
at Bloody Falls, at your feet,

Samuel Hearne, with two spears in her,
you helpless before your helpers.

and she twisted about them like
an eel, dying, never to know.

1968

The Pride

JOHN
NEWLOVE

1

The image/   the pawnees
in their earth-lodge villages,
the clear image
of teton sioux, wild
fickle people the chronicler says,

the crazy dogs, men
tethered with leather dog-thongs
to a stake, fighting until dead,

image: arikaras
with traded spanish sabre blades
mounted on the long
heavy buffalo lances,
riding the sioux
down, the centaurs, the horsemen
scouring the level plains
in war or hunt
until smallpox got them,
the warriors,

image—of a desolate country,
a long way between fires,
unfound lakes, mirages, cold rocks,
and lone men going through it,
cree with good guns
causing terror in athabaska
among the inhabitants, frightened
stone-age people, 'so that
they fled at the mere sight
of a strange smoke miles away.'

2

This western country crammed
with the ghosts of indians,
haunting the coastal stones and shores,
the forested pacific islands,
mountains, hills and plains:

beside the ocean ethlinga,
man in the moon, empties
his bucket, on
a sign from spirit
of the wind ethlinga
empties his bucket, refreshing
the earth, and it rains
on the white cities;

that black joker, broken-
jawed raven, most prominent
among haida and tsimshian tribes
is in the kwakiutl
dance masks too—
it was he who brought fire,
food and water to man,
the trickster;

and thunderbird hilunga,
little thought of
by haida for lack of thunderstorms
in their district, goes
by many names, exquisite disguises
carved in the painted wood,

he is nootka tootooch, the wings
causing thunder and the tongue
or flashing eyes engendering
rabid white lightning,
whose food was whales,

called kwunusela by the kwakiutl,
it was he who laid down the house-logs
for the people at the place
where kwunusela alighted;

in full force and virtue
and terror of the law, eagle—
he is authority, the sun
assumed his form once,
the sun which used to be
a flicker's egg, success-
fully transformed;

and malevolence comes to the land,
the wild woman of the woods—
grinning, she wears
a hummingbird in her hair,
d'sonoqua, the furious one—

they are all ready
to be found, the legends
and the people, or
all their ghosts and memories,
whatever is strong enough
to be remembered.

3
But what image, bewildered
son of all men
under the hot sun,
do you worship,
what completeness
do you hope to have
from these tales,
a half-understood massiveness, mirage,
in men's minds—what
is your purpose;

with what force
will you proceed
along a line
neither straight nor short,
whose future
you cannot know
or result foretell,
whose meaning is still
obscured as the incidents
occur and accumulate?

4
The country moves on;
there are orchards in the interior,
the mountain passes
are broken, the foothills
covered with cattle and fences,
and the fading hills covered;

but the plains are bare,
not barren, easy
for me to love their people,
for me to love their people
without selection.

5

In 1787, the old cree saukamappee, aged 75 or thereabout,
speaking then of things that had happened when he was 16, just
a man, told david thompson about the raids the shoshonis, the
snakes, had made on the westward-reaching peigan, of their
war-parties sometimes sent 10 days' journey to enemy camps,
the men all afoot in battle array for the encounter, crouching
behind their giant shields. The peigan armed with guns drove
these snakes out of the plains, the plains where their strength had
been, where they had been settled since living memory (though
nothing is remembered beyond a grandfather's time), to the west
of the rockies:

these people moved without rest,
backward and forward with the wind,
the seasons, the game, great herds,
in hunger and abundance—

in summer and in the bloody fall
they gathered on the killing grounds,
fat and shining with fat, amused
with the luxuries of war and death,

relieved from the steam of knowledge,
consoled by the stream of blood
and steam rising from the fresh hides
and tired horses, wheeling in their pride
on the sweating horses, their pride.

6

Those are all stories;
the pride, the grand poem
of our land, of the earth itself,
will come, welcome, and
sought for, and found,
in a line of running verse,
sweating, our pride;

we seize on
what has happened before,
one line only
will be enough,
a single line
and then the sunlit brilliant image suddenly floods us
with understanding, shocks our
attentions, and all desire
stops, stands alone;

JOHN
NEWLOVE

we stand alone,
we are no longer lonely
but have roots,
and the rooted words
recur in the mind, mirror, so that
we dwell on nothing else, in nothing else,
touched, repeating them,
at home freely
at last, in amazement;

'the unyielding phrase
in tune with the epoch,'
the thing made up
of our desires,
not of its words, not only
of them, but of something else
as well, that which we desire
so ardently, that which
will not come when
it is summoned alone,
but grows in us
and idles about and hides
until the moment is due—

the knowledge of
our origins, and where
we are in truth,
whose land this is
and is to be.

7

JOHN
NEWLOVE

The unyielding phrase:
when the moment is due, then
it springs upon us
out of our own mouths,
unconsidered, overwhelming
in its knowledge, complete—

not this handful
of fragments, as the indians
are not composed of
the romantic stories
about them, or of the stories
they tell only, but
still ride the soil
in us, dry bones a part
of the dust in our eyes,
needed and troubling
in the glare, in
our breath, in our
ears, in our mouths,
in our bodies entire, in our minds, until
at last
we become them

in our desires, our desires,
mirages, mirrors, that are theirs, hard-
riding desires, and they
become our true forbears, moulded
by the same wind or rain,
and in this land we
are their people, come
back to life again.

1968

America

JOHN
NEWLOVE

Even the dissident ones speak
as members of an Empire, residents
of the centre of the earth. Power
extends from their words
to all the continents and their modesty
is liable for millions. How must it be
to be caught in the Empire, to have
everything you do matter? Even
treason is imperial; the scornful
self-abuse comes from inside the boundaries
of the possible. Outside the borders of royalty
the barbarians wait in fear,
finding it hard to know which prince
to believe; trade-goods comfort them,
gadgets of little worth, cars, television,
refrigerators, for which they give iron,
copper, uranium, gold, trees, and water,
worth of all sorts for the things
citizens of Empire take as their due.

In the Empire power speaks from the poorest
and culture flourishes. Outside the boundaries
the barbarians imitate styles and send their sons,
the talented hirelings, to learn and to stay;
the sons of their sons will be princes too,
in the Estate where even the unhappy
carry an aura of worldly power; and the lords
of power send out directives
for the rest of the world to obey. If they live
in the Empire, it matters what they say.

1970

JOHN
THOMPSON

1938-1976

The Bread Hot from the Oven

Under the ice with its bouldery death's faces
hidden forms begin to churn the tides,
a wink of blood starts the moon's white track,
fish rise
to their eternal lives;

this morning the bread hot from the oven
sounds with voices:
terrible blows struck
below an unimaginable prairie;

deer break from a mesh of dreams
and two bears burn with the dawn,
cursing the earth's white face
in a stony blood dance
that I feel as words I do not know,
of immense weight,
that I would carry with me,
burdens, until

they appear as they are:
the gods of this place,
this household,
words so light, so still
they are heard only at night
when the earth moves
inwardly:

root songs, that our bodies wake
freighted with melancholy
and the joy of something
a moment held
in our empty hands.

1973

The Onion

JOHN
THOMPSON

I have risen from your body
full of smoke, charred fibres;

the light kicks up off
the glazed snow: I have to
turn from its keenness,
its warmth, seeking
darkness, burying ground;

I am without grace, I cannot shape
those languages, the knots
of light and silence:
the newness of being
still, the press
of the snow's whiteness.

Young steers turned from the barn
stand, furry stones, streaked
with dung,
cold light, thin
February snow.

In this kitchen warmth I reach
for the bouquet
of thyme and sage, drifting
in the heat: a world crumbles
over my hands, I am washed
with essences;

I cup the onion I watched grow all summer:
cutting perfectly through its heart
it speaks a white core, pale
green underskin, the perfections
I have broken, that curing grace
my knife releases;

and then you are by me, unfolded
to a white stillness, remade warmth on warmth.

So we turn from our darkness,
our brokenness,

share this discovered root,
this one quiet bread
quick with light, thyme, that deep
speech of your hands which always
defeats me, calling me through strange earths
to this place suddenly yours.

JOHN
THOMPSON

1973

'Now you have burned . . .'

Now you have burned your books: you'll go
with nothing but your blind, stupefied heart.

On the hook, big trout lie like stone:
terror, and they fiercely whip their heads, unmoved.

Kitchens, women and fire: can you
do without these, your blood in your mouth?

Rough wool, oil-tanned leather, prime northern goose down,
a hard, hard eye.

Think of your house: as you speak, it falls,
fond, foolish man. And your wife.

They call it the thing of things, essence
of essences: great northern snowy owl; whiteness.

1978

J. MICHAEL YATES

b. 1938

From THE GREAT BEAR LAKE MEDITATIONS

I persist in a little fabric between me and the world. This is the sleep inside a tent on an airless, sunstung afternoon. The sleep beyond mosquitoes and black flies that close in and in upon the beast that ceases to stir. This is the orange sleep that seeps and clings like mire. The muskeg and the clear streams are going away. The wet sleep comes for me like water on the rise. Snow-caps in the distance are burning. Somewhere in the extinguishing light, the plume of a crowning forest fire. Whatever will enter this canvas crypt can have me. Nothing comes, and I can't rise. The tick of a clock somewhere beneath things diminishes with the last fly that circles outside like a plane coming to rescue the lost in sleep. The mouth of flat blackness is closing. Sleep stiffens through me to the bayous beyond dream. I shall die here in this uncertain growth. Seams of the tent will give, canvas and skin will sink beneath the ash of the fire that has been burning toward me forever. The wind changes. The fire goes green. This is the sleep of mastodons and mammoths; this is not the sleep of winter bears I've buried beneath cornices of words. On the surface of the tar-pit, stillness over the blackness signals the stop of a monstrous metabolism. The undergrowth is zombied in the thin stutter of heat. The coming destruction. The roads I followed here are washing away. This is the Lazarus who returned with no more to show than a yawn, the taste of dying in his mouth, vague hunger, thirst and no recollection of awakening at an earlier dawn. This was the sleep within the tent that I sewed. I entered, shut out the weather and went to sleep for darkness' sake. The afternoon and the insects have waited. I dream I only dream I am awake.

1970

Death of a Young Son by Drowning

He, who navigated with success
the dangerous river of his own birth
once more set forth

on a voyage of discovery
into the land I floated on
but could not touch to claim.

His feet slid on the bank,
the currents took him;
he swirled with ice and trees in the swollen water

and plunged into distant regions,
his head a bathysphere;
through his eyes' thin glass bubbles

he looked out, reckless adventurer
on a landscape stranger than Uranus
we have all been to and some remember.

There was an accident; the air locked,
he was hung in the river like a heart.
They retrieved the swamped body,

cairn of my plans and future charts,
with poles and hooks
from among the nudging logs.

It was spring, the sun kept shining, the new grass
leapt to solidity;
my hands glistened with details.

After the long trip I was tired of waves.
My foot hit rock. The dreamed sails
collapsed, ragged.

    I planted him in this country
1970   like a flag.

There Is Only One of Everything

MARGARET
ATWOOD

Not a tree but the tree
we saw, it will never exist, split by the wind
                    and bending down
like that again. What will push out of the earth

later, making it summer, will not be
grass, leaves, repetition, there will
have to be other words. When my

eyes close language vanishes. The cat
with the divided face, half black half orange
nests in my scruffy fur coat, I drink tea,

fingers curved around the cup, impossible
to duplicate these flavours. The table
and freak plates glow softly, consuming themselves,

I look out at you and you occur
in this winter kitchen, random as trees or sentences,
entering me, fading like them, in time you will disappear

but the way you dance by yourself
on the tile floor to a worn song, flat and mournful,
so delighted, spoon waved in one hand, wisps of
                    roughened hair

sticking up from your head, it's your surprised
body, pleasure I like. I can even say it,
though only once and it won't

last: I want this. I want
this.

1974

November

MARGARET
ATWOOD

i

This creature kneeling
dusted with snow, its teeth
grinding together, sound of old stones
at the bottom of a river

You lugged it to the barn
I held the lantern,
we leaned over it
as if it were being born.

ii

The sheep hangs upside down from the rope,
a long fruit covered with wool and rotting.
It waits for the dead wagon
to harvest it.

Mournful November
this is the image
you invent for me,
the dead sheep came out of your head, a legacy:

Kill what you can't save
what you can't eat throw out
what you can't throw out bury

What you can't bury give away
what you can't give away you must carry with you,
it is always heavier than you thought.

1974

Marrying the Hangman

MARGARET
ATWOOD

She has been condemned to death by hanging. A man may escape this death by becoming the hangman, a woman by marrying the hangman. But at the present time there is no hangman; thus there is no escape. There is only a death, indefinitely postponed. This is not fantasy, it is history.

*

To live in prison is to live without mirrors. To live without mirrors is to live without the self. She is living selflessly, she finds a hole in the stone wall and on the other side of the wall, a voice. The voice comes through darkness and has no face. This voice becomes her mirror.

*

In order to avoid her death, her particular death, with wrung neck and swollen tongue, she must marry the hangman. But there is no hangman, first she must create him, she must persuade this man at the end of the voice, this voice she has never seen and which has never seen her, this darkness, she must persuade him to renounce his face, exchange it for the impersonal mask of death, of official death which has eyes but no mouth, this mask of a dark leper. She must transform his hands so they will be willing to twist the rope around throats that have been singled out as hers was, throats other than hers. She must marry the hangman or no one, but that is not so bad. Who else is there to marry?

*

You wonder about her crime. She was condemned to death for stealing clothes from her employer, from the wife of her employer. She wished to make herself more beautiful. This desire in servants was not legal.

*

She uses her voice like a hand, her voice reaches through the wall, stroking and touching. What could she possibly have said that would have convinced him? He was not condemned to death, freedom awaited him. What was the temptation, the one that worked? Perhaps he wanted to live with a woman whose life he had saved, who had seen down into the earth but had nevertheless followed him back up to life. It was his only chance to be a hero, to one person at least, for if he became the hangman the others would despise him. He was in prison for wounding another man, on one finger of the right hand, with a sword. This too is history.

*

My friends, who are both women, tell me their stories, which cannot be believed and which are true. They are horror stories and they have not happened to me, they have not yet happened to me, they have happened to me but we are detached, we watch our unbelief with horror. Such things cannot happen to us, it is afternoon and these things do not happen in the afternoon. The trouble was, she said, I didn't have time to put my glasses on and without them I'm blind as a bat, I couldn't even see who it was. These things happen and we sit at a table and tell stories about them so we can finally believe. This is not fantasy, it is history, there is more than one hangman and because of this some of them are unemployed.

*

He said: the end of walls, the end of ropes, the opening of doors, a field, the wind, a house, the sun, a table, an apple.

She said: nipple, arms, lips, wine, belly, hair, bread, thighs, eyes, eyes.

They both kept their promises.

*

The hangman is not such a bad fellow. Afterwards he goes to the refrigerator and cleans up the leftovers, though he does not wipe up what he accidentally spills. He wants only the simple things: a chair, someone to pull off his shoes, someone to watch him while he talks, with admiration and fear, gratitude if possible, someone in whom to plunge himself for rest and renewal. These things can best be had by marrying a woman who has been condemned to death by other men for wishing to be beautiful. There is a wide choice.

*

Everyone said he was a fool.
Everyone said she was a clever woman.
They used the word *ensnare*.

What did they say the first time they were alone together in the same room? What did he say when she had removed her veil and he could see that she was not a voice but a body and therefore finite? What did she say when she discovered that she had left one locked room for another? They talked of love, naturally, though that did not keep them busy forever.

*

The fact is there are no stories I can tell my friends that will make them feel better. History cannot be erased, although we can soothe ourselves by speculating about it. At that time there were no female hangmen. Perhaps there have never been any, and thus no man could save his life by marriage. Though a woman could, according to the law.

*

He said: foot, boot, order, city, fist, roads, time, knife.

She said: water, night, willow, rope hair, earth belly, cave, meat, shroud, open, blood.

They both kept their promises.

1978

In eighteenth-century Quebec the only way for someone under sentence of death to escape hanging was, for a man, to become a hangman, or, for a woman, to marry one. Françoise Laurent, sentenced to hang for stealing, persuaded Jean Corolère, in the next cell, to apply for the vacant post of executioner, and also to marry her.

You Begin

MARGARET
ATWOOD

You begin this way:
this is your hand,
this is your eye,
that is a fish, blue and flat
on the paper, almost
the shape of an eye.
This is your mouth, this is an O
or a moon, whichever
you like. This is yellow.

Outside the window
is the rain, green
because it is summer, and beyond that
the trees and then the world,
which is round and has only
the colours of these nine crayons.

This is the world, which is fuller
and more difficult to learn than I have said.
You are right to smudge it that way
with the red and then
the orange: the world burns.

Once you have learned these words
you will learn that there are more
words than you can ever learn.
The word *hand* floats above your hand
like a small cloud over a lake.
The word *hand* anchors
your hand to this table,
your hand is a warm stone
I hold between two words.

This is your hand, these are my hands, this is the world,
which is round but not flat and has more colours
than we can see.

It begins, it has an end,
this is what you will
come back to, this is your hand.

1978

MARGARET
ATWOOD

*Notes Towards a Poem
That Can Never Be Written*

For Carolyn Forché

i
This is the place
you would rather not know about,
this is the place that will inhabit you,
this is the place you cannot imagine,
this is the place that will finally defeat you

where the word *why* shrivels and empties
itself. This is famine.

ii
There is no poem you can write
about it, the sandpits
where so many were buried
& unearthed, the unendurable
pain still traced on their skins.

This did not happen last year
or forty years ago but last week.
This has been happening,
this happens.

We make wreaths of adjectives for them,
we count them like beads,
we turn them into statistics & litanies
and into poems like this one.

Nothing works.
They remain what they are.

iii
The woman lies on the west cement floor
under the unending light,
needle marks on her arms put there
to kill the brain
and wonders why she is dying.

She is dying because she said.
She is dying for the sake of the word.
It is her body, silent
and fingerless, writing this poem.

iv
It resembles an operation
but it is not one

nor despite the spread legs, grunts
& blood, is it a birth.

Partly it's a job
partly it's a display of skill
like a concerto.

It can be done badly
or well, they tell themselves.

Partly it's an art.

v
The facts of this world seen clearly
are seen through tears;
why tell me then
there is something wrong with my eyes?

To see clearly and without flinching,
without turning away,
this is agony, the eyes taped open
two inches from the sun.

What is it you see then?
Is it a bad dream, a hallucination?
Is it a vision?
What is it you hear?

The razor across the eyeball
is a detail from an old film.
It is also a truth.
Witness is what you must bear.

In this country you can say what you like
because no one will listen to you anyway,
it's safe enough, in this country you can try to write
the poem that can never be written,
the poem that invents
nothing and excuses nothing,
because you invent and excuse yourself each day.

Elsewhere, this poem is not invention.
Elsewhere, this poem takes courage.
Elsewhere, this poem must be written
because the poets are already dead.

Elsewhere, this poem must be written
as if you are already dead,
as if nothing more can be done
or said to save you.

Elsewhere you must write this poem
because there is nothing more to do.

1981

Variation on the Word Sleep

MARGARET
ATWOOD

I would like to watch you sleeping,
which may not happen.
I would like to watch you,
sleeping. I would like to sleep
with you, to enter
your sleep as its smooth dark wave
slides over my head

and walk with you through that lucent
wavering forest of bluegreen leaves
with its watery sun & three moons
towards the cave where you must descend,
towards your worst fear

I would like to give you the silver
branch, the small white flower, the one
word that will protect you
from the grief at the center
of your dream, from the grief
at the center. I would like to follow
you up the long stairway
again & become
the boat that would row you back
carefully, a flame
in two cupped hands
to where your body lies
beside me, and you enter
it as easily as breathing in

I would like to be the air
that inhabits you for a moment
only. I would like to be that unnoticed
& that necessary.

1981

b. 1939

dont worry yr hair

dont worry yr eyes
dont worry yr brain man th snow is
cummin th bright burds flyin highr,th
sun is already all ovr yu,

all th words all th mony all th unnecessary
changes, a tree grows inside yu, let it and th bird
red with blue circles,a white arrow on its side,sings
within yr breast, near yr spine, let its wings
spread, yr arms

each day probably sumhow yul get th watr

grow out to sum
piece a land away from th bad business, th amerikan
takeovr,to
ward,into th earth yu cum from, have none of
th bargain with th tanks,th war heads

each day th pebble is more stone,
ium dreaming now of th place that will
soon have me, find me

moving into th dark,it
is like going into a soft jewel. and being ther what at
first yu cud see nothing totally dark, only
th feel of yr feet on th ground guides yu,

being ther, light apears here and ther,flashing,

yr head especially around th back breathes unfolds
opens like a flowr all around yu,

to th light

1971

th wundrfulness uv th mountees
our secret police

they opn our mail   petulantly
they burn down barns they cant
bug   they listn to our politikul
ledrs phone conversashuns   what
cud b less inspiring to ovrheer

they had me down on th floor til
i turnd purpul thn my frends
pulld them off me   they think
brest feeding is disgusting   evry
time we cum heer to raid ths place
yu always have that kid on yr tit

they tore my daughtrs dolls hed off
looking for dope   whun uv my mor
memorabul beetings was in th back
seet lockd inside whun a ther unmarkd
cars

they work for the CIA   at nite they
drive around nd shine ther serchlites
on peopul embracing   nd with ther
p a systems tell them to keep away
from th treez

they listn to yr most secret farts
re-winding th tape looking for hiddn
meening indigestyun is a nashunal
security risk

i think they shud stick to protecting
th weak   eldrly laydees n men childrn
crossing th street   helping sick
nd/or defensless peopul nd
arresting capitalist crooks

insted theyve desertid th poor
n eldrly   nd ar protecting
th capitalist crooks

its mor than musical
th ride theyr taking
us all on

1978

BILL
BISSETT

christ i wudint know normal if i saw it when

were yu normal today did yu screw society
were yu normal today did yu screw society
were yu normal today did yu screw society
were yu normal today did yu screw society
were yu normal today did yu screw society
were yu normal today did yu screw society
were yu normal today did yu screw society
were yu normal today did yu screw society
were yu screw society were yu normal today
were yu were yu are yu screw society normal
did yu blow cock eat cunt make a good
business deal and still relate were yu are
yu happy were yu good just once did yu today
have an existential moment in no time were yu
normal today did yu screw society but found
sum innocent outlets like no one knew or evry
one knew did yu buy sum orange pop sticks green
ones did yu have a treat and were clean were yu
a dirty outlet for a while managin at th same
time to find pleasure in nature and read a thot
conditioning book by a provocative author did
yu get lovers nuts and act on it do it all day
without cumming did yu cum together or sd yu
did lie to each othr but cum on yu both really
know where th action is so that yu werent really
lieing and at th same time same were good to th
children and swinging and confused but at th same
time getting what yu want and no one's killd yu
yet and yu even had a lyrical moment and were
social and controversial and no one even suspects
how yu hate evrything i mean evrything but slosh
brings yu back to love like yu compromisd but

didint have to pay for it and as long as they dont
know what yu compromisd they cant get yu to pay
anyway compromise is old fashiond dialectick and
yu still know where yr going know who yr doing in
were yu abul to be negative and dangerously so but
with it appearing as an endorsement of th positive
virtues of lust and greed and isolation and death
and th full joy of personal romantik freedom were yu
were normal today did yu screw society wr yu normal today
today did yu fuck th world were yu normal today did yu
screw society were yu normal today did yu take society
to bed with yu were yu normal today did yu fuck society
were u i mean were u gloriously intolerant for th
good of yr total soul did yu stick to business
and still retain an awareness of yr karmik destiny
like were yu dangerous for just a while so evryond
know yu mean business and know where th business lies

BILL
BISSETT

1971

DAVID
DONNELL

b. 1939

Stepfathers

There you were in my dream last night,
burly, caught in mid-step, crop-headed or bald,
old car coat splashed with chicken blood,
carrying a shotgun
or was that a blur of shadow I saw?

I followed you into the corridor
but you disappeared, circling,

the stairway ended in everyday light
and a mute caretaker with a terrier appeared.

Old man, you die but you live around.

Pig mouth is pig mouth. Nothing touched clean.

Mercy is baffling.
My final image in the dream is always
the way you slide down the wall
blood all over the tiles, clutching at nothing.

1977

Potatoes

DAVID
DONNELL

This poem is about the strength and sadness of potatoes.
Unknown in Portugal or China, England or France,
untasted by the legions of Hannibal or Caesar,
hardy, simple, variable tuber; plain dusty brown,
North Carolina, New Brunswick, Idaho,
of the new world, passed over by the Indians
who preferred the bright yellow of corn, its sweetness,
the liquor they made from it, pemmican and wild corn mush.
The potato was seized upon by the more spiritual Puritans
while their companions were enraptured
by the beauty of New World tobacco, cotton and squash.

The Puritans recognized something of themselves in the pale
potato. Its simple shape reminded them of the human soul;
the many eyes of the potato amazed them. They split it
in half and saw the indivisibility of man;
they looked at the many eyes of the potato
and saw God looking back at them.
Potatoes like many different kinds of soil, resist cold weather,
store well in cool cellars and are more nutritious than beets.
Potato dumplings became the pièce de résistance of eastern
    Europe.
They developed a considerable number of useful proverbs.
For example: 'Love is not a potato, do not throw it out the
    window'.
Or the famous Scottish lament—'What good is he to me?
For three days he has not even brought me a potato'.

The potato is modest and develops its indivisible bounty
under the ground, taking from the ground some of its color
and just enough skin to resist an excess of moisture.
It can be harvested easily by young boys and girls working
in rows with bushel baskets and pausing at lunch
to lift up their skirts and make love under the fences.
Truckloads of potatoes can be sent to every part of the world.
The French make frites with them. The Russians make vodka.
The Chinese have white and brown rice but all potatoes are the
    same.
Potato flour is not as sweet as corn but makes an excellent bread.
In the cellars of poor farmers all over America
the potatoes sit quietly on top of each other growing eyes.

1980

The Canadian Prairies View of Literature

DAVID
DONNELL

First of all it has to be anecdotal; ideas don't exist;
themes struggle dimly out of accrued material like the shadow
of a slow caterpillar struggling out of a large cocoon;
even this image itself is somewhat urban inasmuch as it suggests
the tree-bordered streets of small southern Ontario towns;
towns are alright; Ontario towns are urban; French towns are
    European;
the action should take place on a farm between April and October;
nature is quiet during winter; when it snows, there's a lot of it;
the poem shimmers in the school-teacher's head like an image
of being somewhere else without a railway ticket to return;
the novel shifts its haunches in the hot reporter's head
and surveys the possible relationship between different farms;
sometimes the action happens in the beverage rooms and cheap
hotels area of a small town that has boomed into a new city;
Indians and Metis appear in the novel wearing the marks
of their alienation like a sullen confusion of the weather;
the town drunk appears looking haggard and the town mayor
out ward-heeling and smelling women's hands buys him a drink;
a woman gets married and another woman has a child;
the child is not old enough to plow a field and therefore
does not become a focus of interest except as another mouth;
they sit around with corn shucks in the head and wonder
who they should vote for, the question puzzles them,
vote for the one with the cracked shoes, he's a good boy,
or the one who jumped over six barrels at a local dance;
the fewer buildings they have, the more nationalistic they become
like a man who has stolen all his life accused of cheating;
above all, they dislike the east which at least gives them form
and allows their musings and discontents to flower into rancour;
musing and rancorous, I turn down the small side streets of Galt,
Ontario, afternoon light, aged twelve, past South Water Street,
not quite like Rimbaud leaving Charleville,
my hands in my windbreaker pockets like white stones,
and promise myself once again that when I get to the city
everything will happen, I will learn all of its history
and become the best writer they have ever dreamed of,
I'll make them laugh and I'll even make them cry,
I'll drink their whiskey and make love to all their wives,
the words tumbling out of my mouth as articulate as the young
    Hector,

366

the corn under my shirt awkward a little rough light brown dry
and making me itch at times

1982

DENNIS
LEE

b. 1939

From 'Civil Elegies'

Nathan Phillips Square, Toronto

1
Often I sit in the sun and brooding over the city, always
in airborne shapes among the pollution I hear them, returning;
pouring across the square
in fetid descent, they darken the towers
and the wind-swept place of meeting and whenever
the thick air clogs my breathing it teems with their presence.
Many were born in Canada, and living unlived lives they died
of course but died truncated, stunted, never at
home in native space and not yet
citizens of a human body of kind. And it is Canada
that specialized in this deprivation. Therefore the spectres arrive,
    congregating in bitter droves, thick in the April sunlight,
accusing us and we are no different, though you would not expect
the furies assembled in hogtown and ring me round, invisible,
    demanding
what time of our lives we wait for till we shall start to be.
Until they come the wide square stretches out
serene and singly by moments it takes us in, each one for now
a passionate civil man, until it
sends us back to the acres of gutted intentions,
back to the concrete debris, to parking scars and the four-square
    tiers
of squat and righteous lives. And here
once more, I watch the homing furies' arrival.

DENNIS
LEE I sat one morning by the Moore, off to the west
ten yards and saw though diffident my city nailed against the sky
in ordinary glory.
It is not much to ask. A place, a making,
two towers, a teeming, a genesis, a city.
And the men and women moved in their own space,
performing their daily lives, and their presence occurred
in time as it occurred, patricians in
muddy York and made their compact together against the gangs
    of the new.
And as that crumpled before the shambling onset, again the
lives we had not lived in phalanx invisibly staining
the square and vistas, casting back I saw
regeneration twirl its blood and the rebels riding
riderless down Yonge Street, plain men much
goaded by privilege—our other origin, and cried
'Mackenzie knows a word, Mackenzie
knows a meaning!' but it was not true. Eight hundred-odd steely
    Canadians
turned tail at the cabbage patch when a couple of bullets fizzed
and the loyalists, scared skinny by the sound of their own gunfire,
gawked and bolted south to the fort like rabbits,
the rebels for their part bolting north to the pub: the first
spontaneous mutual retreat in the history of warfare.
Canadians, in flight.

Buildings oppress me, and the sky-concealing wires
bunch zigzag through the air. I know
the dead persist in
buildings, by-laws, porticos—the city I live in
is clogged with their presence; they
dawdle about in our lives and form a destiny, still
incomplete, still dead weight, still
demanding whether Canada will be.

But the mad bomber, Chartier of Major Street, Chartier
said it: that if a country has no past,
neither is it a country and promptly
blew himself to bits in the parliament john, leaving as civil
    testament
assorted chunks of prophet, twitching and
bobbing to rest in the flush.
And what can anyone do in this country, baffled and

making our penance for ancestors, what did they leave us?
    Indian-swindlers,
stewards of unclaimed earth and rootless what does it matter if
    they, our
forebears' flesh and bone were often
good men, good men do not matter to history.
And what can we do here now, for at last we have no notion
of what we might have come to be in America, alternative, and
    how make public
a presence which is not sold out utterly to the modern? utterly? to
    the
savage inflictions of what is for real, it pays off, it is only
accidentally less than human?

In the city I long for, green trees still
asphyxiate. The crowds emerge at five from jobs
that rankle and lag. Heavy developers
pay off aldermen still; the craft of neighbourhood,
its whichway streets and generations
anger the planners, they go on jamming their maps
with asphalt panaceas; single men
still eke out evenings courting, in parks, alone.
A man could spend a lifetime looking for
peace in that city. And the lives give way around him—marriages
founder, the neighbourhoods sag—until
the emptiness comes down on him to stay.
But in the city I long for men complete
their origins. Among the tangle of
hydro, hydrants, second mortgages, amid
the itch for new debentures, greater expressways,
in sober alarm they jam their works of progress, asking where in
    truth
they come from and to whom they must belong.
And thus they clear a space in which
the full desires of those that begot them, great animating desires
that shrank and grew hectic as the land pre-empted their lives
might still take root, which eddy now and
drift in the square, being neither alive nor dead.
And the people accept a flawed inheritance
and they give it a place in their midst, forfeiting progress,
    forfeiting
dollars, forfeiting yankee visions of cities that in time it might
    grow

whole at last in their lives, they might
belong once more to their forebears, becoming their own men.

To be our own men! in dread to live
the land, our own harsh country, beloved, the prairie, the
    foothills—
and for me it is lake by rapids by stream-fed lake, threading
north through the terminal vistas of black spruce, in a
bitter, cherished land it is farm after
farm in the waste of the continental outcrop—
for me it is Shield but wherever terrain informs our lives and
    claims us;
and then, no longer haunted by
unlived presence, to live the cities:
to furnish, out of the traffic and smog and the shambles of dead
    precursors,
a civil habitation that is
human, and our own.

The spectres drift across the square in rows.
How empire permeates! And we sit down
in Nathan Phillips Square, among the sun,
as if our lives were real.
Lacunae. Parking lots. Regenerations.
Newsstand euphorics and Revell's sign, that not
one countryman has learned, that
men and women live that
they may make that
life worth dying. Living. Hey,
the dead ones! Gentlemen, generations of
acquiescent spectres gawk at the chrome
on American cars on Queen Street, gawk and slump and retreat.
And over the square where I sit, congregating above the Archer
they crowd in a dense baffled throng and the sun does not shine
    through.

1972

The Gods

DENNIS
LEE

I

Who, now, can speak of gods—
their strokes and carnal voltage,
old ripples of presence   a space ago
archaic eddies of being?

Perhaps a saint could speak their names.
Or maybe some
noble claustrophobic spirit,
crazed by the flash and
vacuum of modernity,
could reach back, ripe for
gods and a hot lobotomy.
But being none of these, I sit
bemused by the sound of the words.
For a man no longer moves
through coiled ejaculations of
meaning;
we dwell within
taxonomies, equations, paradigms
which deaden the world and now in our
heads, though less in our inconsistent lives,
the tickle of cosmos is gone.
Though what would a god be *like*—
would he shop at Dominion?
Would he know about *DNA* molecules? and keep little
haloes, for when they behaved?
. . . It is not from simple derision
that the imagination snickers. But faced with an alien
reality it
stammers, it races & churns
for want of a common syntax and
lacking a possible language
who, now, can speak of gods? for random example
a bear to our forebears, and even to
grope in a pristine hunch back to that way of being on earth
is nearly beyond me.

And yet—
in the middle of one more day, in a clearing maybe   sheer
                    godforce
          calm on the lope of its pads
    furred   hot-breathing   erect, at ease, catastrophic
                    harsh waves of stink, the
          dense air clogged with its roaring and
                    ripples of power fork through us:
          hair gone electric   quick
                              pricklish glissando, the
                    skin   mind skidding, balking is
                              HAIL
and it rears foursquare and we are jerked and owned and
                    forgive us   and
              brought to a welter, old
          force & destroyer and
                              do not destroy us!
                    or if it seems good,
                              destroy us.

          Thus, the god against us in clear air.
                    And there are gentle gods—
                              as plain as
                    light that
                              rises from lake-face,
                    melding with light
    that skips like a stepping-stone spatter
                              down to
                                   evoke it
          till blue embraces blue, and lake and sky
                    are miles of indigenous climax—
                    such grace in the shining air.

          All gods, all gods and none of them
                    domesticated angels, chic of spat & wing
              on ten-day tours of earth. And if
          to speak of 'gods' recalls those antique
                    wind-up toys, forget the gods as well:
                              tremendum rather,
          dimension of otherness, come clear
                    in each familiar thing—in
          outcrop, harvest, hammer, beast and

caught in that web of otherness
we too endure & we
worship.
Men lived among that force, a space ago.

Or,
whirling it reins into phase through us, good god it can
use us, power in tangible
dollops invading the roots of the
hair, the gap behind the neck,
power to snag, coax bully exalt into presence
clean gestures of meaning among the traffic of earth,
and until it lobs us aside, pale snot poor
rags we
also can channel the godforce.
Yet still not
abject: not
heaven & wistful hankering—I mean
the living power, inside
and, that sudden that
plumb!
Men lived in such a space.

III

I do say gods.
But that was time ago, technology
happened and what has been withdrawn
I do not understand, the absent ones,
though many then too were bright & malevolent and
crushed things that mattered,
and where they have since been loitering I scarcely comprehend,
and least of all can I fathom, you powers I
seek and no doubt cheaply arouse and
who are you?
how I am to salute you, nor how contend with your being
for I do not aim to make prize-hungry words (and stay back!) I
want
the world to be real and
it will not,
for to secular men there is not given the glory of tongues, yet it is
better to speak in silence than squeak in the gab of the age
and if I cannot tell your terrifying
praise, now Hallmark gabble and chintz nor least of all

373

what time and dimensions your naked incursions
announced, you scurrilous powers yet
still I stand against this bitch of a shrunken time
in semi-faithfulness
and whether you are godhead or zilch or daily ones like before
you strike our measure still and still you
endure as my murderous fate,
though I
do not know you.

1979

FRED
WAH

b. 1939

'Breathe dust . . .'

Breathe dust like you breathe wind so strong in your face
little grains of dirt which pock around the cheeks peddling
against a dust-storm coming down a street to the edge of
town in Swift Current Saskatchewan or the air walked out
into the fields across from Granny Erickson's house with a
few pails of water to catch gophers over by the glue factory
downwind of all the horses corralled their shit and hay smell
whipped over the grass and the smell of prairie water as
unmoved water doesn't move is stale or even rancid but the
air along the prairie road by Uncle Corny's farm first thing
on a clear summer sunday morning and in winter how the
snow smelled like coal when I maybe later in Trail B.C. up
the alley behind our place my mother needed water to melt
on top of the wood cook stove so she sent me out with my
sleigh and a galvanized washtub to collect the snow so dirty
in the city I scraped off the top few inches before I put my
shovel in and then packed it into the tub and back to the
house and stove air hot and steamy pink over the stove my
mother what did she need that water for I don't know but
where somewhere the snow smelled like coal or is it back in
Swift Current the cold so cold it smelled of cold I don't
remember maybe we had oil there we did later in Nelson

and I had to go out into the shed and pump a bucket of oil
from a 45-gallon drum for the stove in the living room but
the shed had a coal bin too coal for the stove in the kitchen
at night coal dust even later filling up Pearson's furnace
hopper every three days move it shovel full across the
basement the dust even later in the summer play anywhere
someone's coal bin settled into my nose and the oilyness of it
on the skin I rode down the hill outside the house on
Victoria on a coal shovel I hit a rock and had the wind
knocked out of me I was dying and couldn't even tell
anyone as they walked by but stood and waved my arms
and flailed the message without air

1981

FRANK
DAVEY

b. 1940

She'd Say

'I'll never reach 40,' my mother would say.
'I have a short life-line,' she'd say,
holding out her palm solemnly
& pointing. 'I went to a fortune-teller
before the war,' she'd say, 'at the Exhibition,
& she took one look at my hand & she gasped
& said "Oh my dear, I'm so sorry,
you shouldn't have come in here," & I said
"What is it, can't you tell me." & she said
"No, I can't bear to tell you,
oh you poor dear," she said,
& she threw her arms around me
& she hugged me just like that,' she'd say,
'& it was only later,' she'd say,
'that Genevieve told me about my life-line.'
'It was the same thing,' she'd say,

'with Dr. McCready, he'd be listening to my heart
& a sad look would come over his face,
& he'd put his arms around me & hold me tight
just for a minute, & afterward
he'd smile as if nothing had happened
& say I was okay, but I always knew
what he'd been thinking,' she'd say.
'I always knew,' she'd say.

'What will you do when I'm gone,' she'd say
when I brought a sock to be darned
or a book to be mended. Or to my dad
as she bustled around the kitchen,
'You're going to have to learn to cook
when I'm gone,' she'd say,
& when he growled 'Don't talk rubbish, honey,'
she'd say cheerily 'I know what you're thinking,
you're going to get yourself
a cute young floozie after I'm gone.'

'I nearly died when I had you,' she said.
'Dr. McCready didn't think I'd make it,' she said.
'He never said so but I could tell
by the way he looked at me,' she said.
'Look at my pot belly,' she said.
'That's what you did to me but it was worth it,'
she said. 'You were wanted,' she said.
'When I told Dr. McCready I was expecting
he put his arms around me & said
"Oh no, Jeannie, you're not,"
& he looked sadly out the window & then said

"Well, we'll do the best we can,
but you're not to have another, you hear,
you be a good girl now, & don't have another," '
& my father would sit silently
when she talked like this,
but sometimes she'd keep going & ask
why he had not yet bought their burial plot.
'You can put me wherever you want,' she'd say.
'You'll have someone else to go in your double plot,'
she'd say. 'She won't want me,' she'd say.
'She'll sure make you toe the line,' she'd say.

& when they argued, or when she & I argued,
'You can count on one thing,' she'd say,
'You won't have me around much longer,' she'd say.
'You'll be able to have your own way soon,' she'd say.
She'd hold out her palm & say 'It's right here,
you can look at it,' she'd say. 'The fortune teller
was really upset,' she'd say.
'She took me in her arms & said "You poor thing,"
& sobbed on my shoulder.' 'I'll never make 50,'
she'd say.

1980

The Piano

I sit on the edge
of the dining room, almost
in the living room where my parents,
my grandmother, & the visitors
sit knee to knee along the chesterfield & in
the easy chairs. The room is full, & my feet
do not touch the floor, barely
reach the rail across the front
of my seat. 'Of course
you will want Bobby to play.'—words
that jump out from the clatter
of teacups & illnesses. The piano
is huge, unforgettable.
it takes up the whole end wall
of the living room, faces me down
a short corridor of plump
knees, balanced saucers, hitched
trousers. 'Well when is
Bob going to play?'
one of them asks. My dad says,
'Come on, boy, they'd like you
to play for them,' & clears
a plate of cake
from the piano bench. I walk between
the knees & sit down

where the cake was, switch on
the fluorescent light
above the music. Right at the first notes
the conversation returns to long tales
of weddings, relatives bombed out again
in England, someone's mongoloid
baby. & there I am at the piano.
with no one listening or even
going to listen
unless I hit sour notes, or stumble
to a false ending.
I finish.
Instantly they are back to me. 'What a nice
touch he has,' someone interrupts
herself to say.
'It's the hands,' says another,
'It's always the hands, you can tell
by the hands,' & so I get up
& hide my fists
in my hands.

1980

GARY
GEDDES

b. 1940

Transubstantiation

The pig stands squarely
in the boarded stall, looking
stupid and out of his element.
My rope is tied in a slip-knot
around his thick neck.

My father asks
if I am ready.

                    The stall is
clean and smells of fresh straw.

Through the cracks blades of sunlight
carve the cool interior of the barn.

GARY
GEDDES

He puts the knife, freshly sharpened,
on a bale of hay at stall's end, opens
the breach of the gun, pushes in a shell
                              (a 22-long)
and closes the breach. He points the gun
at the pig's head and before cocking it
nestles the tip of the barrel
between the pig's eyes. I strain
at the rope as the pig backs off,
flat moist snout extended.

        He asks if
        I am ready.

                The report is loud
in the empty barn and wings begin to beat
overhead in the loft. The new straw
will come soon, to pad the thinning cushion,
and it will come with great excitement
and sneezing.

                Front legs stiffen,
he settles back on his haunches like
the dog at mealtimes. I slacken the rope.

He grabs the left ear
(no, the right) and with his other hand
takes up the knife. Thick well of blood
gushes from the stuck throat,
covers rope.

                It is hot
                and sticky.

I close my eyes and then nothing.
When I am awake again it is hanging
by its hind legs from the loft-pole.
I can see it from my window.
It has become meat.

1973

The Inheritors

GARY
GEDDES

i
They possessed nothing, the
bare essentials
            of land and sky.
When stocks fell their lot was
scant rations, hard looks;
their future, cold nights
and endless miles of track.
They saw mounted police
riding among the strikers
                        with clubs,
childhood friends interned
as communists and agitators,
a Chinaman, dead on his axe,
denied the decency of burial.

Still they hung on, enchanted
by legends, promise of prosperity,
remembered slick con men touring
the Highlands, the literature
of trade and immigration.

ii
We were their dreams,
their careful sand-castles,
must never come to rest
in shacks of tarpaper
and shingles, lie rusting
and abandoned in fields.

We were the inheritors, we
couldn't leave fast enough.

1973

DAVID
McFADDEN

b. 1940

House Plants

It has been a month since I gave up shaving
& already the houseplants are much more alert,
a pleasure to see such delicate strength—
it would be so easy to hurt their little stems
yet they stand so proud & fearless,
their leaves gently cocked
between the sun streaming through the windows
& that other sun streaming through my cloudy thoughts.

Of course when I think an unkind thought
the plants imperceptibly shudder
& when I open a can of pork & beans
or watch TV commercials
or smoke cigarettes
or holler at my wife
or contemplate suicide
the plants become aware of their perilous position
stranded on small islands of potted soil
in an ocean of human supremacy.

They know what a killer I am,
worse than the birds, insects, fungus & harsh weather
they'd be exposed to outside.
Being cut, smoked, trod on, eaten & tossed out
they can accept
& perhaps they know they can't really be killed
but it is much harder for them to accept
my boredom, my bombing of cities,
my incomprehensible evil,

& yet they are forgiving & spring to life
& they are so easily pleased
& even a simple thing like me forgoing
the daily torture of slicing off my facial hairs
has given them new hope,

& now the clouds have covered the sun
& the houseplants continue to shine.

1975

A Form of Passion

DAVID
McFADDEN

This is the form my passion takes.

On a train heading into the night
he sat beside me and spoke as if
he'd known me all my life
yet he was less than half my age.
He was as black as this ink,
his face as perfectly shaped
as one of Shakespeare's better sonnets
radiant with intelligence
and a youthful arrogance
that was not at all obnoxious.

I can't remember what he said
but only that I was swamped with love
for this strange young African
                   and with a feeling
he understood me more deeply than anyone
had ever understood anyone before
or ever would again,
               as if he had
tasted the marrow of my bones and
counted
       the hairs of my head.

I wanted to take him home.
I wanted to adopt him.

And suddenly I who had been suffering
from insomnia for years
fell asleep sitting up in the coach
as softly as a baby,
one moment intensely awake
and the next in the deepest sleep
and when I awoke it was dawn

and he was gone,
            disembarked
at some night-stop on the prairie.

And later, at noon, the train
heading through the northern forest,
a tall blond man appeared
carrying a strange white hat in his hand,
a hat glowing with a life of its own
and delicately marked in an unknown script.
And when he saw me admiring his hat
he said: 'Why are you staring like that?
You have one of your own just like it.
Why don't you ever wear it?'

He looked down at me with much sadness
as if he'd seen some glory in me that had long
been submerged in life's misery.

And when I told him I'd never seen a hat like that
and that I knew I certainly didn't own one
he insisted that I did.

And when I asked him where it was
he mumbled something about luggage
and then he disappeared.

Shaken, I knew I didn't have a hat like that
in my luggage or anywhere
I'd never seen one like it.

1978

DAVID
McFADDEN

Lennox Island

They're more beautiful than the angels of heaven
the beautiful Micmac children of Lennox Island
as all through the long summer they dive dive dive
off the dock into the warm waters of Malpeque Bay.
Sometimes they join hands and leap in en masse
then resurface with a gasp, dark hair streaming
and dark eyes flashing in the sun.
From early morning to early evening they dive,
careful to avoid the poisonous jellyfish
which they sometimes call bloodsuckers
and pick like giant mushrooms and flip onto the dock
to die, to fry in the hot sun like eggs,
the dock coated with fading remains
of the summer's harvest and stains
of previous summers.
                              It's hard to believe
there are children on earth more beautiful
than the beautiful Micmac children of Lennox Island,
aristocratic, oriental, magical and shining with joy.
As for me the water is too full of bloodsuckers
and the current too strong for me to swim
and I remain silent, strained, and wish I could vanish
for fear they'll flee or become somehow tainted
by my clumsy, poisonous presence
and so I strive to become relatively pure
and I invite life to flow through my body
as it flows through the bodies of these children
but I simply become more and more aware
of my powers of destruction and I quietly leave.

And I believe these children are my ancestors
and I believe these children populated the once-sacred earth
and I believe Lennox Island and across the bay
Bird Island, Hog Island, and maybe even part of the
Prince Edward Island mainland
is the birthplace of the human race
and I believe that since that glorious day
we've become more and more stupid in every way.

But I'm not about to immolate myself
because of the imminent death of an ancient race

DAVID
McFADDEN

and I'm thankful fate has given me a glimpse
of all this beauty before it's gone forever.
And on a hill overlooking the dock where the children play
is a curiously twisted hunk of metal.
It is a World War I cannon
that appears to have suffered a direct hit
and there is a plaque to the memory
of the nine Lennox Island men
who were killed in that horrible white man's war
that war that failed to destroy
that widely held belief in Caucasian superiority
except in the minds of non-Caucasians.

And standing quietly watching me
as I try to swallow my foolish tears
is a tall young man of pure African descent
who tells me he's a student from Calgary
who volunteered to spend the summer working
with the 200 Micmac residents of Lennox Island
and he tells me the Micmacs of Lennox Island
are a shy people who desire as little contact as possible
with white occupants of Prince Edward Island
but they're an industrious group of people
who are perhaps the world's best oyster farmers
and he predicted the beautiful children on the dock
would eventually leave Lennox Island
for Summerside, Charlottetown,
or maybe even Halifax or Moncton,
but they would return after a short time
disillusioned, sick in spirit
and spend the rest of their lives on Lennox Island.

1981

b. 1941

Manzini: Escape Artist

now there are no bonds except the flesh; listen—
there was this boy, Manzini, stubborn with
gut stood with black tights and a turquoise
leaf across his sex

and smirking while the big
brute tied his neck arms legs, Manzini
naked waist up and white with sweat

struggled. Silent, delinquent, he
was suddenly all teeth and knee, straining slack
and excellent with sweat, inwardly

wondering if Houdini would take as long
as he; fighting time and the drenched
muscular ropes, as though his tendons were worn
on the outside—

as though his own guts were the ropes
encircling him; it was beautiful; it was thursday; listen—
there was this boy, Manzini

finally free, slid as snake from
his own sweet agonized skin, to throw his entrails
white upon the floor
with a cry of victory—

now there are no bonds except the flesh,
but listen, it was thursday, there was this boy,
Manzini—

1968

A Breakfast for Barbarians

GWENDOLYN
MacEWEN

my friends, my sweet barbarians,
there is that hunger which is not for food—
but an eye at the navel turns the appetite
round
with visions of some fabulous sandwich,
the brain's golden breakfast
>   eaten with beasts
>   with books on plates

let us make an anthology of recipes,
let us edit for breakfast
our most unspeakable appetites—
let us pool spoons, knives
and all cutlery in a cosmic cuisine,
let us answer hunger
with boiled chimera
and apocalyptic tea,
an arcane salad of spiced bibles,
tossed dictionaries—
>   (O my barbarians
>   we will consume our mysteries)

and can we, can we slake the gaping eye of our desires?
we will sit around our hewn wood table
until our hair is long and our eyes are feeble,
eating, my people, O my insatiates,
eating until we are no more able
to jack up the jaws any longer—

to no more complain of the soul's vulgar cavities,
to gaze at each other over the rust-heap of cutlery,
drinking a coffee that takes an eternity—
till, bursting, bleary,
we laugh, barbarians, and rock the universe—
and exclaim to each other over the table
over the table of bones and scrap metal
over the gigantic junk-heaped table:

by God that was a meal

1968

The Thing Is Violent

GWENDOLYN
MacEWEN

Self, I want you now to be
violent and without history,
for we've rehearsed too long our ceremonial ballet
and I fear my calm against your exquisite rage.

I do not fear that I will go mad
but that I may not, and the shadows of my sanity
blacken out your burning; act once
and you need not act again—
give me no ceremony, scars are not pain.

The thing is violent, nothing precedes it,
it has no meaning before or after—
sweet wounds which burn like stars,
stigmata of the self's own holiness,
appear and plot new zodiacs upon the flesh.

1968

The Discovery

do not imagine that the exploration
ends, that she has yielded all her mystery
or that the map you hold
cancels further discovery

I tell you her uncovering takes years,
takes centuries, and when you find her naked
look again,
admit there is something else you cannot name,
a veil, a coating just above the flesh
which you cannot remove by your mere wish

when you see the land naked, look again
(burn your maps, that is not what I mean),
I mean the moment when it seems most plain
is the moment when you must begin again

1969

Dark Pines Under Water

GWENDOLYN
MacEWEN

This land like a mirror turns you inward
And you become a forest in a furtive lake;
The dark pines of your mind reach downward,
You dream in the green of your time,
Your memory is a row of sinking pines.

Explorer, you tell yourself this is not what you came for
Although it is good here, and green;
You had meant to move with a kind of largeness,
You had planned a heavy grace, an anguished dream.

But the dark pines of your mind dip deeper
And you are sinking, sinking, sleeper
In an elementary world;
There is something down there and you want it told.

1969

From THE T. E. LAWRENCE POEMS

The Void

The last truly foolish thing I did was some years ago
When I flew the Hejaz flag from the pinnacle of All Souls;
I knew then that I was becoming an aging schoolboy,
  a master-prig with an ego as big
  as an ostrich egg. A pity,
  for I was still young.

Now I'm gray-haired, half-blind, and shaking at the knees;
There's something almost obscene about the few gold teeth
  I got in nineteen-thirty. What
  have I done, what am I doing, what
  am I going to do?
Days seem to dawn, suns to shine, evenings to follow.
I have burned all my bridges behind me; this is high, dry
  land.

I'm going around shooting the same camel in the head
Over and over; I'm a pilgrim forever circling the Kaaba,
   which has none of its sides or angles equal,
   for whatever that's worth.
Have you ever been a leaf, and fallen from your tree
   in Autumn? It's like that.

Poets put things like shirt-sleeves or oysters
Into their poems, to prevent you from laughing at them
   before they have laughed at themselves.
   I have put an ostrich egg in this one
   to amuse you. I have already laughed.

Where are my noble brothers, my bodyguards, my friends,
Those slender camelmen who rode with me to the ends
   of the desert? When does the great dream end?
   With my right wrist recently broken,
   I write this sad, left-handed poem.

1982

There Is No Place to Hide

Here is a famous world; I'm standing on a stage
With ten spotlights on me, talking about how I detest
   publicity. I stand there like an ass,
   apologizing for having a past, a soul,
   a name (which one?), and then
   back shyly into the limelight.

No. What I'm really doing is standing in an unlit room
Holding a court martial upon myself. Shaw tells me
   that to live under a cloud
   is to defame God. I can neither reveal myself
   nor hide. No matter what I do, I am naked.
I can clothe myself in silk or chain mail, and I
   am naked; everything shows through
   and yet no one can see me.

Can you imagine that posterity will call me wonderful
        on the basis of a few pencil sketches,
        a revolt in the desert,
        and my irresistibly foul soul?
Outside my window, a small tit bird bashes itself
        against the glass. At first I thought
        it was admiring itself in the window.
        Now I know it's mad.

GWENDOLYN
MacEWEN

1982

DON
McKAY

b. 1942

A Barbed Wire Fence
Meditates Upon the Goldfinch

More than the shortest distance
between points, we are
the Stradivarius of work.
We make the meadow meadow, make it
mean, make it yours, but till the last
insurance policy is cashed in we will
never be immune to this
exquisite cruelty:
                that the knots in all our posts remember limbs
they nested and were busy in and danced *per-*
chic-o-ree their loops between,
that the fury of their playfulness persists
in amputated roots.
Remember us
next time the little yellow bastards lilt
across your windshield. No one
no one is above the law.

1980

I Scream You Scream

DON
McKAY

Waking JESUS sudden riding a scream like a
train braking metal on metal on
metal teeth receiving signals from a dying star sparking
off involuntarily in terror in all directions in the
abstract incognito in my
maidenform bra in an expanding universe in a where's
my syntax thrashing
loose like a grab that like a
look out like a
live wire in a hurricane until

until I finally tie it down:
it is a pig scream
a pig scream from the farm across the road
that tears this throat of noise into the otherwise anonymous dark,
a noise not oink or grunt
but a passage blasted through constricted pipes, perhaps
a preview of the pig's last noise.

Gathering again toward sleep I sense
earth's claim on the pig.
Pig grew, polyped out on the earth like a boil
and broke away.
            But earth
heals all flesh back beginning with her pig,
filling his throat with silt and sending
subtle fingers for him like the meshing fibres in a wound
like roots
like grass growing on a grave, like a snooze
in the sun like furlined boots that seize
the feet like his *nostalgie de la boue* like
having another glass of booze like a necktie like a
velvet noose like a nurse

like sleep.

1980

March Snow

DON
McKAY

The snow is sick. The pure
page breaks and greys and
drools around the edges, sucks
at my snowshoe every heavy step saying
fuck it, just
fuck it, softly to itself.

It fails the toothpaste test.
In fact, it makes me think of dentists
frowning, the sag along the jawline as he
hmm as he
mutters something to his nurse
whose complexion's turned to cottage cheese
from too much Harlequin Romance.

So is it possible to
fix a person to her place, to pin her
like a name tag to her
self.
I missed
the atomic fission of her yearning till I looked back

bang into a fiery lake: the snow
suicidal with desire, wearing
his image like a poster of the movie star
she dies to be   the sun
simmering in her flesh her
nerves her burning
bedroom eyes

too bright for mine.
Beside the house scared earth emerges
frawny with sleep, imagines
the atrocity of tulips thrusting up
dog-penis red and raw.

1980

b. 1942

From STEVESTON

Imagine: A Town

Imagine a town running
                              (smoothly?
a town running before a fire
canneries burning

                    (do you see the shadow of charred stilts
on cool water? do you see enigmatic chance standing
just under the beam?

                         He said they were playing cards in the
Chinese mess hall, he said it was dark (a hall? a shack.
they were all, crowded together on top of each other.
He said somebody accidentally knocked the oil lamp over, off
the edge

          where stilts are standing, Over the edge of the
dyke a river pours, uncalled for, unending:

                                   where chance lurks
fishlike, shadows the underside of pilings, calling up his hall
the bodies of men & fish corpse piled on top of each other (residue
time is, the delta) rot, an endless waste the trucks of production
grind to juice, driving through

                         smears, blood smears in the dark
dirt) this marshland silt no graveyard can exist in but water swills,
endless out of itself to the mouth

                              ringed with residue, where
chance flicks his tail & swims, through.

1975

Femina

DAPHNE
MARLATT

you who
      fail,
           subtly seeking, with your face
angled downward to the floor, to cups, to broom
slivers in the cracks, to sea below, to the
hands & feet of people walking in proximity to you.
Who wait, up in your room that sideways to the
street holds certain figures in a gloom.

When the whiteness of light casts its sheen over
your face, you sit reading. & your eyes seem closed
in their downward looking, in the electric
enumeration of eyes of strangers reading you.
& bed posts, glutted with the heads of fishing
corks, which you, as yet, can still hold onto.

All
   evening
         air slowly darkened round the windows
you were caught in, rings, on a glass jar. Coherent
images of light fisted into themselves after the
bulb had gone, just out . . . (*then* the rock cod
drift up thru blankets of the sea to reach you . . .

They flung the door open onto the city. You saw
her framed: her long. bream. skirt. ankle-tied,
heels poised on your fire-escape. The precision of
those heels. Paused, in third position, knees bent,
one fishy sleeve out, to the door . . .

                    O the fabulous
laugh of the sea trapt in a jar (o the tearing of
water.

    You are there
          bristles of the broom are there

The bones of your face are pinned with autographs.

1975

b. 1942

The Snake

1

his green eyes on the homestead of another man
he is not man enough to find his own—
he and his wife form a plan

they move in with an old timer and she cooks
and washes all the clothes
(later attends to sexual needs of both men
the old timer believing: *heaven could never be this good*)

several months later he gratefully transfers his land title
to their name
and the simple heaven continues several more weeks
till he is given the boot—
the story being: *the couple no longer needs a hired man*

thus the homestead is attained

2

they raise wheat pigs potatoes and a son as hopelessly
homely as his old man

to the bewilderment of all the neighbours
the son marries the most beautiful farm girl around—
following the reception and wedding dance
the son's father sleeps with the bride
and later says: *my boy didn't marry her for love
he married her because he couldn't find a hired man*

the old man continues sleeping with her
delighting in her youth and softness
and occasionally treats her to her own husband

she endures this for three weeks
before running away
forever

1976

Chinese Camp, Kamloops (circa 1883)

ANDREW
SUKNASKI

in the photograph he stands alone
under a willow
before the small tent
the shadows are long
likely an evening in early july
his left foot is extended slightly
beyond the other
on the edge of his shadow
at the base of the tree
two washbasins lean perfectly
against one another
like two coins in a child's hand
his clothes are baggy
his arms are flexed
you would like to be romantic
and believe he is reading
a letter from his parents back home
or a letter from some young lady
he possibly dreaming of her small delicate hands
tiny feet
and body smooth and soft as silk
exactly the way it was supposed to be
if your family were rich
and you were a girl
growing skilful at some craft
you constantly sitting
to ease the pain from tiedup feet
knowing the suitors and matchmakers
would always ask
'let see feet . . . how small?'
the oriental myth
the smaller the feet
the softer the body
but no . . . if this young man had a sweetheart
she was likely poor
and walked to work
like the rest of the family
simply surviving
her feet growing naturally . . .
looking closer at the photograph

you become realistic
and realize . . . no
there are no letters for this lonely man
he is only rolling
a cigarette

2
in the second photograph
his two friends
standing ten feet apart
actually pose:
one smiling
and revealing
a missing tooth
. . . the other
an unusually tall man
looking
almost stately
a stern face
that might have been
the face of an emperor
behind them
a simple table
and two stools
in the shade
of a tree

3
by the third photograph
oriental clothes have been worn out
it's likely another summer
the men are wearing cowboy hats
and pointed riding boots
the new clothes fit more snugly
across angular bodies seeming thinner
and solid
as anvils

1978

b. 1942

Portrait

She slipped. Heels over head she landed
in a bucket of blue paint. Fluent as blue,
the day was green—magnificent. How
describe the green after an accident?

That's twice you've rescued me, she said,
bearing a resemblance to a shaky Rembrandt.
I dried her off and she broke into tears,
deftly combing strands of hair in place.

The other rescue was scientific. She
could only see people blurred, a distinction
allowed those with the green eyes of photo-
synthesis in their brains.

Trees also have this problem, I pointed
out, and she laughed hysterically, my sister,
while grandmother politely shuffled
cards and waited to deal them out.

Later I found such advice strangely terrible,
my cat suddenly malevolent around my
beautiful and suddenly ripped to pieces
skirt, my sister, crazy.

And all my teeth ground to little bits
in my pitch and feverish sleep; my sister,
my metaphor for intensity and parlour games,
smashed between two cars at midnight.

1980

'It is her cousin's death . . .'

It is her cousin's death that
she must write about. Dead leaves
on the hanging plant, the window
a container of dead light. Crackle
of leaves, she plucks them off
and throws them to the floor. Falling,
they snap like a synapse in the brain,
a dislocation of the fire to make
a thought.

Night. She sighs and washes the
remaining leaves with wet, kicks the
dead leaves in a pile, looks at her lover
puzzled, then smiles, and pulls off
leaves she's missed.

The kitchen rocks. Her lover's rocking as the
water fills the bottle once again and
washes over the bright red leaves of the
wandering jew. She is everywhere at once, the
darkness is a death, and she must write of
death after tending the dying plant.

'Dear Don,' she will say to the husband
of the deceased; and then she will
pause and stare off at a window where
the dead light gathers behind a dying
plant she watered just now while struggling
for the words to write.

1980

'She lay wrapped . . .'

She lay wrapped in the
tangle of bedclothes around
her lover. He was kissing her
breast, sun falling on her
cries, small birds flying past
the window.

She closed her eyes and let
the pleasure rush from her
stomach, her legs felt like
solid energy. No—not energy,
like an intense conversation
about jealousy.

Why did her lover know
so many people? Why was he
such a friendly person? 'You're mine,'
she said, fiercely to the large
angelic flesh beside her.

1980

PAULETTE
JILES

b. 1943

The Tin Woodsman

This is Hill 49, an arena for bad dreams.
The wind is flaying this ridge to the bone,
peeling up membrane after membrane
of snow from the rocks.
A prismatic ring in the sky
wears the moon like a monocle.

I wonder what it's like under
that mild counterpane
where the low degrees that signify
       NO HEAT
would agree with my metal lips and cheeks
that clang together
and betray me when I speak?

I am not a tone or note;
I harmonize nowhere.
The creaks, the shrieks of alloys upon alloys

are my joints of knees and pelvis
moving in groups
the stiff, sequential troops of rivets.
I'm held up by an armature of nerves,
for which I take pills.
Mechanics come along and tender to my ills
with oilcans and greaseguns.
My eyes are red and full of thumbs.
This is sleep falling on me; snow—
it constitutes a resolution.

And now, Dorothy, they are coming up the hill.
If, like a shotgun, I blew my brains out,
how many could we kill?
Tough luck for you, you pink thing,
all full of corpuscles and organs.
The shotgun hollers in a big balloon of sound
goodbye, goodbye.
Rusting is painless.
I will settle
in the shadow of this red rock
and be metal.

1973

Paper Matches

My aunts washed dishes while the uncles
squirted each other on the lawn with
garden hoses. Why are we in here,
I said, and they are out there.
That's the way it is,
said Aunt Hetty, the shrivelled–up one.

I have the rages that small animals have,
being small, being animal.
Written on me was a message,
'At Your Service' like a book of
paper matches. One by one we were
taken out and struck.
We come bearing supper,
our heads on fire.

Time to Myself

PAULETTE
JILES

It takes time to make
yourself a stranger.

I go through town unknowing
all the people I have met.

Hands unshake themselves, glances
miss each other,
          I take back reams of words.

Conversations run backwards,
     disappearing into my mouth.

Sentences are tape measures rolled up,
     they snap sharply when
the last word slides in.

I roll up the road to my cabin;
this is true decampment.

Then silence walks by with
blessing-gestures;

bless the outhouse, the
junked taxi, the tripole fish-rack,

bless the table and the can of Pepsi.
Bless the pine outside my window bless
the stranger in my midst.

Windigo

No one understands the Windigo, his voice like
the white light of hydrogen, only long.
Some say he carries his head under his arm, for
others it is the race down to the rapids
where the canoes draw close, close to the shore
and he jumps in. You have time for a few last words.

Under the moon he turns pearl grey, the
head chatters amiably about meals. He is the
Hungry Man, the one who reached this wasteland of
the soul and did not emerge. Not whole. Not as you
would recognize wholeness.

Sometimes he wants to be killed, putting his
heart or what there is of it in the way of arrows,
bullets, he wants his soul or what there is of it
to spring heavenward to the village where people
begin again, he too
wants to cross the bridge.
His story is of one who reached starvation
and death and did not make it through, not
as you would recognize making it.
People shoot the Windigo, they
do not pray for him, or it.

MICHAEL
ONDAATJE

b. 1943

Burning Hills

For Kris and Fred

So he came to write again
in the burnt hill region
north of Kingston. A cabin
with mildew spreading down walls.
Bullfrogs on either side of him.

Hanging his lantern of Shell Vapona Strip
on a hook in the centre of the room
he waited a long time. Opened
the Hilroy writing pad, yellow Bic pen.
Every summer he believed would be his last.
This schizophrenic season change, June to September,

when he deviously thought out plots
across the character of his friends.
Sometimes barren as fear going nowhere
or in habit meaningless as tapwater.
One year maybe he would come and sit
for 4 months and not write a word down
would sit and investigate colours, the
insects in the room with him.
What he brought: a typewriter
tins of ginger ale, cigarettes. A copy of *StrangeLove*,
of *The Intervals*, a postcard of Rousseau's *The Dream*.
His friends' words were strict as lightning
unclothing the bark of a tree, a shaved hook.
The postcard was a test pattern by the window
through which he saw growing scenery.
Also a map of a city in 1900.

Eventually the room was a time machine for him.
He closed the rotting door, sat down
thought pieces of history. The first girl
who in a park near his school
put a warm hand into his trousers
unbuttoning and finally catching the spill
across her wrist, he in the maze of her skirt.
She later played the piano
when he had tea with the parents.
He remembered that surprised—
he had forgotten for so long.
Under raincoats in the park on hot days.

The summers were layers of civilisation in his memory
they were old photographs he didn't look at anymore
for girls in them were chubby not as perfect as in his mind
and his ungovernable hair was shaved to the edge of skin.
His friends leaned on bicycles
were 16 and tried to look 21
the cigarettes too big for their faces.
He could read those characters easily
undisguised as wedding pictures.
He could hardly remember their names
though they had talked all day, exchanged styles
and like dogs on a lawn hung around the houses of girls
waiting for night and devious sex-games with their simple plots.

Sex a game of targets, of throwing firecrackers   MICHAEL
ONDAATJE
at a couple in a field locked in hand-made orgasms,
singing dramatically in someone's ear along with the record
'How do you think I feel / you know our love's not real
The one you're mad about / Is just a gad-about
How do you think I feel'
He saw all that complex tension the way his children would.

There is one picture that fuses the 5 summers.
Eight of them are leaning against a wall
arms around each other
looking into the camera and the sun
trying to smile at the unseen adult photographer
trying against the glare to look 21 and confident.
The summer and friendship will last forever.
Except one who was eating an apple. That was him
oblivious to the significance of the moment.
Now he hungers to have that arm around the next shoulder.
The wretched apple is fresh and white.

Since he began burning hills
the Shell strip has taken effect.
A wasp is crawling on the floor
tumbling over, its motor fanatic.
He has smoked 5 cigarettes.
He has written slowly and carefully
with great love and great coldness.
When he finishes he will go back
hunting for the lies that are obvious.

1973

Letters & Other Worlds

'for there was no more darkness for him and, no doubt like
Adam before the fall, he could see in the dark'

> My father's body was a globe of fear
> His body was a town we never knew
> He hid that he had been where we were going
> His letters were a room he seldom lived in
> In them the logic of his love could grow

My father's body was a town of fear   MICHAEL
He was the only witness to its fear dance   ONDAATJE
He hid where he had been that we might lose him
His letters were a room his body scared

He came to death with his mind drowning.
On the last day he enclosed himself
in a room with two bottles of gin, later
fell the length of his body
so that brain blood moved
to new compartments
that never knew the wash of fluid
and he died in minutes of a new equilibrium.

His early life was a terrifying comedy
and my mother divorced him again and again.
He would rush into tunnels magnetized
by the white eye of trains
and once, gaining instant fame,
managed to stop a Perahara in Ceylon
—the whole procession of elephants dancers
local dignitaries—by falling
dead drunk onto the street.
As a semi-official, and semi-white at that,
the act was seen as a crucial
turning point in the Home Rule Movement
and led to Ceylon's independence in 1948.

(My mother had done her share too—
her driving so bad
she was stoned by villagers
whenever her car was recognized)

For 14 years of marriage
each of them claimed he or she
was the injured party.
Once on the Colombo docks
saying goodbye to a recently married couple
my father, jealous
at my mother's articulate emotion,
dove into the waters of the harbour
and swam after the ship waving farewell.
My mother pretending no affiliation
mingled with the crowd back to the hotel.

Once again he made the papers

though this time my mother
with a note to the editor
corrected the report—saying he was drunk
rather than broken hearted at the parting of friends.
The married couple received both editions
of *The Ceylon Times* when their ship reached Aden.
And then in his last years
he was the silent drinker
the man who once a week
disappeared into his room with bottles
and stayed there until he was drunk
and until he was sober.

There speeches, head dreams, apologies,
the gentle letters, were composed.
With the clarity of architects
he would write of the row of blue flowers
his new wife had planted,
the plans for electricity on the house,
how my half-sister fell near a snake
and it had awakened and not touched her.
Letters in a clear hand of the most complete empathy
his heart widening and widening and widening
to all manner of change in his children and friends
while he himself edged
into the terrible acute hatred
of his own privacy
till he balanced and fell
the length of his body
the blood screaming in
the empty reservoir of bones
the blood searching in his head without metaphor

1973

Breaking Green

MICHAEL
ONDAATJE

Yesterday a Euclid took trees. Bright green
it beat at one till roots tilted
once more, machine in reverse, back ten yards
then forward and tore it off.
The Euclid moved away with it
returned, lifted ground
and levelled the remaining hollow.

And so earth was fresh, dark
a thick smell rising
where the snake lay.
The head grazed ribbon rich
eyes bright as gas.

The Euclid throttled and moved over the snake.
We watched blades dig in skin
and laughed, nothing had happened,
it continued to move bright at our boots.

The machine turned, tilted blade
used it as a spade
jerking onto the snake's back.
It slid away.
                The driver angry then
jumped from the seat and caught the slither
head hooking round to snap his hand
but the snake was being swung already.

It was flying head out fast
as propellers forming green daze
a green gauze through which we saw the man
smile a grimace of pain as his arm tired
snake hurling round and round mouth arched open
till he turned and intercepted
the head with the Euclid blade.

Then he held the neck in his fist
brought his face close
to look at the crashed head
the staring eyes the same
all but the lower teeth
now locked in the skull.

The head was narrower now.
He blocked our looks at it.
The death was his. He
folded the scarless body
and tossed it like a river into the grass.

MICHAEL
ONDAATJE

1973

Walking to Bellrock

Two figures in deep water.

Their frames truncated at the stomach
glide along the surface. Depot Creek.
One hundred years ago lumber being driven down this river
tore and shovelled and widened the banks into Bellrock
down past bridges to the mill.

The two figures are walking
as if half sunk in a grey road
their feet tentative, stumbling on stone bottom.
Landscapes underwater. What do the feet miss?
Turtle, watersnake, clam. What do the feet ignore
and the brain not look at, as two figures slide
past George Grant's green immaculate fields
past the splashed blood of cardinal flower on the bank.

Rivers are a place for philosophy but all thought
is about the mechanics of this river is about
stones that twist your ankles
the hidden rocks you walk your knee into—
feet in slow motion and brain and balanced arms
imagining the blind path of foot, underwater sun
suddenly catching the almond coloured legs
the torn old Adidas tennis shoes we wear
to walk the river into Bellrock.

What is the conversation about for three hours
on this winding twisted evasive river to town?
What was the conversation about all summer.

Stan and I laughing joking going summer crazy MICHAEL
ONDAATJEas we lived against each other.
To keep warm we submerge. Sometimes
just our heads decapitated
glide on the dark glass.

There is no metaphor here.
We are aware of the heat of the water, coldness of the rain,
smell of mud in certain sections that farts
when you step on it, mud never walked on
so you can't breathe, my god you can't breathe this air
and you swim fast your feet off the silt of history
that was there when the logs went
leaping down for the Rathburn Timber Company 1840-1895
when those who stole logs had to leap
right out of the country if caught.

But there is no history or philosophy or metaphor with us.
The problem is the toughness of the Adidas shoe
its three stripes gleaming like fish decoration.
The story is Russell's arm waving out of the green of a field.

The plot of the afternoon is to get to Bellrock
through rapids, falls, stink water
and reach the island where beer and a towel wait for us.
That night there is not even pain in our newly used muscles
not even the puckering of flesh
and little to tell except you won't
believe how that river winds and when you
don't see the feet you concentrate on the feet.
And all the next day trying to think
what we didn't talk about.
Where was the criminal conversation
broken sentences lost in the splash in wind.

Stan, my crazy summer friend,
why are we both going crazy?
Going down to Bellrock
recognizing home by the colour of barns
which tell us north, south, west,
and otherwise lost in miles and miles of rain
in the middle of this century
1979   following the easy fucking stupid plot to town.

The Cinnamon Peeler

MICHAEL
ONDAATJE

If I were a cinnamon peeler
I would ride your bed
and leave the yellow bark dust
on your pillow.

Your breasts and shoulders would reek
you could never walk through markets
without the profession of my fingers
floating over you. The blind would
stumble certain of whom they approached
though you might bathe
under rain gutters, monsoon.

Here on the upper thigh
at this smooth pasture
neighbour to your hair
or the crease
that cuts your back. This ankle.
You will be known among strangers
as the cinnamon peeler's wife.

I could hardly glance at you
before marriage
never touch you
—your keen nosed mother, your rough brothers.
I buried my hands
in saffron, disguised them
over smoking tar,
helped the honey gatherers . . .

*

When we swam once
I touched you in water
and our bodies remained free,
you could hold me and be blind of smell.
You climbed the bank and said

this is how you touch other women
the grass cutter's wife, the lime burner's daughter.
And you searched your arms
for the missing perfume

MICHAEL
ONDAATJE

what good is it
to be the lime burner's daughter
left with no trace
as if not spoken to in the act of love
as if wounded without the pleasure of a scar.

You touched
your belly to my hands
in the dry air and said
I am the cinnamon
peeler's wife. Smell me.

1981

VICTOR
COLEMAN

b. 1944

How the Death of a City Is Never More Than the Sum of the Deaths of Those Who Inhabit Its Spaces

A town might abort
in its early stages
as a woman, the weight
carried with difficulty
to & fro in the earth
her body is;
            no longer life
a cancer eats away,

the sac,
undeveloped to its fullest,
breaks simply
and the embryo pushes
the blood it's lived in, breathed,
before;
            travels the passage

as dead
weight,
          beyond
the cervix out
a usual waste
passage: a reverse
fuck

until it came
to me the child
was in it un-
formed of body,
or mind, but child,
insistent ex-
tension of her-
self/myself

              part
of our activity,
part discourse in
the going to
& fro the fore-
skin makes
              had much
to do with
the realisation
of its cells.

          This:
what frightened me;
that I had seen fit
not to recognize
the existence of
what is not *truly*
formed, or formed
by me as
completed activity;

a return, some
horrible payment
I would ask of this dead child
I haven't seen;

                    she
flushed it down the toilet saying
she thought 'it'
looked like a boy;
I pictured it with cock
& balls that weighed on me for days.

1967

Day Twenty-three

> Feel, perceive, notice, suspect;
> be conscious of; be sensible of (to);
> be alive to.
>
> be sensible of kindness.
> be alive to the sense of honour.
> be sensible to shame.
>
> Did you feel the earthquake last night?

1
The ground beneath my feet is cracked . the world
opens to this sense of wracked pain I have.

As the forms land takes
in its perception;
                    ice against
rock to make terminal moraine;
                              this lake
a real idea the land had, has;
I was swimming many years ago
in one that turned me under
took my breath away
a hand across my breathing.

Or the wind dead in the sails of our dinghy
like a mistake we didn't make
to go out on this water,
venture such a calm.

The land knows no day
its time is as the flight
the migrant makes away
from winter into spring,
or the bear holed up
not to freeze his ass in our weather.

2

If the earth breaks up beneath our feet
it is because we will it so, as nature
& light will disease on us.

A man, unable to cope with his own movement
who lies down in disease, so that it might
pass through him as earth through a worm
or water in a river changing what it passes.

What we know is the river
that passes through imagination
eroding what concepts we've no defense for.

I stand a cracked man on a cracked earth
earth into the space that is earth.

1967

BRIAN
FAWCETT

b. 1944

The Hand

Trees,
and the wind,
the moon rising
out of the southwest over the calm lagoon
like a Joseph Conrad story
nightbirds and all that

the traditional things of poetry
at hand.

But the pleasure of it
trickles through my hands,
the old Sense of Beauty
is now perverse, underneath the old delight
a faint stench carries on the wind.

BRIAN
FAWCETT

Conrad's tropic palms are common fir in shadow
are rooted in a dark
that whispers now, like Beauty
and the things we live with every day and take for granted
are rooted in the degradation of the planet
the misery of millions of human beings.

In the mostly private tangle of poetic truth
to force the appearance of the shadows
to slime the Beautiful with facts
like those of the systematic murder in the Congo
of as many as 25 million people
between 1890 and 1910:

facts not secondary to
nor separate from
the leisure to write poems
or watch the moonrise on a summer's evening

the amber wings of a butterfly
my son rescued from a tangle of weeds this afternoon
proudly cupped to show me
in his two small hands.

For him if nothing else
I want to evoke factual disturbances
in the act of thinking and writing
until what I've learned as Beauty
becomes accountable to
the terrible facts of the world

or if those facts are to be partitioned
from the concerns of Art
then Art must be recognized and condemned
as at least an accomplice
in the maintenance of the conditions
that make misery and violence
the dominant experience of most lives.

I want to learn
to turn my hand against mere Beauty
until such facts are a bad memory
unthinkable in the acts of living men and women.

I told my son to let the butterfly go
that it has a message to deliver
in the several days of life it has

that this is no world
to make such beauty captive.

He opens his hands to let it go
it spills out into the weeds once more but then
flits up, takes flight.   See?

I let that story exist
no longer an isolated event of poesy
removed from the 25 million africans
murdered in the economic service of what was set up
by the European powers and the U.S.
as a 'Free State'
under the sadistic control of Leopold II of Belgium
who used the proceeds
to buy the finest art of Europe
repatriating the Flemish Masters
and filling the museums
any number of us
have wandered through in awe.

As the shadows descend across the lagoon
the T.V. news offers footage of another war in Africa
seems genuinely puzzled at the african hatred
of everything we are.

Our best writers casually estimated the Congo death toll
between 10 and 40 million people
uninterested in a variance of 30 million lives
more interested, as poets too often are
in catchy metaphors about
a once dark continent on fire

as if an artful phrase explains away

the unburied bones piled up in every Congo village
explains administrative massacres:
the documented practice of making the congo constabulary
account for bullets used
with severed human hands
meaning not only brutal death for thousands
but should a soldier go hunting for food
and miss his quarry six times
six right hands
usually of women and children
a few of whom survived to be photographed

And now those photographs stand
alongside the beautiful reproductions
of Renoir's rosycheeked children
or the works of the Flemish Masters crowding the walls
of Brussels' galleries.

In this splendid northern dusk
longshoremen unload wine and fruit
from South Africa and Chile

The full moon peaks too early
doesn't want to crown this sky with light.
What lies do the nightbirds sing for us, do
we hear what they really have to tell us?
What matter that butterflies drift across
the moon's slow descent?

Who captains this craft
across the nightmare Beauty hides?

What should I do
with these hands?

CHARLES
LILLARD

b. 1944

Bushed

This morning we found him
    mumbling and eating bushes
        so we tied him to a tree.

He didn't even notice us
    sitting there watching him;
        his mind was elsewhere

and you can be damn sure
    it wasn't raining there
        and the no-see-ums don't thump

as they land on his hard hat.
    In the late afternoon the Otter
        dropped down through the overhead.

He was calm as piss in a bowl
    as we loaded him aboard the plane,
        he even asked us to *drop me a line*.

That was almost two months ago.
    Here on a log, writing this
        I know he's cured, that he's

back with his family
    and looking for work.
        Knowing this doesn't help

doesn't alter that final moment
    when he asked for *some bushes*
        something to nibble, I've got

a long way to go, boys.
    And there he sits, next
        to the pilot, his arms full

of bushes, his eyes moving
        from nowhere to nowhere across
                our faces that lonely stunned look.

1973

Lobo

I could kill you right now.

Your grey brown hunch
nestles into the crotch of this buckhorn
sight; standing still—
long-legged, mangy,
teeth bared to a wind
filled with hunter and horse;
hell, I could blow you into next month.

Cheena curls into the hollow
of my arm; she's
watching you, too; laughing
in her own slow way,
'cause you've lost, Lobo.
She adapted, you went strange.
Now
you're the one filling my sights.

And I am of two minds

to pull this trigger
or raise the barrel,
lever all seven bullets
skyward
and rip the silver lining
from that cloud?

If so,
and I am of this mind,

this wolf will disappear
into the birch . . .

Damn it,
I'm tired of disappearances.
He's done it too many times;
it's always the same story:
the wolf running from the man,
crossing a meadow
to disappear into the jack pine brake,
and the myth of ferocity,
as though
man needed to be afraid of
something.

I would have it otherwise.

Like this:
his nerves should quicken,
wound tight,
tighter
until spastic as the spring
of a two-dollar watch
he would rise above his story;
uncoiled from the shackles of fear,
I could never hit him;
not in this brush,
him moving,
my eyes lost and ears
full of blood.

Now
his teeth girdling my arm,
now the spine-jarring rip
of cloth
now flesh
now the thought that this . . .
this coat was . . .
this was a . . .

But it won't end this way.
He won't lunge, suddenly full of
legend,

legendary,
larger than life
and smarter than all the dogs
sired north of the railhead.

And it won't end,
for your sake or the poem's,
with me squeezing the trigger.
His head rises, leaves
the sight's wrath, and
turns to a bitch trotting
across the meadow.

You aren't the last one, Lobo.
You're not *the* survivor.

1976

BARRY
McKINNON

b. 1944

The North

> the worse it gets, the better—KEN BELFORD

somebodies walked the woods

                    *

in the air, the lines appear, as a grid
cut thru trees

possession is nine tenths of the law
theft makes up the rest

what men have walked these
woods, carried chains
& instruments
            of exactitude

BARRY
McKINNON

to own nothing becomes
achievement

a kind of ownership
not to care

1980

Bushed

I am in a desert
of snow.   each way
to go, presents an equal
choice, since the directions, &
what the eye see's is the same

if there were some sticks, you wld
stay & build a house, or
a tree wld give a place to climb
for perspective.   if you had a match, when
the wind didn't blow, you
wld burn the tree for warmth, if
the wind didn't blow & you had a match

there is this situation where love
wld mean nothing.   the sky is
possibly beautiful, yet the speculation
is impossible, & if you could sing, the song
is all that wld go

anywhere

1980

SID
MARTY

b. 1944

In the Dome Car of the 'Canadian'

The mongoloid boy is astounded
with joy at terrific
white-fanged mountains

The shining makes him cry aloud

Tunnels through stone to him
are mysteries, are happy as the womb
And equally happy to him alone
embraced by folly's equanimity
was his birth in this bright world

He claps his hand over his mouth
and moans with ecstasy
to be swallowed whole again
then borne into the glimmering light

These boats along the Fraser
trailing their glistening sweepers
of logs along the river
are arks of all creation
rocking on the dappled water

Oh passengers, you travellers
may strain your eyes to blindness
but never again you'll see
what he is seeing

As he dances in the aisles, for joy

1981

b. 1944

Roots

—Holy man, ungird your gaberdeen. Rest. Tell us of those days when you sat next to the Sattàn, and each of you stroked the other's beard.

—The other . . . as a brother. Do not hate him. Take him unto you as your own. Many times he let see my face in his eyes.

—O Zaddik, will we all get to see this manshape? How many ladders must we trip on, how many bruises as we cling to the slippery rungs?

—Hold to your young bones, my young scholars. Youth may be crowned—with the same black skullcaps, and married women with others' hair. But he and I clenched the other's hair. And pulled out the thoughts by the light roots.

The Zaddik undid his phylacteries, folded away his smooth faded prayershawl, blessed his bread, his morning drink.— Next year I see you all again!

Now, with the deep fall, the season of the festival of Sukkot, the frail tabernacles trembled beside our ramshackle homes. When we returned after morning prayers, remembering that dark figure at the horizon on the muddy road, we wondered how long the threequarter filled sacks would last. Some potatoes must have shrivelled. And already begun to grow pale green roots.

1970

Before Passover

SEYMOUR
MAYNE

Before Passover there in the old flat
who searched at the underside of curtains,
spiders' dust, for the crumbs of final dinners?

Rummaging for bread in 1919
grandmother gave up on fresh compost heaps,
found instead sweetgrass
roots to feed her brood.

Later in the bustling capital the refugees
found others even trying
to cheat them of the price of passage.

'In Canada bread grows on trees—'
the children fed their big eyes and ears—
'In Canada one merely picks them for the eating!'

Early winter nights later in Montreal
they returned from work and underpay,
their snowy three-sided shadows
marching them into silence.

From afar now hear
the voices of aging women,
smell the shawl hugging
the wizened *bobeh*
who never begged but lived
for the conceptions of the ordinary,
bartering in the bazaars of genes and death.

1981

bp
NICHOL

b. 1944

Two Words: A Wedding

For Rob & Sheron

There are things you have words for, things you do not
have words for. There are words that encompass all your
feelings & words that encompass none. There are feelings
you have that are like things to you, picked up & placed in
the pocket, worn like the cloth the pocket is attached to, like
a skin you live inside of. There is a body of feeling, of
language, of friends; the body politic, the body we are
carried inside of till birth, the body we carry our self inside
of till death, a body of knowledge that tells of an afterlife, a
heaven, an unknown everything we have many words for
but cannot encompass. There are relationships between
words & concepts, between things, between life & death,
between friends & family, between each other & some other
other. We wed words to things, people to feelings, speak of
a true wedding of the mind & heart, intuition & intellect, &
out of this form our realities. Our realities are wedded one
to another, concepts & people are joined, new people
conceived within that mesh of flesh & realities, are carried
forward in the body of the mother, the family, the bodily
love we have for one another. They are creating their own
reality each step of the way, daily, another kind of reality is
born, each new word, person, expanding our vocabulary,
our concepts, new realities are conceived, our old reality
changes, the 'real' grows realer every day. We are marrying
the flesh to the flesh, the word to the daily flux of lives we
know & don't know, our friends grow older & marry, raise
children as you once were children with mothers & fathers
of your own, grow older, so many things you still lack
words for, struggle to wed the inner & outer worlds, the self
to some other self or selves, confess your love & struggle
with one another, together, conscious there is this word is
you, your name, & that you are yet another thing or things
you will never encompass, never exhaust the possibilities of,

428

because you are wedded to the flux of life, because we are bp NICHOL
words and our meanings change.

1978

Gorg, a detective story

For a.a.fair, posthumously

a man walks into a room. there is a corpse on the floor. the
man has been shot through the temple the bullet entering at
a 45° angle above the eyes & exiting almost thru the top of
the skull. the man does not walk out of the room. the corpse
stands up & introduces himself. later there will be a party.
you will not be invited & feeling hurt go off into a corner to
sulk. there is a gun on the window sill. you rig up a pulley
which enables you to pull the trigger while pointing the gun
between your eyes & holding it with your feet. a man walks
in on you. you are lying on the floor dead. you have been
shot thru the temple the bullet exiting almost thru the top of
your skull. you stand up & introduce yourself. the man lies
on the floor & you shoot him between the eyes the bullet
piercing his temple & exiting thru his skull into the floor.
you rejoin the party. the man asks you to leave since you
weren't invited. you notice a stranger in the doorway who
pulling out a gun shoots you between the eyes. you
introduce each other & lie down. your host is polite but firm
& asks you both to leave. at this point a man walks in &
introduces himself. you are lying on the floor & cannot see
him. your host appears not to know him & the man leaves.
the party ends & the room is empty. the man picks up the
corpse & exits.

1980

PETER
VAN TOORN

b. 1944

Shake'nbake Ballad

In 100% surefire arsenic
in snowwhite lye
in lepers' bathwater
in strychnine buttered with lead
in scrapemash off soldiers' bootsoles
in 7 cities' drainmalt
in snot pastry
in wolverine toad and turkey gall
    and in viler things
shake'nbake their envy-schooled tongues.

In pencilpaint and braspy mulepiss
in rabid dogdrool
in long peels of oven grease
in wormpie and roachpaste
in cigarettesog of tavern urinals
in rats' swimming water
in coffinslag and maggotmatting
in plasters of runover skunk
    and in viler things
shake'nbake their envy-schooled tongues.

In battery acid and engine goo
in egglacquered ragrot
in soapfoam and mosquito spray
in flubbery diaperslop
in stiff dishwater
in surgical mustard (morgue scraps)
in cat toad snail and tire wipe
in dead fish and ulcer ooze
    and in viler things
shake'nbake their envy-schooled tongues.

Prince
push all these into a crush
and if you haven't got a strainer handy
use the back of your pants.

And make sure there's enough batter —
roll on pig manure — before you
shake'nbake their envy-schooled tongues.

PETER
VAN TOORN

From Villon

1973

Mountain Study

After rain
dust's down, gone Dutch —
everything naked, wet, clear as Vermeer.
Tires
pulling the adhesive wet off the streets
make a 'frizzing' sound.
Oilspots
those cocky vulgar bits of peacock stain
rolled to all parts of town
like leaves.
Air
lumpy with sound
after the last churchfull of bellcopper
clangs the damp away.
Air, sweet as baby's breath.
Here and there,
the nation's flag
spanking in the wind,
domestic as Odysseus.
Festive, too, the trees
animated with brand new leaves
moving like mobiles.
And closeby,
almost Chinese, the lucrative
rustlines
of old nails on foxskin fenceboards.
Look under your feet,
so nurtured,
segmenty: the limpstrength of worms.
All journalese

in context of these slums. Still,
like puddles,
or those fish spread flat on newspaper,
something for the eye.

1973

TOM
WAYMAN

b. 1945

The Chilean Elegies: 5. The Interior

The smell of potatoes just taken out of the earth.
The problem every carpenter faces, where the wood
nearly fits. The man who secretly wants to leave his wife
and only his fantasies keep his sexual life alive.

These things no government can alter or solve.

The lineup in the small bank branch on East Twenty-ninth
after work on Friday: old boots and the shapeless trousers,
short windbreakers whose sleeves end in hands that clutch
the paper that means life. Other lines
that have worried their way into the faces above the eyes.

These mean an ache for money that lasts an entire lifetime
from busfare each morning through to the tiny pension.
These mean it is luck that rules: the wisps of lotteries, horses,
or entering the pool each payday for the best poker hand
that can be gathered from the company's number on your cheque.

Also, applying when they're hiring: no government
has been able to touch that.

The small towns of the Interior. The railroad towns deep in the
    forest.
What has the government to do with them?

The struggles of the young teacher TOM
WAYMAN
who has arrived to work in the school
mainly of Indians. All the arguing
with the principal, and with the old librarian,
the enthusiasm carried into the desperate classroom.
And the Indians themselves. Their new hall
they built themselves at Lytton, which had to be boarded up
after a month because of the damage. The summer camp
they built twenty miles away in the mountains
where a young boy drowned the second week it was open.
It too is abandoned again to the silence.
Potato chips and Coke the staple food of so many.
And television, television, television . . .

On the Thompson River, or in Parral
the government is not the government of the Indians,
not of the young teacher, not of the townspeople,
not of the lover, the carpenter, the man who digs potatoes in his
yard.

But where a government takes the remotest of steps
to return home to the ground, and when even this small gesture
is embargoed, denounced, plotted against
and at last some incredibly expensive aviation gasoline
is pumped into certain jet fighters donated by another government
existing thousands of miles away
there is a loss that goes deeper than the blood,
deeper than the bodies put into the ground,
that descends to the roots of the mountains
and travels that far down in the crust of the planet
along the continental chains

until all over the world another sorrow is confirmed
in the lives of the poor. Once again
we are made less. There are men and women
who in the cells of the fibres of their being
do not believe the Indians are dying fast enough
do not believe the poor are dying fast enough
do not believe that sickness and hunger,
automobile crashes, industrial disasters
and the daily suicides of alcohol and despair
are ridding the earth of us with sufficient speed.
So they call for the only institution

maintained at the highest possible level of efficiency:
the men with guns and capbadges, willing or conscripted,
whole armies and the tireless police. These are the men
who have made of this planet throughout my life
a vast geography of blood.

So many shot for subversion in Temuco. So many arrested
for drunkenness in Lytton.

And there is not a government in the world that wants to abolish
the factory.

1975

Another Poem About the Madness of Women

It began as a joke: she did not like to leave the house
even to shop for groceries.
Now she wants to be better. On Saturdays
her husband and children drive her downtown
to one set of doors into a department store
and let her off: agitated, but resolved.
They drive around to the opposite side of the building
and wait.

What she has to do is push
between the people on the sidewalk into the store.
She must walk through the crowd, all the faces hurrying and
    stopping,
past the bright displays of merchandise, the cash registers,
until she reaches the doors that open into the other street.

Every Saturday. Until it becomes easier.
There were women in pioneer Iowa, too,
alone in the house all day
who saw from every summer window the corn around the house,
the tall green corn, high as a man, stretching away for miles

in the sunlight, swaying in the light breeze,

TOM
WAYMAN

leaves rustling, whispering, heard
from the upstairs window in the dark, and the next day
whispering, until the woman knew

what stood on the ground everywhere, what surrounded the
   house
whispering and hissing
was alive, and hated her.

Here the electric clock in the kitchen runs
with hardly a hum. When she takes the garbage bags
out to the cans in the back lane she sees nothing but houses.

She knows there is a woman in each one.

1977

Wayman in Love

At last Wayman gets the girl into bed.
He is locked in one of those embraces
so passionate his left arm is asleep
when suddenly he is bumped in the back.
'Excuse me,' a voice mutters, thick with German.
Wayman and the girl sit up astounded
as a furry gentleman in boots and a frock coat
climbs in under the covers.

'My name is Doktor Marx,' the intruder announces
settling his neck comfortably on the pillow.
'I'm here to consider for you the cost of a kiss.'
He pulls out a notepad. 'Let's see now,
we have the price of the mattress, this room must be rented,
your time off work, groceries for two,
medical fees in case of accidents. . . .'

'Look,' Wayman says,
'couldn't we do this later?'
The philosopher sighs, and continues: 'You are affected too, Miss.
If you are not working, you are going to resent

your dependent position. This will influence
I assure you, your most intimate moments. . . .'

'Doctor, please,' Wayman says. 'All we want
is to be left alone.'
But another beard, more nattily dressed,
is also getting into the bed.
There is a shifting and heaving of bodies
as everyone wriggles out room for themselves.
'I want you to meet a friend from Vienna,'
Marx says. 'This is Doktor Freud.'

The newcomer straightens his glasses,
peers at Wayman and the girl.
'I can see,' he begins,
'that you two have problems. . . .'

1981

b. 1946

Turn (a poem in 4 parts)

i
What they are doing is turning
The earth
In ordered furrows.

Where it is blackest and most fit.
Laying muscles of earth
One beside the other.

And tomorrow, they will return
To harvest the rocks.
Rocks that are drawn from a deeper seeding.

That come with the same energy
That allows the willow to spring straight.
It comes thru, as elsewhere.

KEN
BELFORD

ii
Familiar comes the carrion odor of earth.
Douglas, I said, what do you think of all day?
Nothing, he replied. Nothing

Which is difficult to understand,
Considering I have watched them all day
From a larger expanse of rock.

iii
Groaning, the stoneboat
Skids, lurches, approaches,
Draws nearer the edge.

Animals break
With the sound,
Bursting across the clearing.

Nothing, he said. The air smells sweet of death.
Of earth, of flowers. Nothing is impossible.
Gee up, he calls to his horse, following.

iv
The one furrow doesn't turn with the others,
Leads off into the brush. The man is gone
But the boot prints remain. He will never come
    back.

1967

Carrier Indians

KEN
BELFORD

They have no word for conscience.
Instead, say sdzî, meaning
Heart.

Practical people who associate words differently.
For example, marriage, say me — at, sex. Legend has it
When someone you have loved dies, part of your heart dies too.

They burnt the body. Not cremated. Burnt.
From then, to carry the basket of ash. To continue.
To hunt. To trap. Alkoh tsûtgen, let us sing together.

To bear the ashes until a future final marriage.
A band of thieves, and liars.
Stunted, inter–related.

Ugly people with large eyes.
Having nowhere to go:
I am one of them.

1967

ROBERT
BRINGHURST

b. 1946

Deuteronomy

The bush. Yes. It burned like they say it did,
lit up like an oak in October — except
that there is no October in Egypt. Voices
came at me and told me to take off my shoes
and I did that. That desert is full of men's shoes.
And the flame screamed *I am what I am.*
I am whatever it is that is me,
and nothing can but something needs to be
done about it. If anyone
asks, all you can say is, 'I sent me.'

I went, but I brought my brother to do
the talking, and I did the tricks — the Nile
full of fishguts and frogs, the air opaque
and tight as a scab, the white-hot hail,
and boils, and bugs, and when nothing had worked right
we killed them and ran. We robbed them of every
goddamned thing we could get at and carry
and took off, and got through the marsh at low tide
with the wind right, and into the desert. The animals
died, of course, but we kept moving.

Abraham came up easy. We took
the unknown road and ate hoarfrost and used
a volcano for a compass. I had no plan.
We went toward the mountains. I wanted, always,
to die in the mountains, not in that delta.
And not in a boat, at night, in swollen water.
We travelled over dead rock and drank dead water,
and the hoarfrost wasn't exactly hoarfrost.
They claimed it tasted like coriander,
but no two men are agreed on the taste
of coriander. Anyway,
we ate it, and from time to time we caught quail.

Men and half men and women, we marched
and plodded into those hills, and they exploded
into labyrinths of slag. The air licked us
like a hot tongue, twisting and flapping and gurgling
through the smoke like men suffocating or drowning, saying

An eye for an eye, and on certain occasions
two eyes for one eye. Either way, you model me
in thin air or unwritten words, not in wood,
not in metal. I am gone from the metal when the metal
hits the mold. You will not get me into any image
which will not move when I move, and move
with my fluency. Moses! Come up!

I went, but I wore my shoes and took a waterskin.
I climbed all day, with the dust eating holes
in my coat, and choking me, and the rock cooking me.
What I found was a couple of flat stones
marked up as if the mountain had written all over them.

ROBERT
BRINGHURST I was up there a week, working to cool them,
hungry and sweating and unable to make sense of them,
and I fell coming down and broke both of them.
Topping it all, I found everybody down there drooling
over Aaron's cheap figurines, and Aaron chortling.

I went up again to get new stones
and the voices took after me that time and threw me
up between the rocks and said I could see them.
They were right. I could see them. I was standing right
   behind them
and I saw them. I saw the mask's insides,
and what I saw is what I have always seen.
I saw the fire and it flowed and it was moving away
and not up into me. I saw nothing
and it was widening all the way around me.
I collected two flat stones and I cut them
so they said what it seemed to me two stones
should say, and I brought them down without dropping
   them.

The blisters must have doubled my size, and Aaron said
I almost glowed in the dark when I got down.
Even so, it seemed I was pulling my stunts
more often then than in Egypt. I had to,
to hold them. They had to be led to new land,
and all of them full of crackpot proverbs and cockeyed
ideas about directions. Aaron and I
outbellowed them day after day and in spite of it
they died. Some of weakness, certainly, but so many of them
died of being strong. The children stood up to it
best, out of knowing no different — but with no
idea what to do with a ploughshare, no
idea what a river is. What could they do
if they got there? What can they even know how to wish for?
I promised them pasture, apple trees, cedar,
waterfalls, snow in the hills, sweetwater
wells instead of these arroyos, wild grapes . . .

Words. And whatever way I say them, words only.
I no longer know why I say them, even though
the children like hearing them. They come when I call them
and their eyes are bright, but the light in them is empty.

It is too clear. It contains . . . the clarity only.
But they come when I call to them. Once I used to sing to them
a song about an eagle and a stone, and each time
I sang it, somehow the song seemed changed
and the words drifted into the sunlight. I do not
remember the song now, but I remember
that I sang it, and the song was the law and the law
was the song. The law *is* a song, I am certain . . .
And I climbed to the head of this canyon. They said
I could look down at the new land
if I sat here, and I think it is so, but my eyes
are no longer strong, and I am tired now of looking.

1974

These Poems, She Said

These poems, these poems,
these poems, she said, are poems
with no love in them. These are the poems of a man
who would leave his wife and child because
they made noise in his study. These are the poems
of a man who would murder his mother to claim
the inheritance. These are the poems of a man
like Plato, she said, meaning something I did not
comprehend but which nevertheless
offended me. These are the poems of a man
who would rather sleep with himself than with women,
she said. These are the poems of a man
with eyes like a drawknife, with hands like a pickpocket's
hands, woven of water and logic
and hunger, with no strand of love in them. These
poems are as heartless as birdsong, as unmeant
as elm leaves, which if they love love only
the wide blue sky and the air and the idea
of elm leaves. Self-love is an ending, she said,
and not a beginning. Love means love
of the thing sung, not of the song or the singing.
These poems, she said . . .
                    You are, he said,
          beautiful.
1982   That is not love, she said rightly.

Notes to the Reader

ROBERT
BRINGHURST

I: *Have a Good Time*

This is a poem. Take it. Pack it up
the mountain. You will meet a man
who says it is an ice-axe. Give it to him. Tell him

he should take it out to sea until
he meets a man who calls it a harpoon.
Follow. Watch them. Let them fight about it.

II: *Get Laid*

Watch it: it thinks but, no, you cannot quite watch it
thinking. Listen to it singing: no, you can't quite
hear it singing. Smell it: linseed and lampblack: no,
no you can't quite smell it, touch it, taste it. Take it

intravenously and see if it does not have
some effect. Suck it, stick it in your ear, leave it
underneath your tongue like a thermometer or
pocket it or stick it wherever it occurs
to you to stick it. See if it doesn't have some
effect. You may feel it thinking, singing, feel it
humming to itself, yodelling down these treeless
canyons, up these lattices of sound and shadow

following its echo. Follow. Echo it or
swallow it. It is just a voice; you are a whale.

III: *Stand Back*

or up and back. Inanimate
and animate embrace each other,

cling to each other, lean against
each other: treebark, words, water,
rock, nervecord, chromosome and bone.

It is possible to use, to this
purpose, only certain postures.

1975

b. 1946

Mean Drunk Poem

Backward & down into inbetween as Vicki says. Or as Robin
  teaches
the gap, from which all things emerge. A left
handed compliment. Bats, houses of parliament, giants, stones.
What woman, witness to such Thought, does not feel
so described & so impotent

she thinks
she must speak. 'I will take your linguistic prick & you
will take my linguistic prick & together we will gap
this imagined earth together.' She has the feeling,
all her life, that she never makes sense. There is something
else, big & dark, at the edge of what she knows, she cannot
say. She always has the feeling she is translating into
Broken english. Language all her life is a second language,
the first is mute & exists. I get drunk

to lubricate my brain & all that comes out
of my Gap
is more bloody writing. No wonder we cook dinner. Have
  another
kid. Write poetry about the Beloved & kiss ass.
Who cares, as Eleanor says,
who beats whose door down yelling Truth.

The door is only &
always an entrance.

Sing Om as you take the sausage rolls out of the oven.
The Gap is real & there is no such thing as
female intelligence. We're dumber than hell.

1980

Loose Woman Poem

SHARON
THESEN

For Victoria Walker & Penny Kemp

A landscape
full of holes.
Women.
Pierced
ears voices piercing
the ceiling, a little choir
stung by wine:
I Fall to Pieces, and
Please Release Me.
After which I put on my old wedding band
& go to the party.
Next day 222's
& the moon falls out
of my fingernail.
The house smells like oysters
& a moon is on the loose
a woman in the bathtub   another
talking on the phone, their presence
shimmers, I'm fed up
with the wages of sin
put on some Mingus
& hepcat around
how come
it's always a question
of loss, being sick of self
displaced & frantic, chopped out
of the World of Discourse
waylaid
on the Bridge of Sighs, a net
work of connections coming down
to getting laid
or not getting laid & by whom.
Except getting laid
is not the way she thinks of it,
more like
something that her moons
can waylay waylay waylay
in the dark.

1980

Kirk Lonegren's Home Movie Taking Place
Just North of Prince George, With Sound

The beginning: Some landscape & words about nature, that particular landscape & what it harbors: shots of woodpeckers, porcupines, the swamp lilies bears & moose eat, and the three archers, one old guy, one medium guy, one young guy (Kirk) all dressed in camouflage clothing. There's an early scene of Kirk shooting fish with the bow, aiming straight down into the still creek water. The foresty hills roll on into the distance. The sun is shining on a blue volkswagen parked on the dirt road. A big bear comes wandering out of the bush, turns sideways lifting its front feet & sniffing, then ambles away back into the forest. An arrow thuds into the tree it was standing beside: shot of pissed-off hunter having missed his target. These guys sit in the bush for days waiting to kill a bear. They try out different places — stalking the pipeline cut, the sides of roads, standing on tree trunks for hours at a time, bow held down near the knees. At last a bear comes out of the trees. You see the old guy walking quickly toward it putting the arrow in the bow. The bear doesn't seem to notice & all of a sudden the arrow flies right into him. The impact nearly knocks him over, he jumps straight up & then turns a few fast circles, falls down, then gets up & starts running. He goes about 25 yards, then drops, keels right over on his back, paws waving in the air. The old hunter & the medium guy walk over to him cautiously, poke a boot toe at him a few times, & once they're certain he's dead they congratulate themselves. 'Isn't he a beauty!' the old guy says proudly, and he scratches it fondly on the head between the ears & pulls the carcass up toward him like a passed-out girlfriend at a party. They yank out the arrow & begin slicing the bear open right down the middle This is done very gently and with many reassurances like 'ther-r-r-re we go . . .' He opens up the whole diaphragm & shows the camera where the arrow went in inside — sure enough, a hole right through the chest wall & into part of the lung & into the heart. The bear's internal organs are amazingly clean & pure, the bloodiness is on the old hunter's hands. They display the pierced heart by placing it on the dusty ground & pointing to the V-shaped wound with bloody forefinger. Nearby lies the arrow with blood halfway up the shaft. Next scene is hunters posing with trophies next to the car. The medium guy has apparently got himself a brown bear during the trip. It too is sliced right down the middle. The two of them kid around, heaving the corpses upright & putting their arms around them, mugging & posing, cuddling their big dead teddy bears, laughing & happy. The slit middles of the bears look like giant cunts. The heads wobble stupidly on top, teeth bared. That was the end, and what a crazy image of love.

1980

DALE
ZIEROTH

b. 1946

Beautiful Woman

1
Beautiful woman, you crown the hours
and we grow wonderful, we grow secret
in the assumption of our life. How easily
the electric night warms us. Fish
swim past the edges of our bed, oceans
in their mouths. The morning will never come
and break down this fever to be mad in each other's
warm white skin. We go down
like children, we go down into a great moaning
with silence forgotten and floating through the ceiling
like balloons. See me, see me dancing
to your terrible music, woman. The room
is filling with candles, the sun
is inches away: it smells
of your hair and lies writhing in your palm.
See again the sun and the bed wet with warm rain.
Wave after wave it comes, wave
after wave stones
break open at our touch, small bones break free and drift
out of you into me. And the skin
becomes water and salt shuddering
out past fingers—bloodfilled and animal—
towards the centre
of a thick and velvet earth where the sun
burns a hole in the sky.

2
Yet even from this bed
the anger rises day by day
and digs trenches to fortify its seed. So we
swear, accuse, sometimes punch flat-handed
the stubborn skin. You tell me
what it means to wait and work afternoons
with dishes and floors. You tell me
my friends who pace and strut ignore you, or notice
only your sex. How you hate them!
See your tears fly out at them like diamond-headed
spikes. See that it's me you've hit.
Let that sound surround our bed, let it
fill up the room as high as the windows.
Put your hungriest cats to prowl inside my skin.
Let nothing escape: the mouth
will stretch and harden into my best smile.
(You know this is not like a movie, you know
this is not in our dream—yet it continues.)
Everywhere muscles are dying. Out of my throat
you will hear me cursing, you will hear me
roaring. When it is my turn
nothing will change. The mirror
will fall, history will vomit at your name.

3
It is morning and the yellow sun falls
through the window like a stone. In the kitchen
the dishes wait and bits of swollen meat
have stuck to the sides of knives. All around us
broken flesh is aching. Tonight
we will go deep into our powerful
bodies again. Or we will do nothing
and survive just the same. Woman,
wake up and hold me, I have
nowhere else to take my anger. Wake up and let
your hands spread like warmth along my back.
Now that the skin is dead. Now
that both the music and the bruises have gone.
And all that remains refuses to begin
without falling, is
caught and held in the light that spills
off the floor and stains the bed
1973   like wine.

The Hunters of the Deer

DALE
ZIEROTH

The ten men will dress in white
to match the snow and leave the last
farmhouse and the last woman, going
north into the country of the deer. It
is from there, and from past there, that
the wind begins that can shake
every window in the house and leaves
the woman wishing she had moved away
five years and five children ago.

During the day the father of her children
will kill from a distance. With the others
he will track and drive each bush
and at least once he will kill before
they stop and come together for
coffee in scratched quart jars. And
sometimes the November sun will glint
on the rifles propped together in the snow.

In the evening, as they skin and gut,
they talk about the one that ran three
miles on a broken leg and the bitch wolf
they should have shot and how John
the bachelor likes eating more than
hunting and they pass the whiskey
around to keep warm. In the house
the woman makes a meal from pork.

These men are hunters and later,
standing in bright electrically lighted
rooms they are embarrassed with the
blood on their clothes and although the
woman nods and seems to understand,
she grows restless with their talk.
She has not heard another woman in fourteen days.

And when they leave, the man sleeps
and his children sleep while the woman
waits and listens for the howling of
wolves. To the north, the grey
she-wolf smells the red snow and howls.

She also is a hunter of the deer.
Tonight, while other hunters sleep, she
drinks at the throat.

DALE
ZIEROTH

1973

Baptism

In mid-river we join the ancient force
of mud and leaves moving in their journey
down the face of the continent and after
the first dance of leaving
one element for another, we fall quiet,
waiting for the silence to give us a
glimpse of history. In mid-river, it is
still possible to imagine Thompson's world,
without roads or bridges, rivers that
go back beyond white lives into the rocks
that push and fold, fault and break
as the new world rises from
the old.
        Yet this is still our river.
It does not matter that we are not
the first, what we will find today
has been found a hundred times before: it is
the ancient story of men meeting water,
as if there were a time, or faith,
when all of us were rivers, one
strength sliding out of the sky and into
the sea, one direction in us all.

But the river churns here and beats along the shore.
It picks up speed on the outside curve
cutting past the cottonwoods and under the deadfalls
that sweep across the water like the last arm of the land
and the water takes command.
I bend my paddle in my hand and my friend
digs in but there are branches like dead fingers in our faces
and there can be
no avoidance now, water comes up up and the
snag bends us down until my lungs

are in the water they are stones and I am
grabbing for the tree as if it were
my friend while the current sucks on me and my arms
go heavy as lead, a scream
goes dead in my throat, we do not
belong here, it bubbles and swallows
silt, the taste of ice,
there are blue stars somewhere and all the sounds of water
are alive and they pour in my ears,
into my eyes as if the river is already sure
how deep it will carry me,
what it will do with my skin, how it will dissolve
and burst and thin out the blood and I roll over
in a dream of clouds, willows, catch the edge
of a bank beaver's hole, brown mud like gold on my palm,
my feet still pulling for the ocean and then they find
gravel, the river rock, the river
pushes me away and I am shaking in the air again,
shaking for my friend riding the canoe's bottom
like a drunken pea pod, he grinds on the bank
a hundred yards downstream, his boots sucked off,
his body like a hole in the sand.

I breathe in the sun, take it yellow
into the body that spits grey in the river.
The baptism is over.
We have walked away without the grace of
fish or grebes, and the river is still the same.
I sit and watch the water with the oldest eyes of men:
if I trust the river, I will be
caught in it, rolled backwards into the
simplest race of all, the first, and the river is hard, it is
carnal and twists like an animal going blind in the rain,
but it leaves me pouring water from my shoe and then I see
him stand, wave, we have
first words.
Soon our paddles will bite the water but they will not
break it: our place on earth is rich enough,
the sudden rush of birdsong, our own
mid–river laughter as the warmth begins again.

1981

450

b. 1947

'I don't have the energy . . .'

I don't have the energy for another day
like a poor hand of scrabble without vowels . . .
the sun is at my throat

I wonder what sense I am making of human history
getting halfway through the day leaving a poem scrawk

just thinking about why I fail
screws me right in there
we have a sense of tradition

like watery spaghetti . . .

it is the poorer countries that I wonder about; there,
energy abounds. It is their gift to get ahead
to feel lousy doing it; mine
     to slip   and
to have one hell of a banquet:

     roast corpse of the western world, something must fill a hole—
or what is the dirt dying for?

I call this rarefied morality
some days I can shoot it in my veins without my conscience
     flinching
these days I slide off without batting an eyelash.

1979

sex at thirty-one

Is like love at seventeen.   it plies deep
Affords the illusion there is nothing else.

Every few years kicks sand in the face of everyfew years
Love, only a pornography of the heart has a habit of being

Waylaid, it had a habit of suddenly throwing down
Its basket of roses and running. rape, basic call of thing

Changed.   suddenly and love dies like drool on a napkinless chin
Love gives way to one of love's perversions, dry skin

To wetness, even the idea of sex glistens. like the heart
Thinking of where it left its bubblegum. the heart

Is a dry old taskmaker.   its puppies are like the grains
of sand dragged on to a picnic blanket. as the afternoon

Turns into death. count love with a slight chill.   too many
Times love has occurred,   reared its beautiful head.   we are sick

Sick of change.   sick of wind change. sick of lifeguard change
Sick of the tides of the heart.

1979

Life

                        In a sense
it is the exact opposite of what we want   and
that opposite isn't death
                        but fence.
somewhere over the rainbow
you see, it's parabolic.
sometimes stretched out on drugs that make me taller
I sway over two kingdoms of sidewalk concrete   adjacent
but over the line. clothes vanish through the magic agency of
    drugs
naked to my brain my genitals hang like a child's drawing of
    scissors
open large enough only for the beam of life to shine through
I trap the living photon and aim it down, my friends say: Artie,
you have dropped your handkerchief.

1979

wakepick I

tonight i disentangle
soft underwool fibre from coarse hairs
make ready for carding

rain blasts at the membrane window
the mud walls are damp
begin to leak, little by little
onto the sleeping benches

i escape this flood in the work of hands
pretend not to see the paste
of whiteflies trod underfoot
into the soft mud floor
pretend not to feel clammy & cold

we have no use for human fleas
no use for bland horsehair & wool

tonight again i pretend
to be salt
i separate myself again
fine from coarse
die another death tonight

& when i'm dead
i turn to knotweed on the knolls
to starlings in the rain
i turn blood, hair, bone
i turn to stone

in the work of my hands
i turn my fragments up from the floor
blood & bone from the floor
make ready for another rain
tonight again

i disentangle sinew, hair
1981   i turn to stone

changeling VIII

KRISTJANA
GUNNARS

every morning i break trail
down the mountainside
big snowflakes muffle my bootsteps
like cold skin
on invisible faces
trying to talk

i, too, suffocate under my name
i can't live
up to my great grandmother's ghost
i want another easier name

name me weevil
so i can prowl at night
name me grey mountain carpet moth
so i can hide
name me harvestman
i want to scavenge before daylight

i don't want to have to apologize
for the red mites on my legs
name me harvestman because my mother
dreamed bugs when i lay in her
heath, bracken, birch bugs
she dreamed worms, grey & red
with flat tails & ruddy ripples of spine

she dreamed i burrowed through the damp wall
the humus floor
broken & suffocating even then
at the threat of being

born under great grandmother's majesty
under the white headdress

don't give me a hard life
don't make me die young
give me another name
more suitable

name me leech
name me woodlouse
name me a dream i dream
name me broadleaved woods

KRISTJANA
GUNNARS

1981

MARILYN
BOWERING

b. 1949

Russian Asylum

One of the difficulties is in being
alone, not one with anything or one,
not even a dog or witness.
One of the difficulties is in not being able to move,
or breathe or speak—
to do anything, that is.
One of the difficulties is that you are always
going under when they come; you are fogged and weathered
with lack of sleep.
One of *them* fits something in your vein—
your vein swallows it, questionless.

One of the women takes your lover away.
She is kind and
feeds you when you can't hold a spoon.

You're awake all through it, but it doesn't last long.
Be reassured, brother,
believe there is nothing serious, nothing in it.

They walk you along the sea,
they ask after your family. They offer food and when you
push it away, it's you who look foolish,
yes, you do. Your reasons do not pass outside your brain,
not from eyes to speech—
and even if they did, what good would that be?
You're alone, and they help it along

with something good for you—something
painless and sweet.
          Over the official's desk applications roll in;
there are lives, happy lives, and people behind them,
          You could have been any of them,
then.
Oh, it's harrowing this—going under, going down,
writing out love like this.

1980

Seeing Oloalok

'See, nothing has happened to her,' said my guide,
'nothing at all. Time has done nothing;
I can't explain.'

Her weathered face, crowned by long grey hair
that fell across her neck,
was turned aside as if from the right.
The blue tatoos marking delicate spirals on her face
were perfectly clear. Under the shroud of snow her bible
was clutched between her hands.

At first I mistake it for a foetus,
a fine textured material in a thin white membrane
topped with a lump of blood.
'Making love after first sleeping
explains it,' she said.
'You have to eat the cure,' she said
'you can't have it another way,' she said.
She wore a blue dress to lie in bed,
her bridal gown floated away in a flood, she said.
'We are nearly the same,' she said, 'having lost our fathers
both at an early age.'

I am falling down, nearly through the window twice,
seeing Oloalok, then again, curled on the floor.
Is this the worst to happen,

for this to go on, waking all night,
the lights of the settlement made out in the distance?

MARILYN
BOWERING

But as my guide carefully dusted
away the snow:
Her eyes kept watch on her people.

1980

Wishing Africa

There's never enough whiskey or rain
when the blood is thin and white,
but oh it was beautiful,
the wind delicate as Queen Anne's lace,
only wild with insects
breeding the sponge-green veldt,
and bands of white butterflies
slapping the acacia.
The women's bodies were variable as coral
and men carried snakes on staves.

It would do me no good
to go back,
I am threaded
with pale veins,
I am full with dying
and ordinary;
but oh if there was a way
of wishing Africa.

When there was planting,
when there was harvesting,
I was not far behind
those who first
opened the ground.
I stitched in seed,
I grew meat in the earth's blond side.
I did it all with little bloody stitches.
What red there was in me

457

I let out there.
The sun stayed forever
then was gone.

I am scented with virus,
I breed flowers for the ochre
my skin was.
There is no sex in it.
I am white as a geisha,
my roots indiscriminate
since my bones gave way.
It is a small, personal pruning
that keeps me.
I had a soul,
and remember how it hurt
to be greedy and eat.

1980

PIER
GIORGIO
DI CICCO

b. 1949

The Head Is a Paltry Matter

The head is a paltry matter; feed it crumbs, it goes
on singing just the same.
Much too much is made of it; it goggles over a bit of
fresh wind, is perfectly astonished at the touch of love,
doesn't know what to make of itself but crosses, bearing
its own dull weight along paths it imagines have to do
with the heart.
No more of it. I'm giving it nothing to feed on.
Old lump, let it do its crossword of a grave.
You and I have better things to do, namely wrapping arms
around each other tonight, while it hangs around, poor sot,
childlike, finding a little of what it is
that lovers do, the dark between them like a clock
and their lips set to ignite one future after another.

1979

Errore

PIER
GIORGIO
DI CICCO

We talk of old men who have forgotten their
thoughts, of old women with cancer like
sponges at the face. We say how medicine
doesn't know anything, how we can croak
because the mystery in us
gets teeth. Fear opens its little satchel,
a small bat flies off into the head.

       I want to live for many years like a stone.
I want to announce the end of the body's partnership.
I want to enter a small tunnel not big enough
for my flesh,
    I want to arrange a song and dance for me
and death, laughing it up as the bones cart
their old clothes out the door.
    I want to live forever in the eye of a needle.
I have no footprints, I lied about them.
My mother is not getting old. It is a bad joke,
one day she will walk out of the machine of
sinew and heart and say—it is all right, you can come
out now, god is sorry about the wrong wrapper.

1979

Male Rage Poem

Feminism, baby, feminism.
This is the anti-feminist poem.
It will get called the anti-
feminist poem. Like it or not.
Dedicated to all my friends who
can't get it up in the night,
accused of having male rage during the
day. This is for the poor buggers.
This is for me and the incredible boredom
of arguing about feminism, the right
arguments, the wrong arguments, the
circular argument, the arguments that stem
from one bad affair, from one

bad job, no job—whatever; fill in the
blanks _____ _____, fill in the ways
in which you have been hurt. Then I'll
fill in the blanks, and we'll send rosters
of hurt to each other, mail them, stock
them for the record, to say: *Giorgio Di Cicco*
has been hurt in this way x many times.
We will stock closets of Sarah's hurt,
Barbara's hurt, my hurt, Bobby's hurt.
This is where the poem peters out . . . oops!—that's
penis mentality, that's patriarchal bullshit,
sexist diction and *these line lengths are*
male oriented.

PIER
GIORGIO
DI CICCO

       Where did he get so much male rage?
From standing out like a man for a bunch of
years, and being called the dirty word.
'When you are 21 you will become a Man.'
Christ! Doomed to enslave women ipso
facto, without even the right training for it.
Shouldn't have wasted ten years playing
baseball; should have practised
whipping, should have practised tying up the
girl next door, giving her cigarette burns . . .
oops! Male rage again! MALE RAGE—the words ring out—
worse than RING AROUND THE COLLAR, worse than
  KISSED
THE GIRLS AND MADE THEM CRY, jeesus, male rage
in kindergarten. MALE RAGE. You've got
male rage; I look inside myself and scrounge
for all this male rage. Must be there
somewhere. Must be repressing it. I write poems
faster and faster, therapeutically, to make sure
I get most of the rage out. But someone's
always there to say Male Rage—more Male Rage;
I don't leave the house, working on my male rage.

Things may lighten up. My friends may meet
fine women at a party someday and know
what to say to them, like: 'I'm not a Man and
you're not a Woman, but let's have dinner
anyway, let's fuck with our eyes closed and
swap roles for an hour.'

I'm tired of being a man.
Of having better opportunities,
better job offers,
too much money.
I'm tired of going to the YMCA and
talking jock in the locker room.
I'm tired of all the poems where
I used the word 'whore' inadvertently.
I'm tired of having secretaries type out
all my poems for me.
I'm tired of being a man.
I'm tired of being a sexist.
I'm afraid of male rage.
I'm afraid of *my* male rage,
this growing thing, this buddy, this
shadow, this new self, this stranger.
It's there. It's there! How could it have
happened? I ate the right things, said
yes to my mother, thought the good
thoughts.
        Doc—give it to me straight.
How long do I have before this male rage
takes over completely?
               The rest of your life.
Take it like a man.

1982

Flying Deeper into the Century

Flying deeper into the century
is exhilarating, the faces of loved ones eaten out
slowly, the panhandles of flesh warding off
the air, the smiling plots. We are lucky to be mature,
in our prime, seeing more treaties, watching
T.V. get computerized. Death has no dominion.
It lives off the land. The glow over the hill, from
the test sites, at night, the whole block of neighbours
dying of cancer over the next thirty years. We are
suing the government for a drop of blood; flying deeper
into the century, love,

the lies are old lies with more imagination;
the future is a canoe. The three bears are ravenous, not content
with porridge. Flying deeper into the century,
my hands are prayers, hooks, streamers.
I cannot love grass, cameos or lungs.
The end of the century is a bedspread up to the eyes.
I want to be there, making ends meet.
I will not love you, with such malice at large.
Flying deeper into the century is beautiful, like
coming up for the third time, life flashing before us.
The major publishing event is the last poem of
all time. I am a lonely bastard. My brothers and sisters have
had sexual relations, and I am left with their mongrel sons
writing memoirs about the dead in Cambodia.
Flying deeper, I do not remember what I cared for, out
of respect. Oh *Time*, oh *Newsweek*, oh *Ladies' Home Journal*,
oh the last frontier, I am deeply touched.
The sun, an ignoramus, comes up.
I have this conversation with it. Glumly, glumly, deeper
I fly into the century, every feather of each wing
absolution, if only I were less than human, not angry
like a beaten thing.

1982

DOUG
FETHERLING

b. 1949

Explorers as Seen by the Natives

'Man thrives where angels die of ecstacy
and pigs die of disgust'
KENNETH REXROTH

The need to explore
is the reason they give
for coming
with lanterns to push back the dark
clothes and helmets to keep away the sun
weapons to kill with delight
what presumes to kill only for safety
or food—
all things explorers use
to experience without learning
as they trample through our land
And we are eager to assist them

They move too quickly
to notice life best viewed
standing still, but push on
without resistance
conquering what they have just discovered
and we have known all along
We who are not asked,
who curiously follow

Soon they will return to
wherever it is they are from
talking as though they invented
what we show them now
and encouraging others to come
In truth they invent only new names
never content with the old ones we use
We who are only too willing to help

1974

Elijah Speaking

DOUG
FETHERLING

I expected this face but did not predict it,
though there is a way of doing so I am afraid
I never learned:
like sawing a tree exactly parallel with earth
and knowing in advance the route of its collapse

Once the skin on my face was pulled down taut
and tied off at the chin like a sausage end,
but the years have twirled the knot loose
and let the flesh move upward, wrinkling this visage
that was smooth when we were young
My joints do not flex so unobtrusively as then
and recently cold objects have caused pain in my hands
and everyone seems older whom I met before today
and plans get less important but for time

I have lived in focus scarcely at all
for as a child I knew I was no child
as now I know I am not old

1974

MARY
DI MICHELE

b. 1949

The Moon and the Salt Flats

'How I would like to believe in tenderness'
SYLVIA PLATH

The moon is an ivory tusk in the Utah sky
over the salt flats of ultra white.
The ground is a soft wax that receives my steps
and prints their passage. Before the Mormons
the pulse of the earth was white, the sky, marine.
The Indians spoke of it in their red dream language
of clay and old blood. Sailing for me is the angel of
tenderness.

It had been promised in books that if I were good
and prayed to the right gods I would find my heart
netted in blue pacific light, but I'm perched
unsteadily on spindly doubts and can't run.
Winged and yet a magpie whose tail is longer than her body,
I'm clumsy when I don't talk about flying.
They call me bitter tears, Mary means,

without the trace of the sea I hear in *Maria* like a shell.
Only the salt of that forgotten ocean's biography
remains a relic of powdered bone, chalk white,
Saint Sea who still can make the earth's eyes here moist
with a keen nostalgia for it. Tears, the bed of my own making,
dry and only the salt is left behind. Watch me sleep on it.
If I could get a better look at him, I'd go to the moon

switching on her deeper lights, but the moon won't have me.
All ideas are colourless and odourless and stoppered in a vial
so that they can't be dangerous to me at this moment.
My eyes are sea green, my heart is blue.
Is it love that makes the earth pirouette on his axis
and the moon perform her crab-like bow around him?
There's no looking back, *amore*,

1981   we're the only living things growing on the salt flats.

465

DON
DOMANSKI

b. 1950

Three Songs from the Temple

For Jeannette

1

what are we to do with a heaven
that moves beneath stones
and fallen trees?

a heaven
that keeps good company
with vermin and blackbird
and the far off hills
staggering through?

with a lumbering paradise
that sleeps beside a dog's bowl
until fed?

an ether
that muds its nose
and feet?

2

lounging in this day's elevation
heaven sprawls its unearthly hulk
an inch above the pond
to finger its brainwork of flies
and dream of adorations

to dream it is more
than a toad's placid heart

more than a bullhead's
righteous appetite

something other than the distant
misery of foliage
rising up in prayer
along the horizon.

3
all night heaven dances
brimming with its brutal hugs
and tremblings

twisting its bodiless form
above our beds

uprooting us suddenly
from sleep
to endure the full outcome of love

whose reek of pleasure
hangs in the morning air?

1978

Deadsong

For Ion Rusu

I star in the loam

I bed with the moony shapes
with my trapshut head
and dun heart

when I recite this black hole
there is no one here
to listen

when I go to stand up
I can think of no reason
for moving

I lie still
grubbing memory

wearing a lost suit
of clothes
(toeing the grave)
staring into the tuberous sky

three decades
under the weeds

listening to the birds of the air
to the landscape rustle
like a curtain

listening to
the dead drum
the blood camp of dogs
running prey

to the wreckage of light
among the grass blades

where should I go?
where should I go?

my tongue's none the wiser
for death's uninteresting taste.

1978

b. 1951

Out of Control: The Quarry

It is a warm grey afternoon in August. You are in the country, in a deserted quarry of light grey Devonian limestone in Southern Ontario. A powdery luminescence oscillates between the rock & sky. You feel sure that you could recognize these clouds (with their limestone texture) out of random cloud-photographs from all over the world.

You then lean over and pick up a flat piece of layered stone. It is a rough triangle about one foot across. Prying at the stone you find the layers come apart easily in large flat pieces. Pale grey moths are pressed between the layers of stone. Freed, they flutter up like pieces of ash caught in a dust-devil. You are splashed by the other children but move not.

1975

'This is of two worlds . . .'

This is of two worlds—the one diurnal men know and that other world where lunar mottled eels stir like dreams in shallow forest water. Allowing both these mechanisms to continue operating, we slowly remove and replace theiyr parts with corresponding and interlocking nothings. The glass machinery is equally filled with allusion to our aestive carnality, an infinite part of the pattern which regenerates itself with its own repetitive logic.

Triassic afternoons in early October.

Each huge spring bud a transparent chrysalis pregnant with moth wings unfolding into bats. (Every nuance & cartesian plotted in radar-tunnels.) The secrecy of your voice behind me in a crowd, remoras vacuous and cold that lurk in the eddies of your passing.

The air is water.

The skin, neither moist nor dry, is a permeable membrane of cells dividing the summer landscape into pink and blue. Spring aches in the heart and stomach, the surfacing of women in moist soil and moonlight.

1978

b. 1951

The Judas Goat

It was a bad sign I was born under,
half animal, half a cruel joke of nature.
The antlered ghosts of my ancestors were
vanishing; I envied them their shifty universe.

Fate made me plain and bitter,
my shape more symbol than pathfinder or
builder. I wandered from the herd to
escape humiliation—found more misery there
than mystery.

Where I grazed along the wayside
nothing would grow; when I lay down in the
garbage I gave no thought to the flowers.
Skirting the world's edge I thrived on spoils,
glutted my maw, grew reconciled to hunger.

Returning to the flock restored my
dignity. The fat ewes gathered to greet me;
I spoke to them in their own language.
Where I led them to drink there was a warm trough and
plenty to eat. There was a dry place to
lie down; my ease did not betray cowardice.

Lord of everything pleasurable and defenceless,
I woke to their calling resurrected and holy.
There was no need for treachery in their
measure of life; too simple by origin they
followed me to the slaughterhouse.

My power was inimitable and blinding.
When they smelled their own blood they were
no longer afraid. They stumbled and fell
as if my will had supported them. I watched them
weakening, unashamed.

Even their whimpering made me feel ruthless,
the greatness of conquest far greater than
self-sacrifice. But when they lifted their
gentle heads to remind me all would be forgiven,
I turned and looked away.

There on the solitary block I sprawled
rootless and agonizing, Lord God of lolling tongues,
deliverer of carnage.

I prayed I had not become human.

1979

Returning to the Town Where
We Used to Live

I found this photograph.

A woman is reaching towards you.
Your hands seem to meet
where now my own fall uselessly.
Even the air around me is cruel,
and your creaturely eyes
full of a new hunger.

I seem to have been travelling
all my life. Your last letter written
ages ago says nothing has ended.

Returning to the town where
we used to live
I found this photograph.

A woman is leaning towards you.
Your eyes seem to meet where now
I feel only a stranger.
I had wanted to be so much.
I seem to have been travelling forever.

Just yesterday I flew
over the country where you live,
knowing I would never find you,
knowing I never did.

I saw the new moon holding
the old moon in her arms

I wanted to be held
and to hold you like this.

1979

ROO
BORSON

b. 1952

Gray Glove

Among branches
a bird lands fluttering,
a soft gray glove
with a heart.

The land at twilight.
Swamp of black mist.
A first planet. A swordtip.
The bird chanting
in a jail of darkness.

This is the last unclassified bird,
the one one never sees,
but hears when alone, walking.

You can see how far I've gone
not to speak of you.
Birds have made a simple bargain
with the land.

The only song I know
is the one I see with my eyes,
the one I'd give up my eyes
in order for you to hear.

ROO
BORSON

1981

Talk

The shops, the streets are full of old men
who can't think of a thing to say anymore.
Sometimes, looking at a girl, it
almost occurs to them, but they can't make it out,
they go pawing toward it through the fog.

The young men are still jostling shoulders
as they walk along, tussling at one another with words.
They're excited by talk, they can still see the danger.

The old women, thrifty with words,
haggling for oranges, their mouths
take bites out of the air. They know the value of oranges.
They had to learn everything
on their own.

The young women are the worst off, no one has bothered
to show them things.
You can see their minds on their faces,
they are like little lakes before a storm.
They don't know it's confusion that makes them sad.
It's lucky in a way though, because the young men take
a look of confusion for inscrutability, and this
excites them and makes them want to own
this face they don't understand,
something to be tinkered with at their leisure.

1981

Flowers

ROO
BORSON

The sunset, a huge flower, wilts on the horizon.
Robbed of perfume, a raw smell
wanders the hills, an embarrassing smell,
of nudity, of awkward hours on earth.
If a big man stands softly, his wide arms
gentled at his sides, women dissolve. It is the access
to easy violence that excites them.

The hills are knobbed with hay,
as if they were full of drawers about to be opened.
What could be inside but darkness?
The ground invisible, the toes feel the way,
bumping against unknown objects
like moths in a jar, like moths
stubbing themselves out on a lamp.

The women sit in their slips,
scattered upstairs through the houses
like silken buds.
They look in the mirror,
they wish they were other than they are.
Into a few of the rooms go a few of the men,
bringing their mushroomy smell.

The other men loll against the outsides of buildings,
looking up at the stars,
inconsequential.

One of them bends down to smell a flower.
There are holes in his face.

1981

Jacaranda

Old earth, how she sulks,
dark spin-off
wielding wings and swords,
mountain ranges, centuries,
our eyes with their impurities.

474

Dusk. Planets like spilled mercury
and the stars exuding
loneliness, the old battle
for which there are no medals.

ROO
BORSON

Often I look in that mirror
in which things happen over again.
Useless. Or I look
to the teasing water full of days
and clouds that drift like smoke,
and hours when the head sleeps,
an inn for strange guests. If only
we were easier creatures.

But the jacaranda reclines
like a wise thing,
stars crystallizing
beyond its dusky plumes.
Here in the amethyst air of early autumn,
the dryness a talisman,
the moon the egg of a luminous bird,
the jacaranda's wand-like branches
command each thing to be.

The jacaranda with its feathery leaves
blooms clusters of amethysts,
and its winged boxes
lilt toward the green plains bearing
an imploded formula
for jacarandas.

This is the endless catechism of beasts,
each a question and an answer,
on which time
in luminous drops
is raining down.

1981

INDEX OF POETS